JEFF ARCHER

THE MYSTIQUE OF PROFESSIONAL WRESTLING

Edited by Rick Boucke & Linda Carlson

LAFAYETTE, COLORADO

First published January 1999
Reprinted July 1999 (with changes), July 2000

ISBN 1-888580-06-2

Printed in the United States of America

The photographs in this book have been gathered from diverse sources and are used with the kind permission of the photographers or owners that are indicated. No photograph may be reproduced without permission of these owners. While every attempt has been made to trace and credit proper owners, holders of some historic, publicity and other photographs are not known. We wish to extend our apologies to any copyright holder whose photograph(s) may be uncredited or inadvertently miscredited. If any are perceived, please contact the publisher for rectification in any future editions.

Library of Congress Cataloging-In-Publication Data

Archer, Jeff, 1947-
Theater in a squared circle : the mystique of professional wrestling / Jeff Archer.
p. cm.
Includes index.
ISBN 1-888580-06-2
1. Wrestling. 2. Wrestling--History. 3. Wrestlers--Biography.
I. Title.
GV1195.A73 1998 98-45166
796.818'0973--dc21 CIP

Front cover photograph
(Killer Kowalski with author Jeff Archer)
by **Mike Lano**

Back cover photograph
(Killer Kowalski with Jeff Archer and Mike Lano)
by **Ann Archer**

Some previously published materials are included. Such passages are reproduced by permission of their respective copyright holders, including (but not limited to) **Evan Ginzburg, Walter Kowalski, Bill McCormack, Bill Kunkel, Mike Lano, Lanny Poffo, Brian Walsh** and **Wayne St. Wayne**. The author and the publisher of this work gratefully acknowledge the valuable assistance and understanding of the entire cast of ***Theater in a Squared Circle***.

Special thanks to **David Williamson** for many of the historic "card" clippings included in this book.

CONTENTS

FOREWORD

One man's garbage is another man's treasure. If you perceive pro wrestling as buffoonery, merely lowbrow, mock mortal combat, then there's probably not much I can do to convince you otherwise. But if you understand that wrestling—at least when done right—is an art form, then *Theater in a Squared Circle* will provide a fascinating guide through this once-secret world.

By the time you finish this book, you'll understand the pain these great athletes endure to master their craft, as well as the odds against making it in their unusual chosen field. You'll also see them as real flesh-and-blood people—as opposed to the characters they play on TV.

Jeff Archer is the perfect choice to chronicle this entertainment. A journalist and ex-athlete, Jeff loves the game but isn't blinded by the high-tech glamour of late '90s wrestling. He knows it has a dark, seamy side, as evidenced by steroid and drug abuse taking some of our greatest stars. For the first time, a journalist provides a look at all aspects of the sport, from the bottom to the top, as well as at the fans and writers who devote themselves to it.

My introduction to Jeff was "kismet." He saw a plug for my wrestling newsletter from an unknown source on the Internet. He called me, asking for contacts in the industry. Like any "celebrities," wrestlers generally are wary of strangers, and I felt him out over the phone. Archer told me he worked out of his house, made a living as a writer/production editor, and I felt a real "bohemian" vibe. "I just want to make a living with type," he said, simply. He also has a sincere love and appreciation for wrestling, not scoffing at it as mainstream sports journalists like Phil Mushnick and Wallace Matthews have. I got him in touch with some wrestling legends, not realizing that I was the first person that had cooperated with him.

Months later, I visited Jeff at his home and found an eclectic, warm, politically aware individual. I had him typeset and design my father's autobiography, *Hey Cabby!*

And now you hold this 400-page volume in your hands. Be careful, though: most folks will give you the old, "Why does an intelligent person like you like wrestling?"

Some people just don't understand. Enjoy *Theater in a Squared Circle*. It's a gem.

Evan Ginzburg
Editor, *Wrestling Then & Now*

INTRODUCTION

The year 1960 heralded several milestones for my future in sports. I led the Tiverton, Rhode Island, Little League in home runs and RBIs in addition to striking out more batters and winning more games than any other pitcher in the league. That was the year in which I became my team's leading scorer in the Tiverton Junior Basketball League as well. One event occurred, however, which has eclipsed all my other sporting ventures, but I did not realize its importance at the time—I watched my first professional wrestling match on television.

For the next two years, I spent most Saturday afternoons glued to the television set watching the top grapplers at the beginning of the tumultuous decade of the 1960s work at their trade on Boston's Channel 5. The big names in those days were Killer Kowalski, Bruno Sammartino, Bobo Brazil and Haystack Calhoun, among others. I listened to the announcers talk of the famous submission holds that the stars possessed, such as Killer Kowalski's "claw hold" and Bobo Brazil's "cocoa butt." After a few weeks of viewing, it became evident when a star was about to diminish his opponent's slim hope of victory and pulverize him with his final move.

All sorts of valuable information came over the airwaves. The viewer learned that Haystack Calhoun's beard was a lifelong project because he had never touched a razor. Evidently, Calhoun, cast in a hillbilly role, did not have access to a razor in his younger days in the outback of America. When Pampero Firpo ran uncontrollably down to the ring, grunting instead of talking, we discovered that he was from "parts unknown" in the Amazonian jungle. It never occurred to me at the time that a man who was portrayed as a savage and could not talk or be tamed, was civilized enough to show up at the arena on time for his match.

My mother did not share my enthusiasm for professional wrestling. When my friends visited, we would clear the living room of useless furniture (couches, tables, chairs, etc.) and practice applying full-nelsons and scissors holds on each other. There was the occasional knee-drop, but the unwritten rules allowed a high-impact maneuver only if your opponent pulled your hair or hit you in the eye.

In 1962, tragedy occurred in my household. Channel 5 terminated its broadcasts of professional wrestling. Because of my age, I quickly recovered from the cataclysmic cancellation and found new interests.

For about a year, I did not see a match. One Saturday afternoon, while I was watching candlestick bowling on television (Channel 5's replacement for wrestling), the telephone rang. A friend asked, "Would you like to go see a wrestling match tonight at the Providence Arena? Bruno Sammartino is defending his title against Killer Kowalski." I quickly responded, "Yes." There was no doubt in my mind that I had to go and cheer for my all-time favorite wrestler, Kowalski, in his bid to regain the championship belt.

Sammartino won the first fall in the two-out-of-three fall contest. Kowalski regained his composure and evened the match. Finally, after what seemed to be a period of hours and many near-falls for both grapplers, Sammartino pinned the Killer and retained his title.

That was the last wrestling match I saw for years. I decided at the time that I was too old to continue watching professional wrestling, especially when accusations of the sport being "fake" were running rampant among my teenage comrades.

After years of not watching wrestling, an incident occurred which brought me back to the fold. In 1992, I was painting the kitchen of my home in southern California. Decades and continents (I lived in Europe from 1975 until 1983) had separated me from the allure of professional wrestling. While I was painting, I heard a voice on the television state that a World Wrestling Federation program called *WWF Superstars* was about to begin. Normally, I would have changed the station to one which was broadcasting a program that interested me. For some unknown reason, I did not change the channel. About halfway through the program, the announcer, Vince McMahon, stated, "And here comes Bob Backlund. He's making a comeback."

I took a breath while I watched Backlund, a former WWF champ. I had never heard of or seen the former champ and was curious. Backlund was nondescript and easily defeated a "stiff." When the match, which was quite dull, was over, I thought, "So what?"

Despite my lack of enthusiasm with the first professional wrestling match I had seen in almost 30 years, something told me that there was more to this than I saw. For the next few weeks, I watched professional wrestling every Saturday, and it became clear that there was more to the comeback of Bob Backlund than met the eye. In other words, at age 44, I became addicted to professional wrestling. I had been too old to continue watching it years before, yet I was now old enough to become a fan again.

The biggest complaint from those unenlightened people who hold professional wrestling in disdain is that the sport is "fake." When I hear this unimaginative response, I usually ask if the theater is "fake" and am assured that it is not. Then I explain that actors rehearse fictitious plots and reenact them on a stage, yet no criticism is levied against them as being contrived productions. Perhaps the best description of professional wrestling came from one of the sport's superstars, Ted DiBiase. When confronted by an interviewer for a California talk show about the authenticity of professional wrestling, DiBiase stated, "Professional wrestling is whatever you want it to be."

No truer words could have been spoken. For me, professional wrestling means something very different from the sport I watched during my early teenage years. At that time, I was a fan and cheered for victories for my favorite wrestlers. I shared in their joy when they dominated and languished in a state of mild depression when they lost.

Today it is immaterial to me who wins a professional wrestling match. I enjoy all the matches and am amazed by the incredible athletic ability and skills of all wrestlers. More important, however, is the array of in-ring personalities involved. Some wrestlers possess impeccable manners and enjoy the support of the fans, while others are cads, occasionally accused of being mentally unbalanced while they are on the verge of creating a cataclysmic end for the "good guys.” (I must admit that I tend to prefer the actions of the “bad guys.”) Then you have the inevitable switches in which a terrorist bad guy is transformed overnight into a pillar of the community. For every switch like this, there is the perennial hero who loses his marbles and turns into the ultimate beast.

Character portrayals represent the fuel that feeds the wrestling fire. In some cases, the in-ring characters are extensions of their real-life personalities, and at other times, their contrived in-ring antics have a way of becoming a part of their outside-the-ring activities.

This book is definitely not intended to be a history of professional wrestling, although there are historical inferences and sprinklings of history throughout. There are those who have chronicled professional wrestling’s history in a far more comprehensive and detailed manner than I.

Theater in a Squared Circle is intended to be a celebration of professional wrestling as a true American art style. Nothing else depicts our culture in the same manner as professional wrestling. Almost everything that affects our society is brought inside the ropes of a wrestling ring—economics, foreign affairs, presidential scandals, racism, homophobia, beauty, ugliness, greed, benevolence, the merits of breast enhancement . . . you name it and it will be there.

In addition, this is a book which features those involved with professional wrestling who rarely gain notoriety—the jobbers, referees, historians, writers, newsletter (“sheet”) people, photographers, artists and, most importantly, the fans. If it weren’t for these entities, professional wrestling as we know it would not exist.

To sum up, as I enter my sixth decade, I find no other sport or recreation as pleasing and encompassing as professional wrestling, a form of entertainment that has deservedly earned the title of . . . ***The Shakespeare of Sports.***

PRELUDE

Theater in a Squared Circle *is about the people of professional wrestling—the wrestlers, promoters, fans, writers, artists, referees and other characters—who all form a mosaic from which emerges the product of professional wrestling. If you take away one element of the millions of individuals who participate in the sport, there would be no professional wrestling as we know it. The hardcore fan as well as the uninitiated will enjoy the stories inside.*

Glossary

A "mark" is a person who knows little about the inside workings of professional wrestling, whereas one who is versed in these matters is considered "smart." The following is a glossary of wrestling terms which will be used throughout this book. The glossary has been placed at the beginning of the book instead of in the appendix so the "marks" who read this will eventually become "smart."

angle *n.* a wrestling "plot" which may involve only one match or may continue over several matches for some time; the reason behind a *feud* or a *turn.*

blade *v.i. & v.t.* (razor blade) the practice of cutting oneself or being cut with a part of a razor blade hidden in tights, hair or wrappings in order to produce *juice.*

blow up *v.i.* to become fatigued or exhausted. The Ultimate Warrior was said to be one of a number of wrestlers who blows up on the entry ramp.

booker *n.* the individual responsible for *angles, finishes,* hiring and firing in a promotion.

bump *n.* a fall or hit done as a *spot* which sometimes takes the wrestler (or other participant, i.e., referee, manager) out of action.

card *n.* the series of matches in one location at one time.

draw *v.t.* to attract *marks.* *n.* the popularity of a wrestler; the ability to bring in *marks.*

dud *n.* a particularly bad and totally uninteresting match.

face *n. & adj.* (babyface) a good guy.

fall *n.* (pinfall) a referee's count of three with the loser's shoulders on the mat.

feud *n.* a series of matches between two wrestlers or two tag teams, usually *face* vs. *heel*, though face feuds and heel feuds are not unknown.

finish *n.* the event or sequence of events which leads to the ultimate outcome of a match.

green *adj.* not good because of inexperience.

hardway juice *n.* real blood produced by means other than *blading,* i.e., the hard way. One of the possible outcomes of a *shoot.*

heat *n.* enthusiasm, a positive response. The WWF uses a heat machine for its televised shows which make them somewhat of a *work.*

heel *n. & adj.* a bad guy, rule-breaker.

house *n.* the wrestling audience in the building said to be composed of *marks.*

international object *n.* foreign object, something not allowed in the ring. Derived from an order not to use the word "foreign" by the Turner Broadcasting Company.

job *n.* a staged loss. A clean job is a staged loss by legal pinfall or submission without resort to illegalities. *v.i.* to do a job. Sometimes combined with a descriptive adjective (stretcher job, ropes job, tights job).

jobber *n.* an unpushed wrestler who does jobs for pushed wrestlers. Barry Horowitz is probably the best known of these. Sometimes known as *fish*, *redshirts*, *PLs* (professional losers) or *ham-and-eggers*. Steve Lombardi (Brooklyn Brawler) is also a well-known jobber.

juice *n.* blood. *v.i.* to bleed, usually as a result of blading.

kayfabe *n., adj.* of or related to inside information about the business, especially by fans. Origin is "carny" (carnival) jargon talk for "fake."

kill *v.t.* diminish or eliminate *heat* or drawing power. There are a variety of ways to do this, but mostly it is done by having a wrestler do too many jobs. A house can be killed by too many *screw-job* endings.

mark *n.* a member of the audience, presumed gullible.

paper *n.* complimentary tickets. *v.t.* to give lots of complimentary tickets to make a house look good, particularly for a television taping.

pop *n., v.i.* sudden *heat* from a house as a response to a wrestler's entry or hot move.

post *v.t.* to run or be run into the ringpost.

potato *v.t.* to injure a wrestler by hitting him on the head or face causing him to hit his head on something.

run-in *n.* interference by a nonparticipant in a match.

save *n.* a run-in to protect a wrestler from being beaten up after a match is over.

screw-job *n., adj.* a match or ending which is not clean (definite) because of factors outside the "rules" of wrestling.

shoot *n.* the real thing, i.e., a match where one participant is really attempting to hurt another. The opposite of *work* or *fake.*

spot *n.* an event or sequence of events which makes a particular match distinctive; a high-point of a match.

squash *n.* a totally passive *job* where one wrestler completely dominates another. *v.t.* to win a squash match.

stiff *adj.* chops, hits or moves which cause real injury (though perhaps not more than a welting of the opponent). Vader has a reputation as a stiff worker. Not a *shoot*, but almost.

stretch *n.* a form of *shoot* where one wrestler dominates rather than injures the other as a proof of personal superiority.

turn *n.* change in orientation from *heel* to *face* or vice-versa.

work *n.* a match with a predetermined outcome, the opposite of a *shoot.*

workrate *n.* the approximate ratio of good wrestling to rest holds in a match or in a wrestler's performance.

Definitions used in this glossary are provided courtesy of Byron C. Howes [bch@ecsvax.uncecs.edu], under the declared terms of his published rights.

ACT I
THE MYSTIQUE

In the 20th century, a new American art form emerged which has held the imagination of millions of people for decades—professional wrestling. This art form combines athletic and theatrical skills to produce an offspring which appeals to young and old as well as to male and female. Rich people watch grappling at the same time every week as the less affluent members of society. People of all races enjoy professional wrestling. A politically radical, dope-smoking ex-hippie may be in the same arena and seated next to a conservative adult male dressed in a business suit. Professional wrestling is the forum in which people of all persuasions can sit and agree on one thing—the intrigue of the activity that is occurring in the squared circle.

Good guy against bad guy; justice versus inequality; purity against tainted images: these are the themes which professional wrestling thrives on. In case you think that it is predetermined that good always wins out in the long run, you are wrong. In the ring, good guys don't always win.

Combine the good-against-evil theme with individuals who embody one side or the other, and you have professional wrestling. Add complicated plots with the players occasionally dressed in outrageous garb, and you have the "Shakespeare of Sports."

Only a few decades ago, the business of professional wrestling maintained a tainted image. For some reason, non-fans thought that wrestling was a seedy venture. Just look at the classic movie of the 1950s, Requiem for a Heavyweight. *In that film, Anthony Quinn played an over-the-hill, punch-drunk boxer who eventually suffered the most vile form of indignity in his trade—he became a professional wrestler.*

Things have changed. Today professional boxers (still in their prime) as well as professional baseball, football and basketball players actually make themselves available to become a part of the professional wrestling scene, many times in the hopes of becoming a full-time wrestler after their careers in their respective sports have ended. Add to this the list of actors, talk-show hosts and other celebrities who have participated in professional wrestling angles, and you will see that the image of wrestling has changed from that of an ostracized sport to one of glamour in a matter of less than half a century.

Professional wrestling's popularity is at an all-time high. Act I conveys, through history and the words of wrestling fans and participants, the magical hold that the sport has over the public in the United States and overseas.

Scene I

IN THE BEGINNING

When modern-day fans of professional wrestling watch Bret Hart put the "sharpshooter" on an opponent, or Ric Flair reverse a "figure-four leg-lock" and then diminish his adversary to submission, they are not only observing the best in modern sports entertainment, they are also viewing the progression of the world's oldest sport.

Long before man could even speak or coin the term "sport" or "wrestling," he was practicing the art of grappling; however, it was for survival, not recreational purposes, that prehistoric man wrestled. Tens of thousands of years before recorded history began, man had to compete with animals for food. Man was inferior to a vast number of his animal competitors in the battle for provisions, but he was developing an organ which would assist him in beating out larger members of the animal kingdom—a brain.

Eventually, man realized that he could win the struggle for food against larger opponents by putting holds on the animals that would allow our ancient relatives to gain superiority. When these grips were shown to be effective, family members and neighbors would meet to practice them on each other. Consequently, the holds became more elaborate and effective, allowing man to compete in the struggle for survival.

After tens of thousands of years of wrestling animals for sustenance, man developed tools which would assist in either killing his competitors or scaring them away from common necessities. From then on, wrestling was no longer a requisite in keeping the homo erectus species from becoming extinct.

The first recorded evidence of wrestling as a sport was discovered in 1938. Dr. S. A. Speiser led an archaeological team from the University of Pennsylvania and the American Schools of Oriental Research to excavate an area which was once known as Mesopotamia. At Kyafaje, near Baghdad, Iraq, the team found the ruins of a temple in which was a cast bronze figurine that showed two wrestlers, each with a hold on the other's hips. Archaeologists have concluded that the depiction was created by the Sumerian culture of the time. The find has been judged to be over 5,000 years old.

Other ancient societies held wrestling in high esteem as well. Egyptian slabs over 3,000 years old portray wrestlers performing many holds similar to those used today.

Perhaps ancient Greece elevated the sport of wrestling to a pinnacle of awareness more than any other society of antiquity. The Greeks considered discus throwers to be the finest specimens of athletes, while wrestlers ran a close second in the rating of sportsmen in their society.

Almost 3,000 years ago, Greek wrestling received its first standard rules which were established by Theseus, son of the Athenian King Ageus. The earliest Greek edicts allowed wrestling similar to modern-day catch-as-catch-can style, but breaking of fingers, throttling and gouging were permitted. At first, Greek fans were content with the codification of wrestling rules, but eventually they craved more action by their favorite grapplers, and a new form of wrestling—pancratium—was created. In pancratium, no holds were barred. The fans saw wrestlers bite, gouge, strangle, kick and punch each other with regularity.

Modern professional wrestling in theory is based on the catch-as-catch-can style, yet there are some groups attempting to resurrect the pancratium style—called "Pancrase"—and promote it as a no-holds-barred form of wrestling. There are varying reports on its legitimacy: some maintain that it is all without script, while others infer that portions of Pancrase are contrived. Despite the question of authenticity of Pancrase, the ancient pancratium was most likely unscripted.

Wrestling in the ancient world took a major step forward with the implementation of the ancient Greek Olympic Games, which were held every four years in the sanctuary of Zeus at Olympia. The history of the first Olympics dates from 776 B.C. and records show that wrestling and pancratium were vital elements in the competitions.

Greek wrestlers oiled their bodies and sprinkled them with "lucky dust" in their quest for victory. Most of the time, the dust was brought from the wrestler's hometown or neighborhood.

Of all Greek wrestlers of antiquity, many historians maintain that Milo of Croton was the most famous. He was a six-time champion at the Olympic Games and the Isthmian Games, another prestigious Greek festival.

No less a personage than the great Greek poet Homer glorified wrestling and its participants in ancient Greece. He is considered the greatest Greek poet, and his work *The Iliad* is regarded by Greeks to be the pinnacle of Greek literary achievement.

In Book 23 of *The Iliad*, Homer recounted an epic wrestling match between Odysseus and Aias. Various scholars have designated this the greatest wrestling story ever told. The account, which was translated by the late E. V. Rieu, is reprinted here.[1]

> Losing no time, the son of Peleus brought out and displayed fresh prizes, for the third event, the all-in wrestling. For the winner there was a big three-legged cauldron to go on the fire—it was worth a dozen oxen by Achaean reckoning—and for the loser he brought forward a woman thoroughly trained in domestic work, who was valued at four oxen in the camp. Achilles stood up to announce the contest to the Argives, and called for a couple of entries for the new event. The great Telamonian Aias rose at once, and so did the resourceful Odysseus, who knew all the tricks. The two put on their shorts, stepped into the middle of the ring, and gripped each other in their powerful arms. They looked like a couple of those sloping rafters that a good builder locks together in the roof of a high house to resist the wind. Their backs creaked under the pressure of their mighty hands; the sweat streamed down; and many blood-red weals sprang up along their sides and shoulders. And still they tussled on, each

1. *The Iliad,* Book 23 (The Games), Lines 111–222.

> thinking of the fine cauldron that was not yet won. But Odysseus was no more able to bring down his man and pin him to the ground, than Aias, who was baffled by Odysseus' brawn. After some time, when they saw that they were boring the troops, the great Telamonian Aias said: "Royal son of Laertes, Odysseus of the nimble wits; either you or I must let the other try a throw. What happens afterwards is Zeus's business."
>
> With that, he lifted Odysseus off the ground. But Odysseus' craft did not desert him. He caught Aias with a kick from behind the hollow of the knee, upset his stance, and flung him on his back, himself falling on Aias' chest. The spectators were duly impressed. But now the stalwart admirable Odysseus had to try a throw. He shifted Aias just a little off the ground, but he could not throw him. So he crooked a leg around Aias' knee and they both fell down, cheek by jowl, and were smothered in dust. They jumped up and would have tried a third round, if Achilles himself had not risen to his feet and interposed. He told them they had struggled quite enough and must not wear each other out. "You have both won," he said. "Take equal prizes and withdraw. There are other events to follow." The two men readily accepted this decision, and after wiping off the dust put on their tunics.

Critics of modern-day professional wrestling often knock the sport because it has varied from its amateur roots and does not resemble "true wrestling." When one reads the previous account by Homer, however, it is evident that there are many similarities between the wrestlers of Homer's classic and today's grapplers who wrestle for a living.

For instance, when Odysseus and Aias appeared to be at a standstill, a challenge was issued by one of the wrestlers to throw him. Today's pro wrestlers issue similar analogous confrontations when they have reached a stalemate.

The outcome, two warriors grappling until they had little strength and emotion left and then having a draw called, is depicted occasionally in today's pro ranks.

Unlike the nondescript image that purists would like to see wrestlers don today, ancient wrestlers most likely thrived in notoriety. We have seen that they sprinkled themselves with "lucky dust" in their quests for victory. When Dustin Runnels first appeared as "Goldust," he would walk to the ring while golden-colored dust was falling from the rafters. The question remains: Were ancient grapplers flamboyant in their presentation, similar to modern professional wrestlers, or were they mundane and only concerned about their in-ring skills?

For hundreds of years, the Greeks featured wrestling in their prestigious Olympic Games. In addition, wrestling composed a major part of many of their other athletic events, such as the Isthmian, Pythian and Nemean Games.

Eventually, Rome conquered Greece, and the new rulers altered the Greek form of wrestling. They eradicated some of the violent holds used in pancratium and combined their own methods of wrestling with the earlier, more sedate, form of Grecian wrestling. The hybrid outcome heralded the birth of a new sport, Greco-Roman wrestling, in which holds are not permitted below the waist. This fashion of wrestling has survived (with a few changes) to this day.

The Greeks and the Romans were not the only ancient societies that participated in wrestling as a sport. We have previously mentioned that Middle Eastern cultures, such as the Sumerians, possessed a tradition of wrestling when their own history was in its infancy. The same can be said for the ancient Egyptians.

One culture which was in contrast to the Greeks, Romans, Sumerians and Egyptians, also produced wrestlers of note. Ancient Jews were rarely interested in sports, but they did enjoy wrestling. From a period of over several thousand years ago until well into the Christian era, the Jews and their predecessors spawned many excellent wrestlers.

At the inception of the Christian era, wrestling was popular. As in times past, however, wrestling progressed and came to represent different social mores from those of its preceding times of fame. Royalty and their guests were the prime recipients of wrestling enjoyment in European countries. Most monarchs of the day boasted of their great armies, yet a close runner-up in the area of national bragging rights was having a championship wrestler in the ranks of their subjects.

France and England have fought many wars over the centuries, and the Anglo-French rivalry extended to the wrestling mat as well. King Francis I of France, who reigned from 1515–1549, was particularly keen on his country's wrestlers. At about the same time as Francis occupied the French throne, the infamous King Henry VIII ruled England (1509–1547), and he shared his French counterpart's affinity for wrestling.

Unfortunately for Francis, the English wrestlers dominated the French at that time, and the French monarch was not pleased about the results of the matches in the international rivalry. It has been recorded that at one match, King Henry VIII was basking over the seeming ease in which his grapplers were overshadowing the French. Francis could not take any more of the English King's bravado. His temper ignited, and he leapt to his feet in the royal box where he was seated with Henry, then proceeded to grab him. A public royal wrestling match ensued, but the battle was short-lived as bystanders intervened to halt any further action.

With the epoch ages of European discoveries and relocation of citizens to new territories, wrestling became even more popular. The English enjoyed the sport, all the time creating myriad variations in its British development. English towns adopted their own indigenous styles—each one trying to outdo the others in grueling violence. The most famous styles were the Lancashire, the Cornish and the Devonshire.

During the progression of wrestling, the Irish developed a style somewhat more brutal than that of the English. The Scots adhered to the Lancashire style, which was the most tumultuous in England. On the European continent, the French became more subdued as they permitted holds only from the waist up. Their German neighbors developed a style in which the wrestlers performed all of their skills on the ground.

In early America, wrestling was imported with the waves of immigrants. In addition, the colonists observed that the Native Americans participated in their own version of the sport.

The earliest organized wrestling in the United States employed Greco-Roman rules. These rules looked good on paper, but they were rarely enforced, because most neighborhood wrestlers held any rules in disdain and eventually created an Americanized version of the catch-as-catch-can style—a style which was more open to a variety of moves, yet still had a few constraints.

The habit of changing the rules of a sport to fit a locale in America was not solely practiced by participants in wrestling. For instance, early American baseball was imported from England, yet virtually every town in which the game was played in the United States used different regulations.

Around 1900, a Cleveland rolling-mill-worker-turned-wrestler, Tom Jenkins, was an advocate of the more unfettered wrestling rules that had been created by neighborhood wrestlers and was the first professional to call for the newer American catch-as-catch-can style to be used nationally. With his popularizing of this style, the sport grew, and he became an idol for his fans.

Jenkins, a one-eyed wrestler, created a groundswell of new participants in the sport. As the more innovative form of American wrestling became increasingly popular, other wrestlers abandoned the Greco-Roman style and came into the catch-as-catch-can fold.

Jenkins held sway over the American wrestling scene until he met his match in Frank Gotch. In 1905, Gotch dethroned Jenkins and went on to be considered the greatest catch-as-catch-can wrestler of all time up to his retirement in 1913.

Gotch's skills and reputation precipitated an influx of Greco-Roman wrestlers into the catch-as-catch-can camp in an effort to beat the seemingly invincible Gotch. The only wrestler to beat Gotch was Freddy Beall, who threw Gotch against a ring post during a match in 1906. Gotch was knocked out and Beall easily pinned him. To show that his only loss was a fluke, Gotch easily routed Beall in a rematch.

Upon Gotch's retirement in 1913, the sport of professional wrestling went into decline. No wrestler was able to come to the forefront and take over the leadership of the sport as Gotch, and Jenkins before him, had.

Various wrestling aficionados maintain that professional wrestling's golden years consisted of the three decades from 1890 to 1920. Others, however, can put forward the argument that these times were but the formative years of professional wrestling and that after a hiatus of a few decades, the new-look professional wrestling would come to grasp the imagination of not only the United States but the world.

*** ***

Scene II

A NEW BALL GAME

After the demise of professional wrestling in the early part of the 20th century, the sport wore many hats and was promoted in differing manners. It was not until the 1940s that professional wrestling again became a mainstay with the American public. By that time, the sport had changed so much that it appeared to be a completely new version of grappling.

Scene II outlines the progression of professional wrestling from the 1940s until today. In no way is it meant to be a definitive history. There are wrestling historians who can chronicle in an accurate manner the actual times and dates of events. We only want to highlight certain aspects and bring you up to the current time in wrestling's history.

In the 1920s and 1930s, professional wrestling was fragmented. Various promoters showcased matches in arenas, but many wrestlers plied their trade on the carnival circuits. These were usually tough, strong individuals who fought against each other as well as members of the public who wanted to try to beat the pros. The carnival atmosphere of professional wrestling is still with us today. We can see this with the various promotions that use fireworks to lend a circus-like atmosphere to what was once considered to be an athletic competition.

Professional wrestling prior to 1920 was perceived by many as not worked (staged). But some historians have published articles stating that professional wrestling, even during the glory years of Gotch, was a work in which the match results were predetermined.

One thing is certain, however. During the 1930s, wrestling started its change from being a strict sport to sports entertainment. The promoters saw that creating certain feuds would enhance ticket sales, so they began to script certain matches, and the fans would want to see the rematches between two "enemies."

Initially, producing a worked product did not drastically alter the look of professional wrestling. The wrestlers were still big, strong, tough guys who banged each other around, only this time to a slightly structured script.

The new style of professional wrestling started to become popular after World War II. By then, various promoters were involved under a loose agreement of "territories." This ensured that everybody received a piece of the financial pie.

There were problems, however. There were as many "world champions" as there were promotions. At times, the promoters were in deep competition, instead of enhanced cooperation. In 1948, a group of promoters met with the idea of unifying titles and wrestling history, while protecting each other in their respective territories.

At that time, the National Wrestling Alliance (NWA) was formed. Prior to this, there was a so-called national organization called the National Wrestling Association. It virtually became a part of the NWA with a scheduled title unification match between Lou Thesz of the National Wrestling Association and Orville Brown of the National Wrestling Alliance. Brown was injured in a car accident and was not able to compete, so Thesz was given the NWA title.

For years, the NWA held sway as the top professional wrestling organization. There were others, and there was a certain amount of cooperation among the NWA and various units over the years. These agreements held the sport together.

The NWA produced many legendary champions and performers. Many wrestlers of the time belonged to other organizations, but the best still wrestled against NWA talent, adding credence to their careers.

In the early 1950s, technology assisted in making professional wrestling a major part of the American psyche. Television was in its formative years, and it needed programs to snare the public. Wrestling supplied the perfect product. One camera could film all the action. By the mid-1950s, professional wrestling held a national audience of people who did not have to leave their homes.

One wrestler in particular saw the potential of the medium of television and exploited it to its fullest—Gorgeous George. He was the predecessor to today's grapplers who use a costumed gimmick combined with an abrasiveness that creates a figure who is hated by the fans. With the amount of money and technology available today, professional wrestling promotions would be hard-pressed to create an electrifying ring entrance that would even duplicate, let alone surpass, Gorgeous George's approach to the squared circle.

After Gorgeous George changed the face of professional wrestling, other grapplers began to develop unorthodox or outrageous personas. This period of professional wrestling was the beginning of the sport's "Golden Age."

In 1963, Buddy Rogers lost the NWA championship to Lou Thesz. Some northeastern promoters did not agree with the decision to make Thesz the NWA standard-bearer, so they did not recognize him as the champ. From these dissenters emerged a new organization led by Vince McMahon, Sr.—the World Wide Wrestling Federation (WWWF).

Buddy Rogers eventually became the WWWF champion, but he quickly lost the title to Bruno Sammartino. Rogers allegedly had suffered a heart attack prior to his match with Sammartino and took a break from grappling.

In 1979, the WWWF became the WWF (World Wrestling Federation). The moniker change was only that. The front office and ownership remained intact.

In the early 1980s, Vince McMahon, Sr. relinquished control of the WWF to his son Vince, Jr. Vince, Sr. died in 1984.

With the advent of new leadership in the WWF came new strategies. Vince McMahon, Jr. began to attain talent from other territories. His acquisitions made for a strong WWF, but depleted various other groups. The common term used at this time was "raiding." Today there is still heated debate about his tactics. Some maintain that McMahon ruined wrestling by dismantling the territories, while others state that McMahon elevated wrestling to another level—giving wrestlers a chance to reach national stardom.

After the WWF changed the structure of professional wrestling, it became the major league of the sport. By then, the NWA was only a shadow of its past self. In 1988, Jim Crockett sold Jim Crockett Promotions to superstation WTBS in Atlanta. Crockett's promotion was the mainstay of the NWA. Today the NWA is still in existence, but as a combination of small independent groups that does not resemble the NWA in its heyday.

For a few years, the WWF was the only major league. During the mid-to-late 1980s, McMahon changed the face of the product of wrestling. Again, he had his supporters and his detractors about the direction wrestling took with his guidance. Instead of grizzly looking veterans, the new heroes wore costumes and used preposterous names. The feuds were enhanced by outside-the-ring plots. Hulk Hogan became a household name. When he beat Andre the Giant in 1987 at the Pontiac Silverdome in Detroit, the world began to take professional wrestling seriously in marketing terms. A record 93,000 people were in attendance at that match.

For a few years, the WWF remained unchallenged, but the upstart WTBS station, owned by billionaire Ted Turner, was beginning to change. The station's showing of NWA matches included the subtle name-change to WCW from NWA. By the beginning of 1991, WCW was entrenched in the wrestling world, but still at a much lower level than the WWF.

Within a couple of years, however, WCW had attained a lot of former WWF stars. In other words, the Atlanta-based organization used similar tactics to McMahon's of the 1980s in establishing a talent base. If you watched a WCW card in 1994, you would not be remiss in thinking you were watching an old WWF card.

By the mid-1990s, the WWF and WCW were almost at parity. After the initial raiding of WWF talent, WCW began to establish its own cache of wrestling talent. Today WCW has many stars who have never stepped in the ring with the WWF—The Giant, Chris Jericho, Chris Benoit, Stevie Ray, Buff Bagwell, Sting and Saturn, among others. Five years ago, it had very few homegrown performers.

One other major event that virtually pushed WCW to equality with the WWF was the signing of Hulk Hogan in 1994. Hogan had been a WWF mainstay for years, and his name was equated to "professional wrestling." By 1993, he was on the outs with WWF management and made a career change.

Today WCW and the WWF are the major leagues of professional wrestling. The two organizations differ in their presentations. Both have supporters and detractors, and many wrestling fans watch both with the same amount of reverence.

With the advent of two major leagues of wrestling, other aspects of the sport began to change. Many new independent organizations began to emerge. These new promotions did not attempt to pass themselves off as major leagues. They saw a void where smaller groups could promote matches and at the same time almost be a minor-league-feeding system for the big two. In addition, WCW and the WWF could loan their wrestlers to the groups as well as take grapplers from the groups on a temporary basis. The chaos of the post-territory days seems to have subsided.

WCW attempts to present an image similar to that of wrestling during the sport's Golden Age. Many of the group's performers grapple in Spartan wrestling attire of boots and trunks. There are those who utilize outrageous garb, but overall, the promotion is closer to the wrestling of the 1950s than the WWF is.

The plots and angles in WCW mirror many of those of the Golden Age—a feud develops and is sustained over a period of weeks or months. The basic element of a WCW feud is normally, "I'll kick your ass." The wrestlers will often make reference to what has been said about them and then inform the opponent that he will not be safe until they settle the score. Similar plots hatch on schoolyard playgrounds.

The WWF, however, has taken the gimmick to new heights. Anything goes in the area of plots—wrestlers accused of having sexual relations with other wrestlers' wives; The Undertaker constantly rising from the dead; the Parade of Human Oddities, which includes midgets, giants and a masked man with bumps protruding from his head; women stripping almost naked in the ring; and even a wrestler who came within seconds of having his penis chopped off by a wrestling manager—John Wayne Bobbitt came to his rescue just before the sword hit the flesh. The current in-vogue saying in America's schoolyards is "Suck it!" This statement is made while making a hand gesture toward the crotch. How did this transpire? A WWF group called Degeneration X created this ritual. One of its members, X-Pac (formerly the 1-2-3 Kid), is an expert in urology. He has, at least twice, urinated on *Monday Night Raw*, the nationally televised weekly WWF show—once on a wrestler's motorcycle and another time in a wrestler's boot.

As we approach the end of the 20th century, professional wrestling is far different from the sport that started the century. In fact, it is far different from professional wrestling of only a couple of decades before.

The wrestlers themselves mostly are well-defined bodybuilder types who look almost too perfect to be human beings. Wrestlers dress as clowns, animals, undertakers, punk-rockers and virtually anything else you can make a human being up to be. Old-time fans hate the new-style wrestling, and many vow never to watch the sport again but, like an alcoholic or drug addict, few stick to their promises of withdrawal.

Professional wrestling can be insane, goofy, inarticulate, obscene, action-packed, hypocritical, greedy, unpredictable, ruthless, stupid, creative, reactionary, brilliant, homophobic, racist, enlightened, vulgar and entertaining.

It has never been so popular.

*** ***

Scene III

THE SHAKESPEARE OF SPORTS

Professional wrestling has been described in many ways. Among the terms used to depict pro wrestling are: "sport," "soap opera," "comic theater," "sports entertainment," "choreographed gymnastics" and "mindless violence." Let's look at professional wrestling from the standpoint of it being "theater in a squared circle."

All the elements for a theatrical production are in place. Wrestling includes drama, comedy and tragedy. There are lighting and choreographics. The crowd is seeing live entertainment with no chance for second takes if a performer makes a mistake. Unlike conventional theater, however, a wrestler can jeopardize his career, health or even life if he executes a move and is off by a few centimeters. In traditional theater, embarrassment is the only offshoot for a missed line.

The components for wrestling theater are simple—a character and an angle (plot). Over the years, these two ingredients have kept professional wrestling alive and well.

Let's look at the characters. In the past we saw such colorful personalities as Haystack Calhoun, a 600-pound hillbilly who never wore shoes or shaved in his life. Pampero Firpo was a wild man from parts unknown in the Amazon. Killer Kowalski was the meanest and most ruthless man on the Earth. Hans Schmidt was A HARDCORE NAZI. These wrestlers were part of the sport's Golden Age, and today fans speak of them in nostalgic terms. Now let's look at the real people behind their roles. Firpo became a postal employee after wrestling and is still working for the United States Postal Service. Calhoun died at age 49 and was not a hillbilly—he wanted to be a professional wrestler when he was a youngster and followed his dream. Kowalski, one of the world's most gentle human beings, worked for Ford Motor Company as an engineer and took up wrestling full-time when Ford would not give him a six-month leave of absence. Schmidt, the unrepentant Nazi, was actually a French-Canadian from Montreal.

The one common aspect for all the above wrestlers is that they were masters at making the audience believe their ring roles. They took a character and elevated it to the absurd, ensuring a crowd response.

On the other side of the coin, the Golden Age of wrestling was filled with good guys who were just as impressive in their portrayals of the goodness of humanity as the heels were in their dastardly depictions. Lou Thesz was the consummate wrestler and mentor. He was the kind of person whom every mother would want her daughter to marry. Bruno Sammartino was the epitome of an underdog taking on villains and always winning in the end. Bobo Brazil was the frontrunner in the fight for equality for black Americans. In the ring, he had to endure hardcore racism, but he, like Sammartino, dominated in the end.

Today's heroes and villains look different from those of the past, but the messages are the same. In addition to the costume changes, many modern characters change quickly from babyfaces to heels and vice versa. Hulk Hogan has been both. For years, he dressed in yellow and red, and prompted his fans (Hulkamaniacs) to take their vitamins and say their prayers. In 1996, he shocked the wrestling world by turning into the vilest villain imaginable. He then told his Hulkamaniacs that they were stupid for listening to him in the past. With his turn came a costume change. The red and yellow changed to somber black.

Bret Hart was a babyface for years. While making his entrance, he would shake the youngsters' hands and eventually give a lucky child a pair of his sunglasses. In 1997, he turned heel, and now all he gives the fans are dirty looks and vile insults. His black and pink attire changed to mostly black with a little white.

The underlying factor of the character portrayal of wrestlers is good vs. evil—cowboys vs. Indians; cops vs. robbers; Americans vs. foreigners and so on. Over the years, virtually every aspect of life has been "represented" inside the ring.

Take the Iranian hostage crisis, for instance. In 1979, the government of Iran held 252 Americans hostage in the U.S. Embassy in Teheran. Shortly after, the Iron Sheik made his ring debut in America. He is an actual Iranian, and his ring persona included much U.S.-bashing. At the time, he was the ultimate heel.

Let's go to 1991. The United States fought Iraq in Desert Storm. Prior to the beginning of hostilities, Sgt. Slaughter, the epitome of American greatness, a military drill instructor, changed sides and supported Iraq. His two managers were portrayed as Iraqi colonels. Actually, one, Col. Mustafa, was the Iron Sheik, an Iranian. In reality, Iran and Iraq were not on the best of terms. They had just finished a war in which over two million people died, so it was ironic that the WWF should use an Iranian to portray an Iraqi colonel. Vince McMahon did not let the facts get in the way of a good angle. After all, what's the difference between a Persian and an Arab? They both have dark skin.

The nationalistic angles in wrestling gained their beginnings after World War II. Many heels of the day were Germans or Japanese. The wrestlers who played the parts were dastardly heels, despite the fact that the closest to Germany that the Germans had ever been was New York City, and the less-than-human Japanese wrestlers ironically had absolutely no Asian accent when they spoke their unmistakable English with a heavy American intonation. As in today's angles, the fans did not take these questionable inaccuracies into account. They booed the heels like they had just arrived from Berlin or Tokyo.

Feuds, over the years, have varied in length. Some have lasted one or two matches. Many last a few months and are some of the best-known because the audience has a chance to savor every nuance and progression in the feud as the angle develops. Some feuds last years. Killer Kowalski and Bruno Sammartino were mortal enemies for 17 years. Once, Kowalski was asked what kind of worker Bruno was when he was wrestling someone else. He said, "I don't know. I never saw Bruno wrestle anyone else. Every time he and I were in the same building, we wrestled each other."

Today's feuds and angles generally last a few weeks or months. This is enough time to build up the angle and for the promoters to make adjustments as they go along. Every so often, an angle is a dud from the beginning and is terminated, usually with no fanfare and no explanation to the fans of its demise.

The feuds and angles of the Golden Age were quite simple—the good guy vows to kick someone's ass because he made life difficult for him through deceit and dastardly deeds.

From the beginning of the 1990s, the angles have become more complicated and contemporary. The basic "I'll kick your ass" theme is still there, but the bad guys have elevated their shenanigans. Take Papa Shango, for instance. He would wrestle his opponent and, at an opportune time, usually when he was getting the merde kicked out of him, he mysteriously implanted a green slimelike substance on his opponent, rendering him helpless. No explanation was ever given about the substance or how Papa Shango delivered it. It just happened.

Papa Shango used a mysterious substance to halt his opponents, yet some figures possessed enigmatic characteristics which made them appear to be immortal as they defied the laws of physics. Over the years, The Undertaker has risen from the dead several times. At times, he has disappeared for months after being stuffed into his own casket by a bevy of bad guys, only to reappear with a vengeance.

The Ultimate Warrior also possessed supernatural powers. He appeared and disappeared through clouds of smoke. His voice was heard in arenas, but he was not there. He had the power to transmit his voice through the air to the designated venue without aid of modern technology. It just happened.

Let's go to the theme of cowboy vs. Indian. Later in this book, there is a scene about Cowboy Bill Halliday and his bouts against Chief Jay Strongbow. At least, in professional wrestling, the Indian was usually the good guy and the cowboy the heel, rendering more accuracy to history than Hollywood ever did.

As with the Nazis and Japanese, ring Indians many times were not what the promotions said they were. Chief Jay Strongbow had about as much Indian blood in him as did Winston Churchill. He was an Italian-American. Various other lesser-known Indian characters, who had no Native American ancestry, have graced the ring over the years.

One modern Indian actually was an Indian—Tatanka. His real name is Chris Chavis. For the first portion of his WWF tenure, he was the loyal Native American who wrestled for the pride of his people. His opponents were the worst of the worst. IRS humiliated him by tearing apart his feathered headgear that was given to him by Chief Jay Strongbow. Tatanka's leadership role for Native Americans was short-lived. He met his mentor, Strongbow, in the ring and after a hug and handshake, Tatanka proceeded to beat the hell out of Strongbow and tore apart his Indian feathers. Why did he do this? Greed. He had sold out to the Million Dollar Man, a new ally who was once a hated adversary.

Religion has come into play in professional wrestling. At the time of the outing of various charlatan TV evangelists, the WWF hatched its own version—Brother Love. He was a sleazy individual who was always drooling. Love's red face looked like that of the local wino after a day's drinking. He allied himself with the scum of wrestling, all under the guise of preaching love. He only loved money and the favors the bad guys could do for him.

Another religious angle occurred during the Stone Cold Steve Austin and Jake "The Snake" Roberts feud. In mirroring reality, Roberts, who, in real life, had been an alcoholic and drug addict, returned to the WWF and relayed the message of doom for those who were addicts. He began preaching and making biblical comments. Stone Cold finally won the last bout of their feud and stated to Roberts, "Let me quote you something from Austin 3:16. I just kicked your ass." By the way, Austin's sacrilegious statement became the logo for the best-selling T-shirt that the WWF has ever produced.

Professional wrestling is not above taking a real tragedy and exploiting it on the screen. Brian Pillman unexpectedly died while he was receiving a big push in the WWF. The night after his death, his wife was interviewed for *Monday Night Raw*, the WWF's leading cable TV show. It was tacky.

When Louie Spicolli died suddenly, the feud between him and Larry Zybysko did not end. A few days later, Zybysko tastelessly criticized Spicolli on television. Maybe no one told Zybysko that the feud was a work and should have stopped with Spicolli's death.

The line between reality and fantasy is many times blurred in professional wrestling. Sometimes, however, there is a blatant distinction that embarrasses the wrestling promotions and can lead to serious implications. For example, when a wrestler is supposedly hurt to the point of not being able to continue, there are "medics" by the handful at ringside within seconds. They surround the wrestler and carefully put him on a stretcher, all the time playing to the emotions of the fans.

On the other hand, when a wrestler is truly seriously hurt, a recovery team is hard-pressed to come to ringside in a timely manner. In 1998, Buff Bagwell took a piledriver off the top rope and landed on his head, compressing part of his spine. He was motionless in the middle of the ring. This was a real, life-threatening injury, and there was no way to immediately get him out of the ring. WCW began to show reruns of the previous week's show. After a few minutes, Bagwell was still in the ring, and the fans were still watching the reruns. Eventually, medics finally did arrive and carried the injured wrestler out.

This confusion of reality and fiction can contribute to a serious injury elevating before help is on the way. Perhaps Bagwell's injury will serve as a wakeup call so the promotions always have legitimate medical help available to respond in seconds, not minutes, in the event of real injuries.

Television is almost everything to professional wrestling today. Years ago, television was used much in the same way it was for other sports—an event was televised to show the inevitable outcome of a winner and loser. The history occurred as the event was happening. Today, however, the angles and feuds are determined by television, and the history is predetermined to enhance TV ratings.

WCW and the WWF are extremely popular on television. Recent ratings show that five of the top cable TV shows are wrestling productions from the big two promotions. Weekly, the number one- and number two-rated programs are wrestling programs. Professional wrestling has taken over a portion of the cable TV industry. All the angles are aimed at the viewers of two shows—*Monday Night Raw* for the WWF and *Monday Nitro* for WCW.

There is an extension to the weekly shows—pay-per-view cable TV events. Both promotions show several a year, including the highly popular *Fall Brawl, Bash at the Beach* and *Road Wild* for WCW, and *Wrestlemania*, the *Royal Rumble* and *Summerslam* for the WWF.

The angles that keep viewers glued to their seats during *Nitro* and *Raw* become elevated close to the time of an organization's pay-per-view event. Again, we see a funneling of the angles pointing in one direction. In other words, television dictates the length and depth of angles and feuds, where, in the past, television merely showed the results of the feuds for the viewers.

Today's angles for professional wrestling mirror society. An organization will find a subject and then escalate it to the absurd. At first when the organizations, particularly the WWF, began to become more hardcore, there was a small outburst of protest from moralists, but even that has subsided with the enormous popularity of contemporary themes.

Nationalism is in vogue again. Bret Hart, a Canadian, began to criticize the U.S. At his matches, fans screamed at him and booed. The inevitable sign appeared at one of his matches—"Nuke Canada." Hart switched from the WWF to WCW, so the WWF had to find a new America-basher. Admirably, Tiger Ali Singh from India filled the void. He now ridicules the American public for not having any taste or intelligence. The signs in the audience display the fans' dislike of Singh's anti-American message.

Another of Hart's anti-American successors is Alex Wright, a young and competent wrestler who hails from Germany. For a couple of years, Wright was a mid-level babyface performer. In 1998, he turned heel and gave WCW a counter to the WWF's Singh. Wright began to call Americans stupid while extolling the virtues of German mental superiority. His message was no different from that of nationalistic (supposed) German professional wrestling heels of the 1950s. Ironically, the heel-turn helped elevate Wright's in-ring status, and he became a just-below-main-event wrestler with WCW, appearing weekly on WCW *Monday Nitro*.

Homophobia arose with the transformation of Dustin Runnells into Goldust. The new character took to the ring dressed in a shiny gold outfit. He acted effeminate, but all the time he still was an astute wrestler. One of his "moves" was to kiss his opponent on the lips, and when the adversary showed signs of disbelief and disgust, Runnells would gain victory in the confusion.

Throughout Runnells' tenure as Goldust, fellow wrestlers gave him such oral accolades as pervert and weirdo. During an interview in which Goldust touched Vince McMahon's shoulder, the head man told the wrestler, "Get your filthy hands off me, you pervert" (a gesture dating directly back to Gorgeous George).

Signs in the audience reflected the homophobia running through the fabric of American society—"Goldust is a faggot; Goldust is queer." Those are a couple of the less volatile messages the fans sent to Runnels.

Memories are short, however, in wrestling. After a few months, McMahon told the fans that Goldust is not gay. He is just an eccentric. Now the fans cheered the same wrestler with the same outfit, who only a few short weeks before was disgusting. McMahon had a memory lapse as well: he forgot what he had called Goldust during the aforementioned interview.

A source of creative humor comes from the TV announcers. For years, Bobby Heenan was the nemesis of Gorilla Monsoon and then Vince McMahon in the broadcasting booth. Heenan always stuck up for the bad guys and his persona came off as less than sincere. He was a dastardly companion for the good guys at the announcer's table, always scheming how to thwart them in their activities.

Heenan eventually went to greener (as in money) pastures with WCW. He is still a superb heel announcer, yet his sharp edge has been honed, and at times he almost comes across as a normal guy.

When Heenan left the WWF, a wrestling veteran took his place—Jerry "The King" Lawler. Lawler's character is far above anything else that wrestling had ever seen or heard. He is the ultimate slimeball, bad guy, liar and thief.

Lawler has been involved with so many angles that it would take a book just to list them all. For instance, he had a feud with Bret Hart because he always criticized Hart's parents. He became quite base when he made reference to their ages and physical appearance.

From his introduction to WWF fans until today, Lawler always has had something up his sleeve. Ironically, when he suckers someone into the ring and the plan unfolds for that wrestler's demise, no one is available to come to the rescue of the unwitting dupe.

Lawler is without peer in the art of the insult. Once, Bob Holly was wrestling, and Lawler was merciless on him about his Alabama heritage. Finally, Vince McMahon, then a babyface announcer, asked Lawler, "What is wrong with people from Alabama?" to which Lawler responded, "This guy's so southern he's related to himself."

James Cornette could be considered a runner-up to Lawler in the insult department, although his time behind the microphone has been much less than the King's. When Scott Hall was wrestling in the WWF as Razor Ramon, he was a babyface. Hall's set statement at the time was that he was "oozing machismo." One time, he was making his ring entrance when Vince McMahon stated, "Here comes Razor Ramon, oozing machismo." Cornette countered with, "He's oozing something, but penicillin will take care of that."

Sometimes individuals in wrestling possess physical characteristics which make them open game for both the babyface and the heel announcers. Paul Bearer is a chubby individual who for years was a babyface manager for The Undertaker. Recently, he went through a heel change and now is the enemy of his former protégé. At the Slammy Awards (WWF version of the Academy Awards) of 1996 he was still a babyface. Lawler and McMahon both made reference to his physical appearance—McMahon: "If he's as smart as he is grotesque, he must be Einstein." Lawler: "Is that Paul Bearer's face, or did his butt grow a nose?"

The concept of professional wrestling has changed little in the past 50 years. Feuds and angles propel the sport. Today's angles are contemporary and more comprehensive than the angles of yesteryear, but they are still angles.

There is one aspect of professional wrestling that has changed immensely from the Golden Age, however—perception. The celebrity aura of the 1990s has reached deep into wrestling. Instead of shunning the sport, athletes in various sports are lining up to become grapplers after their own careers wind down. Steve McMichael, former NFL star, is now a mainstay in WCW. There was no shame involved in his decision. Kevin Greene is still an all-star performer in the NFL, but in the off-season, he participates in professional wrestling.

Football is not the only sport from which future pro grapplers will come. Dennis Rodman, a premier rebounder in the NBA, has already transformed his unorthodox basketball career and lifestyle to a ring characterization. He has wrestled at several WCW pay-per-views as a lowly heel in cahoots with the most despicable wrestling group, the NWO led by Hollywood Hulk Hogan. An NBA comrade of Rodman, Karl Malone, a lifelong wrestling fan, has taken to the ring in a babyface role. Both have indicated that they might want a professional wrestling career when they retire from basketball.

Other celebrities have become involved with wrestling in the 1990s. Instead of looking at their participation in shame, they actually regard it as career-enhancing. Among those who have been part of wrestling angles are: Pamela Anderson, Jay Leno, Pete Rose, Mike Tyson and William Shatner. None had to take part in a wrestling angle solely for the sake of money. They performed because they wanted to.

Professional wrestling can be very eloquent in its presentation. Some of the plots are deep and comprehensive, while others are base. One thing is certain: current angles keep millions of people eagerly awaiting in anticipation for the following week's conclusion of an angle. Usually, however, instead of seeing the end of an angle, the next week's show invariably will enhance the angle and complicate it so the fans will have to wait another week to see its conclusion—a conclusion that never comes.

Professional wrestling is the ultimate soap opera. No other sport can begin to come close to wresting for intrigue. Then again, no other sport pre-writes its history or conclusions. Shakespeare had the luxury of creating plots without paying homage to actual history and became the most famous writer in the English language. In this sense, professional wrestling is the "Shakespeare of Sports."

*** ***

SCENE IV

LIKE TRYIN' TO TELL A STRANGER ABOUT ROCK 'N' ROLL

Whether any adult American wants to admit it or not, most have been affected by professional wrestling. Very few members of the post–World War II baby-boomer society can claim that they have never seen a professional wrestling match, and fewer still, if they are telling the truth, can assert that they did not enjoy professional wrestling in their younger years.

Television was in its infancy when professional wrestling first graced the airwaves. Those days represent mystical times for today's population that is over the age of 40. Let's take a few individuals and read what they have to say about those less stressful and more idyllic times.

NAME: Phil Paulson AGE: 49
OCCUPATION: University professor
FAVORITE OLD-TIME: Gorgeous George, Larry Hennig, Ricky Starr
FAVORITE MODERN: Bob Backlund, Psycho Sid

Today, Paulson is 6'4" tall and weighs 300 pounds. At age 14, he was as tall as he is today, but a few inches slimmer in the waistline.

Phil Paulson was born and raised in Clayton, Wisconsin, a small town of 325 residents in the northern part of the dairy state. He stated that the postmaster knew not only the names of every resident of Clayton, but the names of all the dogs and cats of the town as well.

In 1952, Paulson's father, the owner of a small business that sold tractors, bought the first television set ever seen in Clayton, an RCA Victor with a small, round screen. Before long, over 100 people packed the shop's office to watch professional wrestling on Thursday evenings. Paulson said, "I and the other kids would sit on the floor while the adults stood up to watch the matches."

According to Paulson, Clayton had its own version of the classic village idiot of medieval times in a slightly retarded individual designated by the townspeople as "Johnny Dollar the Scholar." One evening, as the crowd was assembled in the smoke-filled office, Paulson's father heard noises coming from the front of the store. He ran out and quickly hollered, "Johnny, what the hell are you doing?" He saw that Johnny was attempting to cut down a pillar that was holding the building up. Johnny explained, "I bought a new saw and wanted to see if it worked." By now, most of the wrestling fans had come to the front of the store to see the reason behind all the commotion. After the chaos subsided, one townsperson expressed his feelings to the would-be Paul Bunyon, "Johnny, you fool. You ruined the whole match!"

Within a couple of years, other residents of Clayton had purchased television sets, and the close-knit community came to experience interesting new situations. According to Paulson, "My neighbor would be screaming and hollering, and everybody in town at first thought he was beating up his wife. In those days, one never approached a family about such matters. You just tried to ignore it. Eventually, you would hear her screaming too. She would say, 'Go ahead and hit him. Beat the living shit out of him,' and then you would hear the kids screaming, so we thought he was beating the kids.

"Finally, somebody had the balls to approach him and ask if he was beating his kids. The town drunk, 'Beer' Rubin, came into the barbershop one day and asked Rogers what the hell was going on in his house every Thursday night. Rubin then elaborated by inquiring whether Rogers was beating up his wife and kids. Rogers took the towel off his head and queried, 'Beer Rubin, are you crazy? That's when I watch professional wrestling.'"

Paulson enjoyed fighting as a teenager and perceived his high school football career to be an extension of his recreational brawling. He said, "In football, I perfected a cross-body block that resulted in career-ending injuries to at least 15 players. I was a mean son of a bitch."

At age 18, Paulson migrated to Minneapolis, Minnesota, to try his hand at working in a big city. He moved into the YMCA because of its reasonable price for room rentals. On his way to the gym to work out, Paulson used to pass a door on which hung a sign that read "Wrestling Room." One day, while in the weight room, Paulson saw two people enter the wrestling room. He went to the door and could hear them slamming each other, and when he peaked in, he saw them practicing all sorts of acrobatics, so he entered the room and sat on a bench to watch the two wrestlers.

According to Paulson, "One of the wrestlers asked me, 'Hey, what do you think? Are you enjoying yourself?' I asked, 'Do you want me to leave?' and he replied, 'How would you like to become a professional wrestler?' I answered, 'Yeah,' and he extended an invitation to 'show me the ropes.' He had a devilish look in his eyes, and I knew something was up. He said, 'In order to become a professional wrestler, you must learn to endure pain.' I told him, 'I can handle a lot of pain.'

"He really messed me up. After a 20-minute workout, every muscle in my body ached for a week. I thought every bone in my body was broken. I had to crawl to the locker room and take a shower on all fours.

"As I was dragging myself out of the wrestling room, I asked somebody, 'Who is that?' pointing at the person who had just turned me inside-out. The bystander, perplexed at my lack of knowledge of the identity of my tormentor, said, 'That's Pretty Boy Hennig.' I then went to my room and slept for 18 hours."

Unknown to Paulson at the time, Pretty Boy Hennig was one of the world's premier, and meanest, professional wrestlers. His son, Curt, has been one of modern day's top wrestlers for the past decades, grappling under his own name as well as "Mr. Perfect."

Despite his experience with Hennig, Paulson retained his admiration for professional wrestling. With his indoctrination into the squared circle, however, he decided to choose another field of employment. Paulson concluded, "I decided against becoming a professional wrestler and took an easier profession—two months later, I was a soldier on the way to Vietnam."

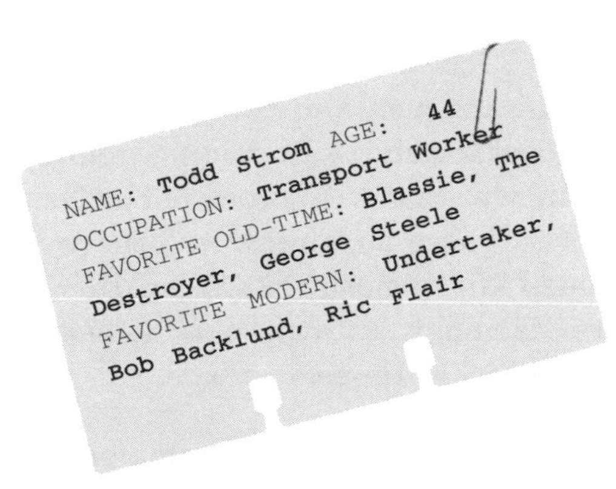

NAME: Todd Strom AGE: 44
OCCUPATION: Transport Worker
FAVORITE OLD-TIME: Blassie, The Destroyer, George Steele
FAVORITE MODERN: Undertaker, Bob Backlund, Ric Flair

Todd Strom was 12 years old when he awoke to the allure of professional wrestling. One day, he was watching a local broadcast and saw Hardy Kreutzkamp introduce a card which he promoted from the E-Street Gym in San Diego. Within minutes, Strom was hooked.

Eventually, wrestling gained a larger audience on the West Coast as Los Angeles station KTLA began to broadcast matches. (Dick "Whoa Nelly" Lane was the show's presenter and later became a legendary wrestling broadcaster.) Strom now could watch two wrestling shows a week, all the time developing an unquenchable thirst for the sport.

When he was 14 years old, on Wednesday evenings, Strom and about a dozen friends would converge on the house of a comrade and begin a bizarre pre-match ritual. "We used to buy up all the toy slot cars in the neighborhood, stuff the cars with newspapers, set them on fire and run the cars into the fireplace. When the cars reached the kerosene-soaked wood, they ignited the fire," Strom said. He used the term "Anarchy City" to describe the venue and events of Wednesday evenings.

"Anarchy City flourished for a few years until one of the group was drafted into the army," Strom added. After that, he would still occasionally watch wrestling at home, and he and his friends would wrestle in his yard and put all the holds they saw on television to good use. "In school, we'd piss off the gym instructor. He wanted us to wrestle Greco-Roman style, and we'd throw figure-four leglocks and hammerlocks on each other."

After high school, Strom's interest in wrestling waned, but it did not disappear. He talks of the shows emanating from the Olympic Coliseum in Los Angeles that were promoted by Gene and Pat LeBell. Strom said, "These guys were it. They were the giants of the West Coast." Nostalgically, Strom talks about various regional wrestlers of the day, stating, "Wild Red Berry was berserk. He was Psycho Sid 18 times over."

Like most adult male Americans, Strom became serious after his teenage years and had to execute mundane tasks, such as working and making a living, so professional wrestling took a back seat to other pursuits. In the late 1980s, he was channel surfing on his television set when something caught his eye—Piper's Pit, a portion of a WWF broadcast in which Rowdy Roddy Piper vented his views to the world. According to Strom, "That snapped me to attention. This was a whole new dimension—a wrestler having his own part of the show." Piper's Pit turned Strom on to a new generation of wrestlers. He told of being impressed with Jim "The Anvil" Neidhardt, the Hart Foundation and Jake "The Snake" Roberts.

Since rediscovering professional wrestling, Strom has not looked back. Today, he enjoys the matches as much as he did while he watched them at Anarchy City; however, he has stopped his unorthodox method of lighting fireplaces. Instead, he sits on a comfortable couch; uses his remote control to tune his stereo, color TV; opens a beer and relaxes for the next hour or two as he enjoys watching the best of contemporary sports entertainment.

Milton Simms grew up and obtained his introduction to pro wrestling in Red Bank, New Jersey, in 1959. According to Simms, "I saw Haystack Calhoun. My father was into wrestling and got me interested."

Simms points out how wrestling in the late 1950s and early 1960s differed from today's version, "In those days I watched wrestling every Saturday morning. The act was in the ring, not outside. There weren't any colorful announcers in my neck of the woods. Some wrestlers had costumes, but very few. It was still like watching wrestling matches from out of the '30s."

Simms also brings up other major differences between wrestling then and now that many fans may have overlooked. "In those days, most main matches were two-out-of-three falls. Also, there were a lot more women's matches, although the women weren't as attractive as they are today. There was a lot of midget wrestling, too."

Wrestling represents more than just entertainment to Simms. He and his father were close, but lived thousands of miles apart, so they maintained a keen telephone relationship. In 1995, Simms' father unexpectedly passed away. Simms said, "My father and I used to argue about who were the more skillful wrestlers. Until he recently passed away, we would argue over the phone about the same subject. It was a 35-year ongoing debate."

Simms' affinity for wrestling reached its pinnacle during the Bob Backlund era of 1978–1984. He recalls all of Backlund's adversaries and how the six-year champ defeated all comers until the Iron Sheik put an end to Backlund's reign in December 1983. After the Backlund era, Simms stopped watching wrestling, but almost a decade later, he began to watch again. The main reason for his return was an article about wrestling he was commissioned to write for a sports magazine. Simms had remarried and discovered that his second wife's brother-in-law had been a professional wrestler in the 1960s and early 1970s. He wrote a superb piece about the travels and experiences of a journeyman wrestler.

With his interest piqued, Simms now began to analyze wrestling from the previous era and today. "What went on in the '80s is totally different from today. There are many more running rivalries today, such as Bret Hart vs. Owen Hart, Razor Ramon vs. The 1-2-3 Kid and Diesel vs. The Undertaker."

In late 1995, Simms enjoyed his first live professional wrestling match. He attended a card at the San Diego Sports Arena that totally amazed even him, a veteran wrestling fan. "There was so much more to watching it live. It's like reading *Mad* magazine. There is so much going on in the background."

Simms went on to say that today's holds are more diverse than those of yesteryear. "There are many more holds today. However, some holds, such as the sleeper, were not particular to only a few wrestlers. In the old days, everybody and his brother used the sleeper."

Simms began to mention Argentine Rocca, when a voice from another room (his wife's) injected, "He (Rocca) was my grandmother's favorite. My grandmother made us watch wrestling. We only had one channel. We knew all the wrestlers, but Rocca had real flair, jumping off the ropes." Simms continued to give his comparisons between the old days and today. "I think there were more so-called rules being enforced back then. In addition, there were more mismatches; you know, a stiff being beaten easily by a name wrestler."

To conclude, Simms related Bob Backlund's two careers which spanned two professional wrestling eras. "The new Backlund (post–1993) is much more exciting. Yeah, I liked the old Backlund (1978–1984), but we were in a different period then. Today his entire personality is better. He was more boring back then. He came out and did his job. Backlund's character back then would not go over today."

Frank Morrow has appeared weekly on Public Access TV since 1979, as the presenter of an award-winning political commentary, *Alternative Views*.

Despite a life-long insatiable appetite for politics, professional wrestling has, at times, played a part in Morrow's life. According to Morrow, "I used to go to wrestling matches back in the mid-1930s with my parents. When I was about four years old I would jump up and down on the seats and yell, 'Kill him! Kill him!'" He remembers that the action in the ring was not as flamboyant as that offered to today's fans. "I can recall that one wrestler would put a hold on the other and hold it for a few minutes. There were no acrobatics like today."

In the late summer of 1951, Morrow was hired for his first job in radio at KACK in Tulsa, Oklahoma. Ironically, the station owner, Sam Avey, also owned the Tulsa Coliseum and at that time began to promote professional wrestling shows. Morrow was not involved in the wrestling aspect of Avey's empire, but he recalled talking to a wrestling announcer who was thinking about quitting. According to Morrow, "He told me he was tired of having blood spilled on him."

After a few years of disk jockey duties at KACK, Morrow was given the assignment of interviewing various personalities, and at times wrestlers were on the other side of the microphone. His first interview with a grappler came in 1956, and he started at the top, interviewing Gorgeous George.

Morrow was not a wrestling fan and had never heard of the famed wrestler with the golden locks. According to Morrow, the interview began on a sour note. "I asked him when he was going to get his hair fixed. He got pissed off and said, 'I already got it fixed.'" When asked about his impression of Gorgeous George, Morrow responded, "He was a lot bigger in person than he looked in the ring."

After his first interview with a wrestler, Morrow became more accustomed to talking with the professional grapplers. His favorite personality was Farmer Jones.

Morrow had to pick him up and give him a ride to the studio. "He couldn't fit in the front seat of my VW van. I had to open the side doors. When we began to move, the car tilted." After four decades, Morrow still remembers Farmer Jones and his easygoing persona. "Farmer would always say, 'I love to get in and scramble with those boys.'"

After he had interviewed a few wrestlers, Morrow began to become aware of the big names and their reputations. He had heard the name Ed "Strangler" Lewis quite a few times, and his fame piqued Morrow's interest. Morrow stated, "I heard he developed this choke hold."

Morrow never interviewed Strangler Lewis, yet he did meet him. "I was a nighttime disk jockey at the time. The studio was down in the basement of the building. You could hear the rats running around. One night at about 11:00, the buzzer rang, and I went to the door to see who would be there at that late hour. A big threatening figure stood there. His neck was bigger than his head. He asked threateningly, 'Where is Sam Avey?' I told him I didn't know, and he said, 'Tell him that Ed "Strangler" Lewis is looking for him.' I said, 'Yes, Sir!'" When talking about his chance meeting with Lewis, he recalled, "I came to attention fast." Despite many years of broadcasting experience behind him and meeting and interviewing world famous authors, political activists, journalists and government officials, Morrow still remembers Ed "Strangler" Lewis vividly. He concluded, "I'll never forget that neck."

Charles Haley has been a full-time fan since he saw his first live match at the age of 10 years. "I thought it was funny: good guys and bad guys. From then on, I went regularly with guys who had bigger brothers who would take us."

After a few years of attending live bouts, professional wrestling left town, but the departure of wrestling was only a slight drawback for Haley. "After live wrestling left San Diego, I always watched it on TV. As I got older, I started watching the WWF."

Prior to the WWF's rise in television dominance of wrestling, Haley watched a local channel to view the latest in wrestling entertainment. "When I was younger, I watched it on Channel 6. The matches were from the Olympic Auditorium in Los Angeles—The Destroyer, Mr. Moto, Tricky Ricky Starr, Bruno Sammartino, Killer Kowalski. Guys like Killer Kowalski, they were the original wrestlers. Those guys are the ones who taught the young guys coming up."

Another favorite of Haley's was Fred Blassie about whom he stated, "Blassie was so rude to everybody. He just knocked the hell out of anybody. He'd smack you. He'd go after kids. He didn't care. If you pissed him off, he didn't care who you were. You could be a priest and he'd still smack you. I saw this guy knock the hell out of everybody. All I remember is Fred Blassie hitting somebody. He'd hit you with canes; he'd cold-cock you. If your head was turned one way, he'd smack you the other way. Blassie was one of the most hated wrestlers ever. I hated him more than any wrestler I could think of."

A pinnacle of Haley's wrestling fandom came when he saw Gorgeous George for the first time. He recalled, "I thought Gorgeous George was great. I saw him live and loved him. He was cool."

Like most lifelong wrestling fans, Haley makes a distinction between the old-timers and those who grapple for a living today. "I think the older wrestlers were more physical. Today they're bigger and stronger, but back then, they were pure entertainment. You'd go home after a match and want to wrestle. We built our own ring, me and my younger brother."

The admiration of professional wrestling has transcended generations in the Haley family. There is a possibility that the reverence for the sport may be genetic. Haley said, "My grandson and I watch it all the time now. It's just like soap operas for other people. People ask, 'Why do you watch that stuff?'" Haley must put up with the jeers his friends sometimes aim at him. "Most of my friends laugh and say 'You know that's fake, don't you?' I tell them that it's choreographed, but I'm never going to stop watching it."

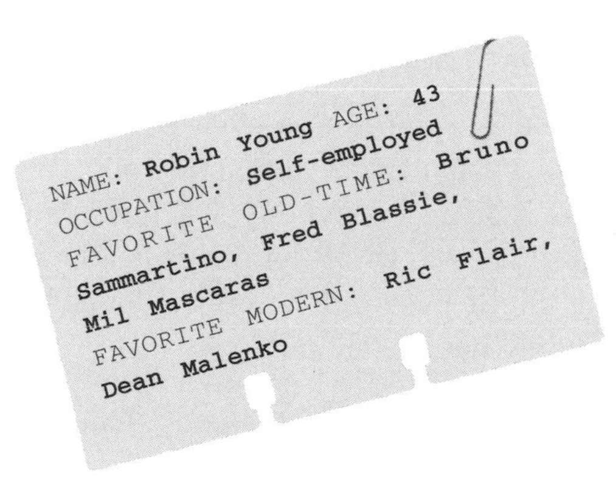

Robin Young has had a diverse career that includes theater, product marketing, physical training. His knowledge of all three have led him to develop a different perspective on wrestling from that of many fans.

He worked in marketing on Wall Street, an experience which taught Young how easily people can be persuaded, therefore creating a distaste for some of wrestling's marketing ploys. His theatrical knowledge has made him astute in discerning between horrible or superb plots, something the average wrestling fan is not encouraged to do by the promoters. Young's physical training background has created an admiration for those wrestlers who are athletic, yet he is adamant in his critique of those grapplers who use artificial means, such as steroids, to enhance their looks and performances.

The enchanted moment of Young's introduction to professional wrestling occurred in late 1969 while he was a 14-year-old junior high school student living in New York City. He said, "I was just turning the channels when, lo and behold, I suddenly saw this monstrous figure with a huge hairy chest, talking into a microphone. I turned the volume up, sat there and watched. The man with the huge chest was Bruno Sammartino, and the man interviewing was Bill Cardille." In recalling his introduction to professional wrestling, Young described the scenario as, "a no frills production. It was a ring and a relatively small studio audience. The ring announcers were ex-Lower East Side tough guys who had developed that slightly affected broadcast voice. It had so much color to it.

"The next week I tuned in, and it was even better than the first week. Within three weeks, I was completely addicted. I was fascinated and was asking everybody I knew about wrestling. Nobody seemed to know a whole lot about it. I heard the rumors that wrestling might not quite be on the level, but at that time I certainly didn't believe them."

Although Young was only in his early teens, he began to analyze the reasons behind his admiration of professional wrestling. Most wrestling fans of his age were only interested in the noncerebral aspects of wrestling, such as who won and who lost. According to Young, "It appealed to me as almost total escapist fare. I was working out myself in those days, and I saw these big muscular guys. For me, they were supermen. I didn't equate them with the human race. I thought they were something way beyond; far more evolved. In terms of suspension of disbelief, I was a perfect mark because I wanted to believe and I found it very easy to believe the story lines and behaviors, no matter how outrageous—a German with armbands and gestapo boots; the crazy Japanese guy throwing salt in his opponent's eyes. I believed in all that."

Within a couple of weeks of his introduction to pro wrestling, Young discovered another televised wrestling promotion. "It was on a UHF station, hosted by Ray Morgan, an elderly man with glasses who was lovable and easy to respect and believe. There was none of the tongue-in-cheek commentary in those days. They were low key and basically described what was happening in the ring. It wasn't as self-serving as it is today."

Robin Young's passion in life was professional wrestling until he began to notice changes in the sport he loved. "I wasn't thrilled with wrestling by the mid-1970s. By the time Sammartino was back in for the second title reign, he had lost a great deal of magic for me. Bruno was 20 or 30 pounds lighter and had changed his overall appearance.

"The opponents were not as colorful. People like Spiros Arion and Nikolai Volkoff were not exciting competitors. In the earlier days, there were guys like The Sheik, Tanaka, and Koloff. During Bruno's second title reign, it was getting more ordinary. The new people coming up were not as exciting as the old-timers. I was weaned on guys like Sammartino and Blassie. Blassie was like a movie star with incredible glamour and magnetism. He was larger than life."

Today's wrestlers do not have the same appeal for Young as those of the sport's "golden era" had. "I don't see anybody with incredible charisma today. I was a huge fan of Gorgeous George and of Ricky Starr, a ballet dancer who jumped around in a ring. I love that stuff. They were absolutely incredible. Starr was a genius at inciting the crowd.

"I think one of the problems with the sport today is that it has become so generic. Every match is the same. The guys master three or four ridiculous maneuvers and that's it. There's no individuality.

"Look at an old card from the '50s. In the first match, you might find a flyer like Ed Carpentier; in the second, you might have Dick Beyer, a mat wrestler; in the next match, Ricky Starr may be doing his arrogant ballet dancer/heel persona; and the next match might be Kowalski in a savage, bloodlust bout. Everything today is basically the same—same moves, same level of energy, nothing distinctive."

Despite Young's criticism of the current version of grappling, one question remains: if contemporary professional wrestling is so mundane compared with the "golden era," why is the sport more popular today than at any time in its history? Young speculated, "It's so popular for the same reason that movies are so popular—people have gotten progressively more stupid. People pay to see a huge blockbuster that is basically a piece of junk. It's popular, but it's not good filmmaking.

"In the past, they tried to keep a certain level of integrity. The promoters wanted to educate the public. Today if you abuse the hell out of the fans, they keep coming back for more. It's a very interesting study in psychology, mass psychology in particular."

Many of today's fans who prefer the style of professional wrestling which was in vogue in the 1950s and 1960s can tell you of their favorite stars of yesteryear, but few can give conclusive reasons behind their affinity for the "golden age." Young, however, is very precise and insightful into why he puts the old days in a higher elevation than today's rendition of professional wrestling. "Aside from the aestheticism and the angles and the moves in the ring, there was a fundamental greatness to a lot of the old-timers. I think Ricky Starr was better than anybody today at all. Look at any pro today and he isn't as good as Ricky Starr. Don't forget, he's only ONE guy from the '50s. There aren't any workers today as good as Dick Beyer (The Destroyer). There aren't any as good as Killer Kowalski. There aren't even any workers as good as The Sheik.

Each and every one of those guys was greater than anybody today. There were a lot of great individuals in the game."

CONCLUSION

It's hard to find anybody who claims to have negative memories of professional wrestling in his or her preteen and early teenage years. However, many of these same people as adults question the sanity of adult fans with full mental capacity.

The naysayers have it all wrong. Being a professional wrestling fan over the age of 14 puts one on another plateau which the uninitiated cannot comprehend. The 1960s rock 'n' roll group The Lovin' Spoonful aptly described the feeling in their 1965 hit song "Do You Believe in Magic?" when they sang,

. . . it's like tryin' to tell a stranger about rock 'n' roll.

Scene IV concludes with an account by Evan Ginzburg, a New York City English teacher. Ginzburg's fanaticism about professional wrestling exceeds that of the average rabid fan. He is the founder, editor and publisher of the monthly newsletter *Wrestling Then & Now.*[1] In the December 1995 issue[2] he spilled his guts about his introduction to, and subsequent adoration of, professional wrestling:

> Unlike director Quentin Tarantino, let's start at the beginning. I'm 12 years old and channel surfing. Manually. No remote back then. Nothing to watch. Until I discover proud Italian Indian Jay Strongbow taking a "pounding"

1. See Act II, Scene II.
2. © 1995, Evan Ginzburg. Reproduced by kind permission of Evan Ginzburg.

and war dancing his way back to victory. I was hooked. Immediately. Passionately. Irrevocably.

Watching that static-filled Spanish station (commercials in Spanish—wrestling English) became the highlight of my week. It didn't matter that most of the bouts were "squashes" (with an occasional tag title thrown in); when you're a total "mark," every match was interesting. Every opponent had the chance of coming back—even if Johnny Rodz had lost 2,000 straight.

I was dumb. It was wonderful.

As time went on, I learned of other wrestling shows; they became a part of the addiction. Wrestling from California's Olympic became one of my passions; I could care less that, it too, was in Spanish. Tolos didn't speak Spanish! Possibly the greatest heel of my time, he'd get on drooling, snarling, screaming; a primeval force. Unstoppable. "Can I use my glove?" he'd scream into the camera years before O.J. Simpson made gloves ominous. And that harmless looking golf glove took on powers beyond my comprehension, as I imagined him clamping that claw on Victor Rivera or Blassie or whomever he was carrying on about. He was maniacal. Magical. To this day, thousands of wrestlers later, he remains one of my all-time favorite heels.

And there was Florida. And Gordon Solie. Solie made any match sound like it was the World Series and Superbowl rolled into one. And with cherished clips from house shows, some of the bouts were just that! The Funks vs. The Briscos. Race and Rhodes. The heat emanated from that TV set. Sizzling. I'd beg my mother to stay up late to watch as it was on at 11:30 at night. And even though I'd be tired in school the next day, she always relented. For it was wrestling. It was religion.

THE MAGAZINES . . .

They were cheap. They were bloody. They generally didn't tell a word of truth (the great *Ring Wrestling* being one of the few exceptions), and they were mine. To study. To cherish. To keep forever. It was a larger-than-life world of crazy. Sheiks and blood-lusting, tooth-sharpening Blassies. And for a 12-year-old, comic-collecting kid, it was a world of real-life superheroes and villains. These men didn't eat and sleep. They fought and bled. And plotted. And sought revenge. And turned on their partners. It was a life of constant drama and action, tragedy and triumph. For a scrawny kid it was almost too exciting to bear.

NIRVANA . . .

June 24, 1974. I can still remember the date. It's like losing your virginity. My first match! I'll never forget it. My heart pounded. The building literally vibrated as the Valiant Brothers worked over Tony Garea as he desperately fought to make the sizzling "hot tag" to his anxious partner Dean Ho. Was it really possible to experience this excitement for only $4?

The answer was YES! Every month. And Tolos was coming to fight Bruno on the next show. John Tolos! The maniac. And each month afterwards there would be something or someone just too amazing to fathom. I'd stare at those tickets on my dresser. Write out the lineups in my notebook at school and study them harder than any textbook.

And when I went to sleep at night, I'd dream about Dawn DeAngleo, the first girl I had a crush on, and Bruno Sammartino. Who else was there?

FINDING OUT . . .

I remember standing outside Madison Square Garden on many occasions, just hoping, praying for a glimpse of one of my heroes. Or even more intense, one of the villains.

It was, as David Letterman said, "More fun than humans should be allowed to have." But there was one catch. The "big kids," those very annoying "big kids" kept telling me wrestling wasn't real.

Sacrilege! How could they even think such a thing? I was offended. Angered. Outraged. Wasn't Bruno Sammartino a holy figure beyond refute? How could HE get involved with anything that wasn't on the "up and up?"

But the more they explained it, the more it made sense. Hey, I was a bright kid. I even skipped eighth grade! And in spite of my elaborate explanations to them as to how very wrong they were, I eventually realized how sadly, tragically right they were. I was disillusioned. I was upset. But it was "in my blood." I got over it.

THE SHAME . . .

There always has been and always will be a stigma attached to being a wrestling fan. Admit it. Live with it. Deal with it.

"You mean you like that WWF stuff?" they'll ask you, disbelief and almost disdain in their tone.
"Uh, no."
"Then what do you like?"
"Well . . . um . . ."

It's hard to explain a Terry Funk and how he's "different." Or a Sabu.

So how do you rationalize to the uninitiated that an inordinate amount of your time is spent catering to a hobby that appeals to nine-year-olds and sometimes DUMB nine-year-olds at that?

Take it a step further. How do you explain spending hundreds of hours a year on a newsletter and annual that attempts to honor a sport that most people mock?

And how do you rationalize that on many vacations you'll visit some wrestling event, or as I did, make a "religious pilgrimage" to a shutdown Olympic Auditorium in Los Angeles "just to see the place?"

The answer is, you can't. So don't bother going into too much detail. If they look at you like you have two heads, it's their problem. Tell 'em the wrestling you like isn't like that Hulk Hogan stuff and let them ponder why a perfectly intelligent adult would enjoy something they "know isn't real."

After all, it's their loss, folks. It's their loss!

*** ***

INTERMISSION

For your visual stimulation, ladies and gentlemen, we now offer you a collage of professional wrestling highlights—
from the past to the present.

Please enjoy this feast of grappling gratification, while we prepare the stage for the remaining acts.

The Promotion

Mike Lano

Bret Hart, addressing the crowd

The late Owen Hart, signing autographs

Mike Lano

courtesy of Mike Lano

Fred Blassie, dripping blood
(inset: A WCW ad featuring Goldberg vs. Curt Hennig)

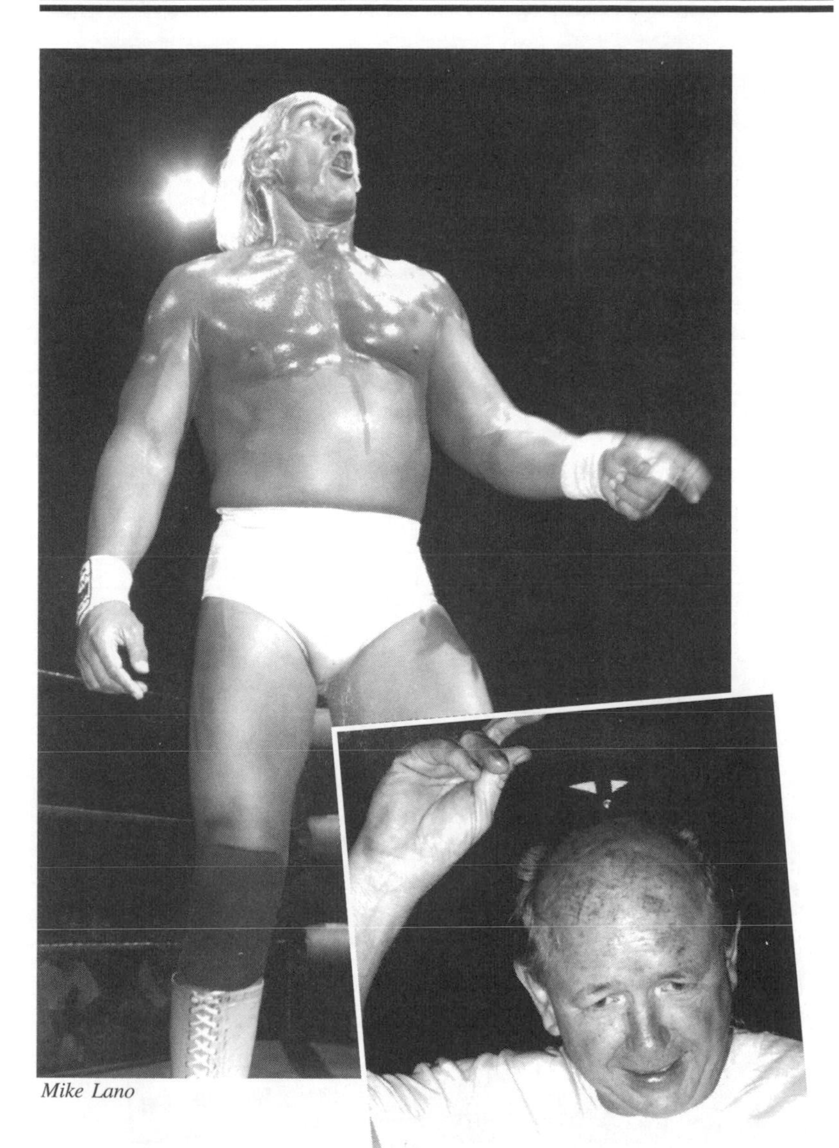

Mike Lano

Mike Lano

top: Hogan, making a ring comeback

right: Dory Funk, showing battle scars

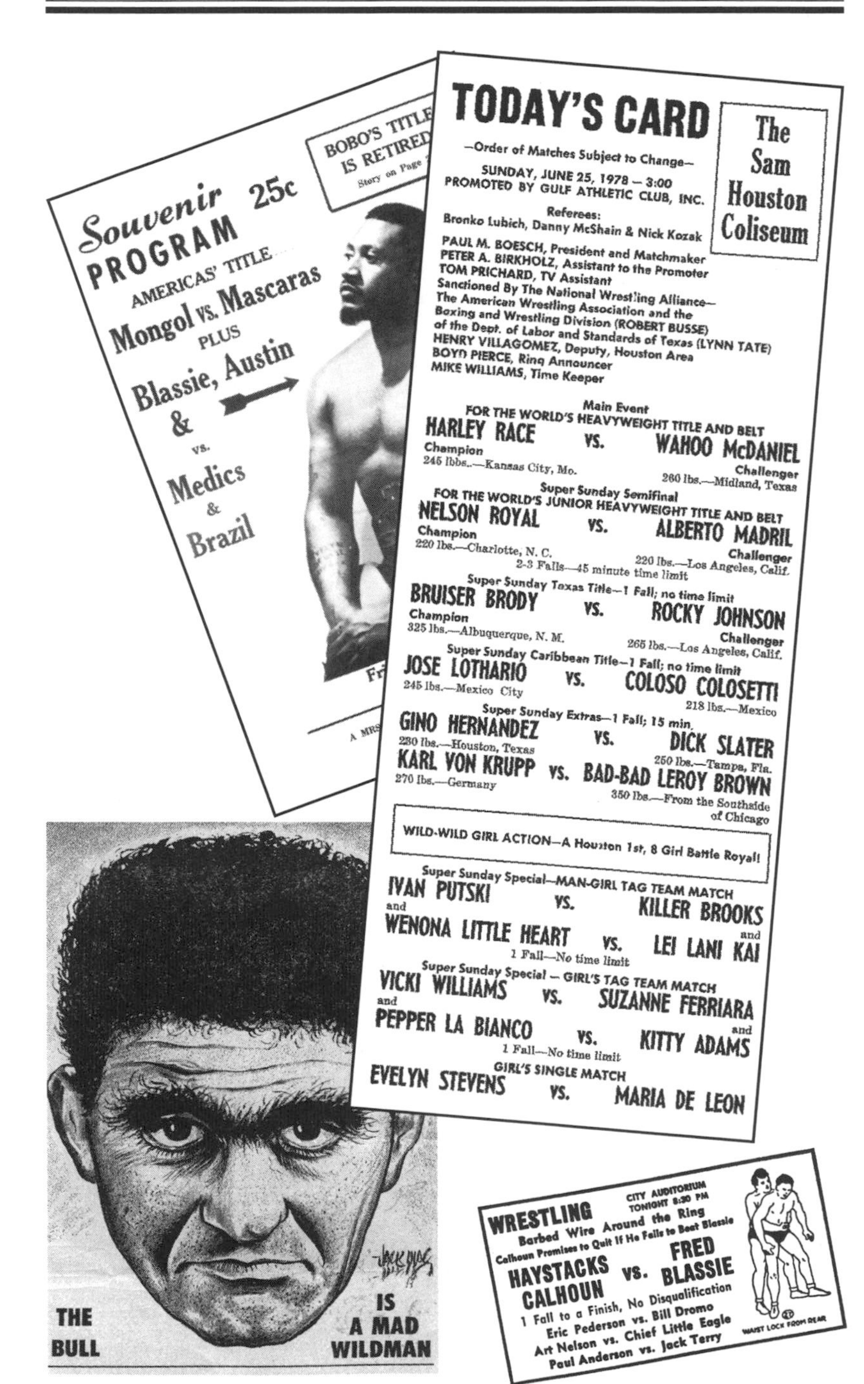
BOBO'S TITLE IS RETIRED
Souvenir PROGRAM 25c
AMERICAS' TITLE
Mongol vs. Mascaras
PLUS
Blassie, Austin
&
vs.
Medics
&
Brazil
TODAY'S CARD
—Order of Matches Subject to Change—
SUNDAY, JUNE 25, 1978 – 3:00
PROMOTED BY GULF ATHLETIC CLUB, INC.
The Sam Houston Coliseum
Referees:
Bronko Lubich, Danny McShain & Nick Kozak
PAUL M. BOESCH, President and Matchmaker
PETER A. BIRKHOLZ, Assistant to the Promoter
TOM PRICHARD, TV Assistant
Sanctioned By The National Wrestling Alliance—
The American Wrestling Association and the
Boxing and Wrestling Division (ROBERT BUSSE)
of the Dept. of Labor and Standards of Texas (LYNN TATE)
HENRY VILLAGOMEZ, Deputy, Houston Area
BOYD PIERCE, Ring Announcer
MIKE WILLIAMS, Time Keeper
Main Event
FOR THE WORLD'S HEAVYWEIGHT TITLE AND BELT
HARLEY RACE vs. WAHOO McDANIEL
Champion
245 lbs.—Kansas City, Mo.
Challenger
260 lbs.—Midland, Texas
Super Sunday Semifinal
FOR THE WORLD'S JUNIOR HEAVYWEIGHT TITLE AND BELT
NELSON ROYAL vs. ALBERTO MADRIL
Champion
220 lbs.—Charlotte, N. C.
Challenger
220 lbs.—Los Angeles, Calif.
2-3 Falls—45 minute time limit
Super Sunday Texas Title—1 Fall; no time limit
BRUISER BRODY vs. ROCKY JOHNSON
Champion
325 lbs.—Albuquerque, N. M.
Challenger
265 lbs.—Los Angeles, Calif.
Super Sunday Caribbean Title—1 Fall; no time limit
JOSE LOTHARIO vs. COLOSO COLOSETTI
245 lbs.—Mexico City
218 lbs.—Mexico
Super Sunday Extras—1 Fall; 15 min.
GINO HERNANDEZ vs. DICK SLATER
230 lbs.—Houston, Texas
250 lbs.—Tampa, Fla.
KARL VON KRUPP vs. BAD-BAD LEROY BROWN
270 lbs.—Germany
350 lbs.—From the Southside of Chicago
WILD-WILD GIRL ACTION—A Houston 1st, 8 Girl Battle Royal!
Super Sunday Special—MAN-GIRL TAG TEAM MATCH
IVAN PUTSKI and WENONA LITTLE HEART vs. KILLER BROOKS and LEI LANI KAI
1 Fall—No time limit
Super Sunday Special – GIRL'S TAG TEAM MATCH
VICKI WILLIAMS and PEPPER LA BIANCO vs. SUZANNE FERRIARA and KITTY ADAMS
1 Fall—No time limit
GIRL'S SINGLE MATCH
EVELYN STEVENS vs. MARIA DE LEON
THE BULL IS A MAD WILDMAN
WRESTLING
CITY AUDITORIUM
TONIGHT 8:30 PM
Barbed Wire Around the Ring
Calhoun Promises to Quit If He Fails to Beat Blassie
HAYSTACKS CALHOUN vs. FRED BLASSIE
1 Fall to a Finish, No Disqualification
Eric Pederson vs. Bill Dromo
Art Nelson vs. Chief Little Eagle
Paul Anderson vs. Jack Terry
WAIST LOCK FROM REAR

Mike Lano

Ric Flair

Mike Lano

Mike Lano

Legendary wrestling managers:
Lou Albano & Jimmy Hart

Mike Lano

Public Enemy in action

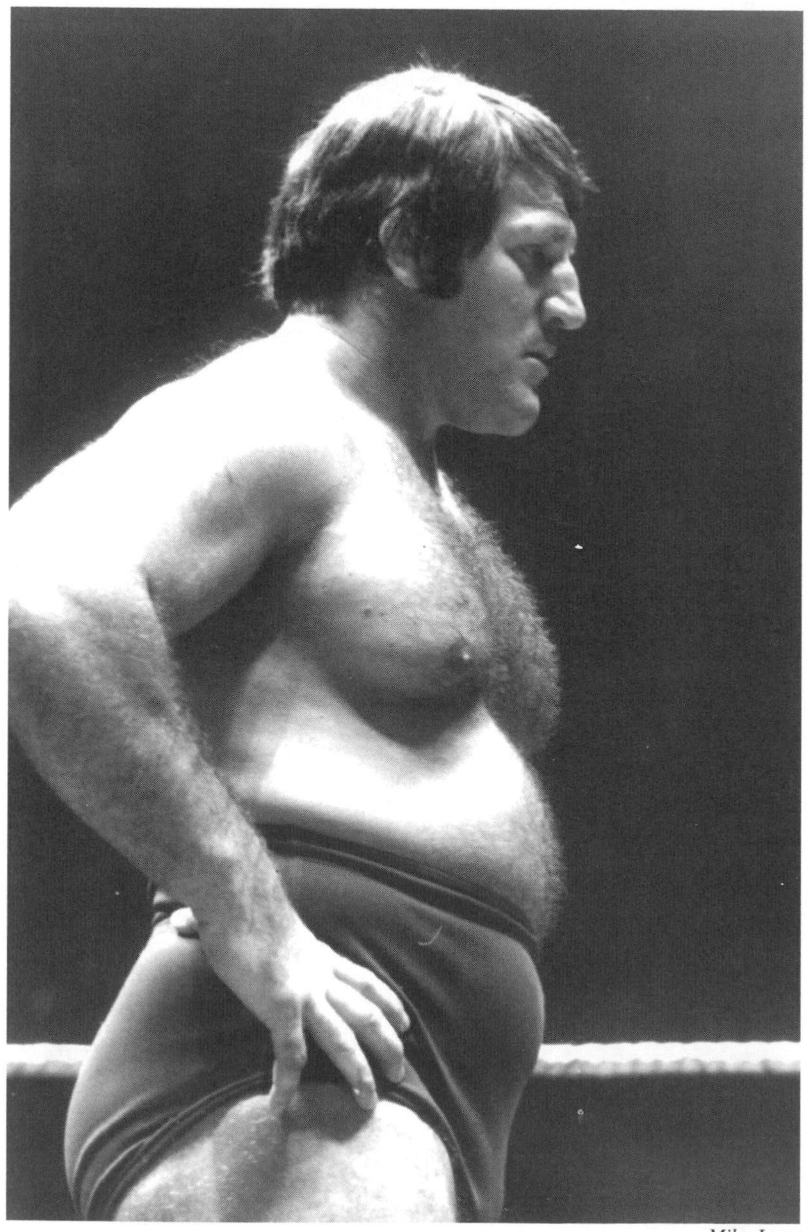

Mike Lano

Bruno Sammartino in one classic pose . . .

Mike Lano

. . . and another

A 1998 *Monday Nitro* card featuring the current crop of WCW stars

Mike Lano

Psycho Sid at a WCW SuperBrawl

Mike Lano

Mike Lano

above:
Shane Douglas

right:
The
Valiant Brothers

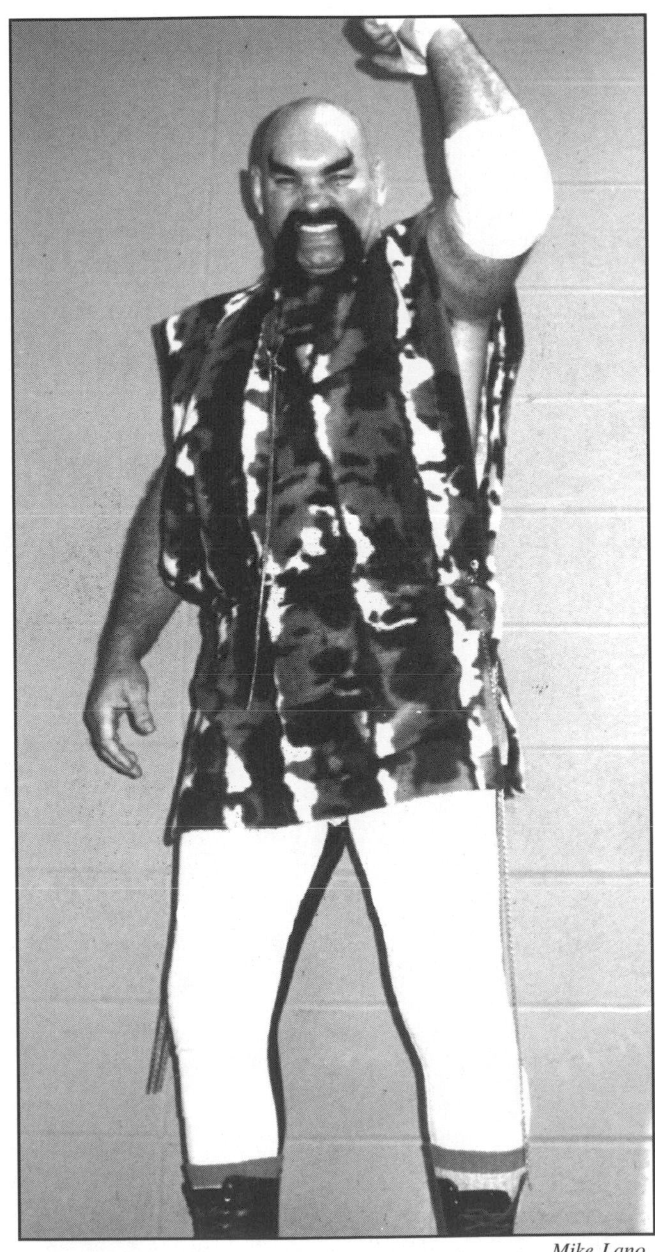

Mike Lano

Ox Baker

Mike Lano

Jimmy Snuka

Terry Funk and Chief Jay Strongbow

Mike Lano

Lynne Gutshall, courtesy of Lanny Poffo

Hogan & Randy Savage – Outraged!!

courtesy of Mike Lano

Stars of their day, in a Battle Royal

***   ***

ACT II
THE PLAYERS

Start to talk about Hulk Hogan, Bret Hart, Stone Cold Steve Austin or The Undertaker, and all wrestling fans will know enough about these grapplers to hold an hours-long conversation. How about Bill Sprague or Bryan Walsh or Tiger Khan? Only a cult following knows that they are professional wrestlers.

The business of professional wrestling is deep and intricate. For every Hulk Hogan, there are hundreds, if not thousands, of wrestlers who work in virtual anonymity. Behind the scenes, there are hundreds of writers who chronicle the events in the squared circle through different means, from historical to social. Various people, wrestlers and non-wrestlers alike, have taken pen or brush to hand and created world-class art which depicts professional wrestling. At every match, programs are being sold which had to be designed, printed and distributed by fans of professional wrestling. Very few entrepreneurs in the wrestling business take on a venture solely for the profit motive. Most are ardent wrestling fans.

Act II is dedicated to those in the trade, from performers in the ring to the guy who sells programs, who receive little or no notoriety. These individuals keep the machine of professional wrestling churning. Without them, there would be no Hulk Hogans or Bret Harts, and there never would have been a Lou Thesz, a Killer Kowalski or a Bruno Sammartino. In essence, they could be called the "unsung heroes" of professional wrestling.

Ironically, the stories of these behind-the-scenes people rival those of the stars in their humor, breadth and imagination. In other words, they embody the human spirit as well as those tales told by the more visible people in the trade. Hulk Hogan may have been world champion several times over and his face is known to millions, but he never wrestled the carnival circuit in Germany like Bryan Walsh. Bret Hart never wrestled on a card and later the same evening, after the match, changed into his police uniform to go to his "regular" job like Bill Sprague did.

The depth of the personalities involved in professional wrestling is immense. The stars of the sport supply the visible aspects of wrestling, while other players embellish wrestling with a spirit that transcends the sport itself.

Scene I

THE JOURNEYMEN

Most professional wrestling fans watch an event, either on TV or live at the arena, in the anticipation of seeing the big-name stars. When Hulk Hogan goes down the runway, the heel receives insults, threats and an array of garbage aimed at him. On the other hand, Stone Cold Steve Austin or The Undertaker will be showered with praise and handshakes. For every Hogan or Austin, there are hundreds of wrestlers who appear, almost anonymously, for just a minute or two in a match. They usually end up being carried out of the ring after being massacred by the name wrestler. Some of these wrestlers are lifetime "jobbers" who accept their plight in the sport and are only too thrilled to be a part of professional wrestling, while others use their gimmick as a stepping-stone in hopes of someday receiving a proper push and being part of the structure of the sport at its top end.

There are various words used to describe these wrestlers, the most common being "jobber." Other monikers are "journeyman" or "veteran." This chapter will highlight the careers of several journeymen and their experiences while being involved with wrestling.

THE BROOKLYN BRAWLER

"I don't have a job.
I just play for a living."
— The Brooklyn Brawler

If you watch WWF matches on TV, you have probably seen the Brooklyn Brawler announced as the opponent of one of the stars. He enters the ring with tattered blue jeans and a New York Yankee shirt that is torn in several places. His presence is formidable.

For the first minute or so, the Brawler actually gets a few licks in. You may think that you will see a competitive match; however, within a few minutes, the star usually gets his timing down and leaves the Brawler sprawled out in the middle of the ring in a semiconscious state.

The Brooklyn Brawler is Steve Lombardi of Brooklyn. He has been wrestling professionally since 1981. His role in wrestling differs from that of most journeymen in that he, at times, has been given a push by the World Wrestling Federation. In 1997, for example, the Brawler, who had not won a match for months, if not years, in the WWF, won a battle royal earning him a title shot at Madison Square Garden. He lost that challenge in a couple of minutes. In other words, the WWF occasionally elevates his status in the organization.

Lombardi did not play sports during his childhood. He stated, "I was just on the streets." He graduated from high school and attended St. Francis College, where he majored in biochemistry.

When he was a senior in college, he attended his first live wrestling match. After that, he was hooked. According to Lombardi, "I was given tickets to a wrestling match at Madison Square Garden. I had only seen wrestling on TV. A year later, I was wrestling at Madison Square Garden."

Unlike most journeymen, Lombardi has spent his entire career with one organization—the WWF. "I've been with the WWF all along. I wrestled in Japan for small companies, and I wrestled for other little outfits in the U.S. on the side, but that was all through the WWF."

Many wrestlers admit that their grueling schedules do actually present opportunities that may not have existed had they not been in their chosen professions. Lombardi added, "I've been all over the world. I've wrestled in New Zealand, Australia, Japan and India. I've wrestled in China. I've wrestled almost everywhere in the world except in Russia."

With the coming-of-age of WCW in the 1990s, the traditional wrestling scene was thrown into a frenzy. Wrestlers had two "major leagues" instead of one, and both the WWF and WCW had revolving doors in which talent consistently switched sides. Lombardi, however, did not become involved in the bidding war for talent. He stated, "I have a high respect for Vince McMahon. He's one of the greatest people I've ever met. I think Vince McMahon is a tremendously fair person. I don't even look at him as a boss. I look at him as a friend. I think the WWF is a tremendous company, but I don't look at it as a company, I look at it as a family."

While other wrestlers have benefitted greatly from the ongoing battle of the two giant wrestling organizations, Lombardi sees the rivalry as a one-sided issue. He said, "WCW is not trying to excel. They're just trying to beat another company and they're failing at it. I have nothing against anybody at WCW. It's good for the wrestlers to have other places to go, but they're grasping at straws."

Many wrestlers have to have an identity created for them when they began grappling. A few, however, actually bring their outside-the-ring personalities inside the squared circle. Lombardi is one. According to him, "I went from the streets to the ring. I didn't have any training in the ring. I was a kind of roughhouse person. I didn't have a gimmick. I mean the ripped clothes, I don't walk around with ripped clothes. As far as being from Brooklyn, being from the streets, growing up in a rough neighborhood, hanging around with, I don't know what you'd call them, street hoodlums, that's all legit."

Many people are surprised to discover that Lombardi studied biochemistry in college. Sometimes he is asked if he is a bright individual. That, to Lombardi, is all a matter of perception. He answers those who are curious about his intelligence with, "Compared to Einstein, I'm not too bright."

When talking of his won-loss record, Lombardi again puts the subject into its proper perspective. Because many fans only see him putting over the stars on TV, they assume that he rarely wins. Lombardi countered, "I've won matches. I got one match here that I was watching the other day where I beat Terry Taylor in Madison Square Garden in front of 23,000 people. Bobby Heenan was managing me.

courtesy of WT&N

The Brooklyn Brawler, by Jason Conlan

"Most people only see the television matches. The house show matches are different. I have quite a few wins. Winning and losing does not matter to me. If a person beats me, he's gotta earn that win. He's not going to walk away with an easy match. I'm not lazy in the ring. I like to work hard."

The Brooklyn Brawler's list of opponents transcends wrestling generations. One could probably make a wrestling Hall of Fame from his adversaries. Lombardi stated, "I've wrestled just about everyone from Andre the Giant to Hulk Hogan. I've wrestled Sammartino, Chief Jay Strongbow, George 'The Animal' Steele and Bobo Brazil. Some of these guys were in their 50s. I've wrestled almost every age."

Most wrestlers can tell about a few opponents who were tougher than the average star. Lombardi made the distinction as he stated, "The Iron Sheik was really tough in his day. Today

Razor Ramon is pretty tough. That finishing move he has, the Razor's Edge, is pretty devastating. I didn't like taking that."

Lombardi is not looking to sell his talent to a higher bidder. He is content to be involved with the WWF and hopes that his career has a few more years left before he hangs up his boots. He concluded, "I'll stay in the business as long as they'll have me, I guess. I love the sport totally—100%. I don't have a job. I just play for a living."

BILL SPRAGUE

"I had the natural ability to make people hate me just by coming out of the locker room and standing there."

— Bill Sprague

Bill Sprague of North Easton, Massachusetts, could be called the consummate journeyman wrestler. His ring career spanned 10 years, after which he chose a less dangerous profession—a policeman. According to Sprague, "I started professional wrestling in 1975. It was one of the things on my list. I had gotten out of the service where I was a member of the SEALS team. I went out on the rodeo circuit for two years and then joined the police department. While I was with the police department, I got into wrestling. My brother, the Giant Zebra, wrestled all over the country for many years.

"I wrestled for 10 years, until I got diabetes and began to smarten up. My training was primarily from my brother. A group of us just began to train with a few top old-name pros as teachers, and we went on for about seven or eight months.

"When I began to wrestle, I was a babyface. Only after a few years did I become a heel. One night, the promoter asked me to be a heel because the original one did not show. It was in Buffalo, New York, I believe. The fans did not know me as a babyface, and the heel persona worked like magic. From that moment on, I did not want to be a babyface. I had the natural ability to make people hate me, just by coming out of the locker room and standing there. I was going under the name of Cowboy Bill Halliday, so I just changed all my outfits to black."

When Sprague began to wrestle, he was associated with the New England Wrestling Federation. Shortly after, the WWF called and asked him to attend a television taping. According to Sprague, "I got some chances to drive down to Pennsylvania for the WWF. They used to do a lot of their tapings there, just outside Philadelphia. They put me over fairly well there.

"The Big Cat, Ernie Ladd, was my first fight. Usually, it was just a swerve with a guy like him if you're an unknown, but the match went so I held my own. Ernie smoked a cigar all the time. He had me in a headlock and told me to take the burning cigar out of his mouth and crush it on his chest. I did, and that was the turnaround for the whole thing. It was a great match. I ended up being thrown out of the ring."

Sprague recalled his career with the WWF and other New England-based promotions, "I probably wrestled about 150 matches for the WWF. Some were as far away as Pennsylvania or Buffalo and some were in Montreal, Canada. Actually, Montreal was for Rudy Kaye, but it was kind of on-a-loan basis from the WWF. All the rest were for local groups like the New England Wrestling Association. They were not all as Cowboy Bill Halliday. Once in a while I would wear a mask and be one of the Masked Destroyers. In certain areas, like New York or Brooklyn, they had me go as Irish Paddy Shapiro. I had a shamrock on one side of my trunks and a Star of David on the other. That was a lot of fun. The best part was trying to get out of the ring and getting a taxi because there was a wild crowd."

Because of the proximity of location, Sprague and Killer Kowalski eventually crossed paths on a professional basis. According to Sprague, "Kowalski and I live near each other. He had a wrestling school in one of the rooms at the YMCA in Salem, Massachusetts. I would go up there a lot and work out with him. Occasionally, I would work his shows, and we got into some good fights at the shows. He would be the referee and I would take a swing at him. He'd pick me up and throw me down. We had quite a few things going like that. We had a good relationship.

"When he throws his kicks, he puts a lot of aplomb behind them. The thing is, if you need a minute's rest, you do not get it. You would try to get out of the ring but just couldn't. He'd go out and throw you back in. The man had legs and wind. He's a vegetarian and a health fanatic. The man could wrestle when he's a hundred, I swear. In addition to his wrestling prowess, he's a very nice man. I'll never forget that he gave autographed pictures to my kids when they were young."

Sprague met many big-name wrestlers in his decade in the ring. One, in particular, sticks out in his mind. He stated, "I wrestled Hulk Hogan when he first came into wrestling. I think he was called the Atomic Kid. He had the hair shaved like an atomic cloud on his chest. I remember wrestling him up in Vermont or New Hampshire several times. He was not Hulk Hogan then."

All wrestlers have their stories about their favorite opponents, and Sprague is no exception. He wrestled George "The Animal" Steele many times and has fond memories. Sprague reminisced, "One time I was wrestling George Steele and told him my back was starting to kill me. I said, 'George, throw me out of the ring to buy some time.' He responded by biting the referee.

courtesy of Bill Sprague

**Bill Sprague (standing)
and Chief Jay Strongbow**

"Steele used to recite poetry and enjoyed the outlandish life of a professional wrestler compared to his normal life. He was naturally strong and never lifted weights.

"For a while, I promoted my own matches. I lugged the ring around and set it up. George Steele, whom I used at several events, used to have a habit of eating the turnbuckles. When you run an operation on a shoestring budget, things like this end up costing you money that you don't have. Steele, however, would always slip me $20 at the end of the night if he ate a turnbuckle."

Some wrestlers from Sprague's time criticize the modern style of professional wrestling, while others begrudgingly admit that today's version is okay. Sprague, however, is a big fan of the current rendition of professional grappling. He said, "First of all, I stand 6'4" tall and was a big guy in my time. Nowadays, I walk in there and see these guys, and I'm up to their shoulders. There are some big men.

"The wrestlers today are a lot more daring. It shows because there are a lot more injuries today. It has changed a lot. It is so outlandish that it's terrific. But, all in all, the people in my time and those before my time were just as happy as they are today watching wrestling, except today we have so much better media coverage."

One of Sprague's claims to fame is a stint in which he wrestled an over-the-hill Chief Jay Strongbow on a regular basis in the Salisbury (MA) Arena. According to him, "We wrestled every Monday night for an entire summer. It turned out to be the main event—the Cowboy vs. the Indian. We wrestled in cages; we wrestled with ropes; we wrestled every possible way, even with our legs tied together. It was a back and forth ongoing battle."

An unexpected occurrence a decade ago forced Sprague from the police department, but he developed his own business shortly after. He concluded, "I had a heart attack 10 years ago on the police force. I went two out of three falls with two armed robbers, but I'm doing well today. I manufacture fireworks and have my own fireworks company. We do the airbursts and all the entrance rockets and things like that. I've done everything from Michael Jackson to Disney on Ice. Right now, I've got to go back out to a big 100-show contract in Colorado. I travel around doing indoor and outdoor pyrotechnics."

TIGER KHAN

"As soon as I stepped out there, little kids started cursing and throwing things at us. It was a great feeling."

— Tiger Khan

Tiger Khan does not fit the same mold as the previous wrestlers in this chapter. Indeed, the term "journeyman" may not apply to him yet. He is still a young wrestler with aspirations of being a household name with either the WWF or WCW. This is the story of a young wrestler and the pitfalls of trying to grasp the next rung on the wrestling ladder.

Khan is 25 years old and was born in New York City, where he resides today. His parents hail from India via Trinidad, yet Khan is American in culture and lifestyle.

As a youngster, Khan did not participate in sports. He had other interests. He explained, "I did not like watching or playing sports. I was more into electronics and stuff like that. Before wrestling, I was into studying and reading about animals and dinosaurs. Most kids would play baseball, but I'd go get motors from the hardware store and always try to build things like helicopters, but we never had all the materials to actually propel one."

In the middle of his childhood interests, Khan discovered professional wrestling, with the assistance of his father, who was a wrestling fan. According to Khan, "My father would always watch wrestling every Saturday morning. He would always try to get me to watch it, but I was never interested. I was into cartoons and stuff like that.

"One morning, he actually forced me to sit down and watch it. I don't think I really got into it right there, but the next week he did the same thing. After that, it was a continuing storyline that caught my eye. It wasn't just wrestling. After the second week of being forced to watch it, I began to watch it voluntarily."

With Khan's newly acquired affinity for professional wrestling came a dilemma, however. He enjoyed it so much that at the age of 13 he declared that he wanted to be a professional wrestler, and his parents realized that they had created a monster. They wanted no part of his career choice. Khan said, "In the beginning, they were totally opposed to me becoming a wrestler. When I was 13, I had decided that this is what I wanted to do with my life and by the time I was 16, I only weighed 140 pounds.

"Eventually, when I was 16, I saw a listing of wrestling schools, and two of them were in Brooklyn. I decided to check on the first one because it was run by Johnny Rodz, a former WWF star. He stated in the advertisement that his school videotaped your training sessions.

"My father took me down to his school. Johnny took a look at me and said, 'Look, kid, go to school, graduate and come back.' He was telling me I was too young. That's the last thing you want to hear when you want to do something.

"Being a little discouraged, I went home, but I was determined. I thought that if I had to wait, I was going to wait. Later on, I saw another school in the same location but with training on different days. It was Bobby Bold Eagle's school.

"My father took me down there again. We introduced ourselves to Bobby Bold Eagle, and this time I knew I had a shot because his son, who was about 14 years old, was in the ring. He told me that I would have to pay and come down, and he would teach me. The only obstacle now was an ominous document that he wanted my parents to sign. It stated, among other things, 'The school is not responsible for death, dismemberment, or paralysis.' With much apprehension, my parents signed.

"At the time, my parents were reluctant about my wanting to be a professional wrestler. Today, however, they are 100% behind me. I couldn't have done it without their support."

In July 1989, Khan began a two-year training program with Bobby Bold Eagle. After the first year, the 17-year-old student was ready for his first match. According to Khan, "Three other students and I were booked for a tag-team match at a Boys Club in New Jersey. We all drove down and wrestled that night and had the best match on the card. There were over a couple of hundred fans, mostly little kids. I was shy in the beginning, but wrestling has a way of taking the shyness out of you. As soon as I stepped out there, little kids started cursing and throwing things at us. It was a great feeling. I really enjoyed the attention. For the first time in my life, I felt completely comfortable in a situation in which I was not among friends or at home."

Khan's first match left a positive indelible mark on him that has remained to this day. His next contest, however, showed him how seedy the world of independent wrestling promotions can be. Khan explained, "The first big show I ever did was for an independent promotion in Pennsylvania. It was not a huge promotion, but they did have TV. The original agreement was for me and three other students to do a tag-team match. We knew each other, so we wrestled well and blew all the other guys on the card away. They realized that they couldn't have us around because we made their guys look bad.

"After our match, something odd happened. They called me and my tag-team partner aside and told us that we would have to wrestle again, this time against their tag-team champions. We got squashed. It was really disgusting. It was pretty obvious that they wanted to teach us a lesson. Sure, we were young and green, but we worked our asses off."

Khan has worked for over 20 independent promotions since his professional debut. At this level of wrestling, the promotions vary greatly—some are good, some not so good. One in particular, Pennsylvania Championship Wrestling (PCW), sticks out in Khan's mind as being an astute organization. His work there was rewarded in November 1997, when he gained the group's championship belt. He held the title until June 1998. Khan calls PCW "by far the most professional, organized promotion on the East Coast."

In 1995, Khan attempted to elevate himself to the next rung on the wrestling ladder. He moved to Atlanta and entered the WCW training school, the Power Plant. After two months in the program, unforeseen circumstances made it necessary for Khan to return to New York. He explained, "After two months, I had a lot of financial difficulty. I ended up having to break my lease in Atlanta and moving back to New York. Part of the reason I moved back is because of a new promotion—Coast To Coast Wrestling. I was supposed to get work with them. I decided that the Power Plant couldn't make me any promises and that I could go back to New York to wrestle. After the first show, Coast To Coast went out of business."

The canceling of a promotion after one card is not atypical in the wrestling business. There are myriad stories about small, independent promotions and their not being totally on the up-and-up. This, to the uninitiated, appears to be horrendous, but professional wrestlers have to endure such travesties, particularly when they are just beginning their careers. According to Khan, "I'm used to it by now. From the first year of my training, a guy promised me a tour of Africa. You end

courtesy of Tiger Khan

Tiger Khan

up getting excited, and it ends up with the tour being canceled. There was always some bullshit excuse. It's typical in this business."

One thing is certain in the professional wrestling business. With the death of one promotion, another is not far from being hatched. Shortly after the demise of the one-card Coast To Coast promotion, another independent group set up shop. Khan said, "I met up with a friend of mine whom I'd known years ago, and it turned out he came into a whole bunch of money. In January 1996, he started the Ultimate Wrestling Federation (UWF). Herb Abrams, the UWF promoter, sent a letter saying that the name UWF was already in use, so the organization changed its name to Ultimate Championship Wrestling (UCW). Our first show was in April 1996."

Khan had a good run with UCW, which used to bring in name wrestlers such as King Kong Bundy, Bruce Hart and Jim Neidhardt, among others, but the organization eventually folded. At least the organization, unlike many other independents, treated its wrestlers fairly.

Many young wrestlers are mesmerized by being in the ring and their desire, at times, leads them to be mistreated. Khan stated, "A lot of promoters get a 'sold show' in which they're guaranteed a certain amount of money. They get the cheapest undercard they can. They'll tell a kid that if he works for $25 that night, they will book him for the rest of the summer. It's totally bullshit because the promoter knows that there are no other shows coming up. It happens a lot."

Politics runs rampant in professional wrestling. Sometimes it's better to be a good politician than a good wrestler, and Khan is well aware of the system. He mentioned, "I've been in the business for nine years. I have to see it to believe it. I have come to the conclusion that the independents are for brushing up your skills. I don't think you can make it with the independents alone. The bottom line in this business is and always will be 'who you know.' It's not about talent. It has very little to do with talent. Eventually, talent comes into play, but breaking into the business, getting your foot in the door, is all about who you know and who's going to vouch for you."

Eventually, we all contract the ugly disease of adulthood. Prior to that, however, many human beings perform routines solely for the purpose of having fun. Khan remembers those days vividly. He and his comrades used to perform a special ritual while driving in two cars on their way to their matches. He concluded, "When I started out, we never cared about the money. We traveled mostly on weekends when there was a lot of traffic. Being kids and being bored like we were, we would pretend that one car had hit the other and we'd all get out. There would be 10 of us and we'd have this big fight, right in the stalled traffic. We were wrestlers, so everything we would do looked real. We would be slamming each other on the hoods and bumping on the ground. We were really convincing. We did that many times. It was really fun. When the traffic began to move, we would just stop, get back in the cars and drive away. Usually, a crowd had assembled, and they would be outside their cars looking at us driving away while they were still holding up traffic."

BRYAN WALSH

"I was a small guy going into the land of giants."

— Bryan Walsh

You would think that someone who is 5'11" tall and weighs about 185 pounds would not put professional wrestling at the top of his list of chosen careers, but Bryan Walsh has been in the ring for over 15 years now and would have it no other way. He has wrestled for dozens of independent promotions in several countries and also for the WWF and WCW. Millions of fans have seen him get demolished on television by the giants of the big two professional wrestling promotions.

Walsh was born in Pawtucket, Rhode Island, and has been a wrestling fan since he was in the fourth grade when he was introduced to wrestling magazines and the television shows *All-Star Wrestling* and *Big Time Wrestling*. His first memories are of Chief Jay Strongbow and Bruno Sammartino.

When Walsh was still in elementary school, he received the opportunity to attend his first live match. He reminisced, "I kind of cheated my way in to see my first live match. My sixth grade teacher, Mr. Romely, held a raffle in the classroom. The kids wrote down numbers on a piece of paper and put them into a hat. The teacher picked six numbers out of the hat to go to Jack Witchi's Sports Arena in North Attleboro, Massachusetts. I wrote my number down twice and, funny enough, he picked it and I went to see my first live show. I hate to say it, but I kind of cheated because I was so desperate to go. It was Larry Zybysko and the Wolfman, and the second main event was Chief Jay Strongbow and Butcher Paul Vachon. I can see it today."

From the fourth grade on, Walsh knew that he was going to be a professional wrestler. However, he was well aware of the drawback of his lack of size in his chosen profession. Walsh said, "It was a difficult decision to make because of my size. When I broke in, it was the time in which steroid-use was becoming rampant. I was a small guy going into the land of giants."

Walsh began wrestling in earnest in junior high school. Unfortunately, his high school did not have a wrestling team, and he had to call a halt to his amateur wrestling career. Walsh

courtesy of Bryan Walsh

Bryan Walsh, early in his career

added, "My high school did not have a wrestling team. Ironic enough, the athletic director used to be the coach of some guy who turned out to be amateur world champion. The reason we did not have a team was that the school did not have finances to buy mats and equipment."

The lack of a high school amateur wrestling program did not make Walsh's interest in wrestling wane. He was still an avid fan of professional wrestling and after graduating, Walsh began to attend live matches on a regular basis, a habit which led him to his first attempt at becoming a professional grappler. According to Walsh, "I attended cards at Madison Square Garden. Every month, I used to take the train from Providence to New York. After a card, I was waiting to cross the street and saw Little Beaver, a midget wrestler, almost get hit by a car as he was trying to dodge traffic. By the time he came over to my end of the sidewalk, I began talking to him about New York drivers.

"We hit it off. I told him I was from Rhode Island and that I wanted to be a wrestler. He then told me about a school in Montreal, Canada, which was really a bingo hall with a boxing ring in it. I went there and found the school. I got in the ring, worked out for about a half hour or so, took an arm drag, broke my ankle and wound up back in the hotel. I'll never forget that night. Here I was, 18 or 19 years old, and I had broken my ankle but didn't go to the hospital for it. I was in agony. There was so much pain that the sheet that was over my body was killing my foot.

By the time I woke up in the morning, I had to take a leak real bad. I got out of bed and had to walk down the hall on my knees, and I could just make it over the urinal. I took the bus back to Providence and got in a taxi cab. The driver took me to Miriam Hospital where I got my foot x-rayed. It was broken. They put a cast on it, and I went home from there. My mother, who did not know that I went to Montreal, was furious with me.

"I had a bedroom full of wrestlers. I had Bruno, Chief Jay Strongbow and the Valiant Brothers. They were everywhere in my room. I didn't have wallpaper; I had wrestling posters. That's how much I was into it.

"I was only 19 and bounced back pretty quick. My mother and father wanted me to give up the idea of becoming a wrestler, especially after my broken ankle, but I wanted to keep going."

For the next year, Walsh continued to work out at various gyms. One night, while working out, another gym patron, Mike Woods, and Walsh began to talk about wrestling. Woods had performed in martial arts films in Thailand and told Walsh about Killer Kowalski's wrestling school. Walsh wrote the address on a piece of paper and took action the following day. He said, "I got on a bus and went there. This was about a year after the incident when I broke my ankle. I met Killer Kowalski and was amazed by his presence."

Walsh joined Kowalski's school, but soon ran into another problem—finances. According to Walsh, "At the time, I was working in a delicatessen. I was making minimum wage and the school cost about $1,200 to join. I joined and he let me pay in installments, but soon I had used up my $300 worth of lessons. I didn't have another $300 to give him, so I explained it to him. He worked out a deal with me where he would keep training me and I would pay him when I was ready to do shows. I'll never forget how relieved I was when he told me that."

About four months after he renewed his deal with Kowalski, Walsh received his first call. A scheduled performer at a Kowalski-run show canceled when his parents fell ill. Kowalski then gave Walsh the nod. Walsh added, "That was the Oktoberfest in Worcester, Massachusetts, in 1983. My first opponent was a longtime friend, Bob Shoop, who worked as Bob Van Winkle. We did a 20-minute draw. That was the first time I ever wrestled on a card, and I'll never forget it."

With his appetite whetted, Walsh began his career in earnest. He said, "I tried to develop my body. I had always been working out. I kept training and training and going to school, doing more and more matches. As time went on, I was developing into a pretty good worker in the ring. Eventually, Walter (Kowalski) made me his champion."

Walsh began to work for other promotions as well as Kowalski's. From 1983 to 1987, he worked the northeast, primarily as a babyface.

Eventually, Walsh wrestled in the WWF. He was called when the organization was in the area and needed a few workers for their television tapings. Walsh added, "My first match in the WWF was with the help of Walter. He put a word in for me and got me the work. The WWF started using some of his guys when they were in the northeast. My first WWF match was with the Quebecers."

Before Walsh wrestled for the WWF, he had toured Europe. He then returned to the U.S. and was amazed at how the wrestling scene had changed in such a short time. He said, "I couldn't believe being in the locker room for the first time. I had been wrestling in England and was accustomed to 'normal' size guys. At the time, the tag-team WWF champs were the British Bulldogs. They were monsters. They weren't tall guys, they were just HUGE."

Walsh's European stints were rewarding and diverse. He recalled, "I wrestled for two promoters in England—Dale Promotions and Martin Promotions. In England, we wrestled everywhere. We also wrestled all over Scotland and Wales. The most common venues were leisure centers or town halls. I never wrestled right in London, but I wrestled in Croydon, a London suburb, many times."

Walsh at first was unaccustomed to the British version of professional wrestling in which wrestlers grappled in rounds, similar to boxing. After he mastered the system, however, Walsh liked the variance from the American version and fit right into the flow of British professional wrestling. He was popular and well received by the fans.

Germany was another story, however. Walsh wrestled for Gerd Zollnick and his wife, who were owners of the German Wrestling Federation (GWF). He said, "They ran tournaments every now and again, but it wasn't anything steady."

The venues in Germany varied considerably from those in Great Britain. According to Walsh, "The places were a bit bigger. We actually wrestled in discotheques, but the main places were hockey rinks. We wound up in a lot of hockey rinks."

Walsh now was beginning to resemble a "regular" on the European professional wrestling circuit. He had overcome various culture shocks and deviations in lifestyles. What happened next, however, changed all that. Walsh stated, "I was wrestling in a 10-day tournament in Hamburg. We just could not draw a crowd, so after five days, the tournament got canceled. I was the only American on the card and decided to fly back to the United States.

"One of the bookers, Dave Morgan, who later became a good friend of mine, took a liking to me, and we kind of became friends in those five days. When he asked me where I was going from there, I told him I was going to fly home. He suggested that I try and wrestle with him on the fairgrounds, which is very different from professional wrestling. It seemed weird, but I said okay. I did not want to go home yet and loved wrestling in Germany. At that time, many wrestlers in America were on steroids, and I didn't even have a way of hoping to get in the locker room in the 'big leagues.' In Germany, I was a pretty well-known wrestler. A lot of people who loved wrestling knew my name and who I was. I enjoyed that little bit of notoriety, so I said I would stay and do the fairgrounds with him."

Walsh knew nothing about wrestling in fairgrounds other than the stories he had heard about carnival wrestling years ago in the United States. Morgan, his new comrade, gave him an outline of what to expect, but this was still all new to Walsh, who explained, "The fairgrounds is exactly what it says. It is a huge fairgrounds. We traveled around from place to place. I started in Berlin at a regular fairgrounds that had carrousels, Ferris Wheels, dobby horses, bumper cars, roller coasters and all the other rides. There was this one tent that was called the 'Sports Show.' That was run by Nicky Schultz. They would do a little demonstration on the platform on top of the stairs. Families would be walking by and all of a sudden see boxers punching a punching bag and wrestlers doing different exercises warming up for a match. When enough people had gathered in front to watch, they would stop the music. Then Nicky Schultz would challenge anyone in the audience to come up and knock out one of his boxers. If you could, you would earn 500 deutschemarks. In addition, if you could pin Dave Morgan, or make him submit, you would get DM500.

"I was in the crowd in street clothes. My job would be to raise my hand saying that I wanted to wrestle. Nicky would set it up, and we would have a really nice match. I told them that I was on vacation in Germany from America. The barker would then tell the audience that I was a wrestler in college. Actually, I never went to college. People came in and saw our show and they loved it."

Once Walsh had begun to wrestle Morgan, it was necessary to create the illusion of parity so the show could continue. Walsh added, "The first match would be two rounds. Usually, I would have the upper hand at the end of the match, and everybody thought I was robbed when Morgan was declared the winner. Then I'd go back outside and challenge him for a three-round contest. We'd do that, and he'd pull a dirty trick on me. I wouldn't win again, but I wouldn't lose either. By the third time, we'd do a five-round, nonstop, no-ringing-the-bell-between-rounds match. Usually, I would win some money.

"By that time, someone would see little me beat this Dave Morgan in a wrestling match, and then the straights came. Someone who wasn't part of our team would come up and challenge Morgan, who was a five-time British amateur champ and had knowledge of most martial art forms. He was really good. At 53 years old, it was amazing to watch this guy take guys who were bodybuilders and thought they were rough and tough. He could have legitimately done me at any time, but he liked me. We were friends. He thought I was good for the show. I never saw him lose. He could grab any part of the body and make you submit, but he didn't go out of his way to hurt people."

Professional wrestlers in the United States have a grueling schedule, sometimes over 300 nights a year. Walsh may not have exceeded their annual amount of contests, yet while on the fairgrounds circuit in Germany, he was called upon to grapple more than once a day. He added, "The most shows I ever did was in Stuttgart at a folkfest. We did 14 shows in one day. This was the biggest carnival place we ever did. We would start at noontime and work up until one or two in the morning. People would not leave this place. They had four or five beer halls which were tents that seated over 2,000 people each."

Ironically, Walsh's German experience became intermingled with his future WWF tenure. His first match for the WWF was with the Quebecers tag-team, of which Carl Ouellette was one-half. "I knew Ouellette in Germany," Walsh said. "He had come to wrestle there, and we actually worked out in the same gym, the Powerhouse Gym in Hamburg. The manager introduced me to Ouellette. We got talking and became acquaintances. Then, before you know it, I came back to the states and there's Carl along with Jacques Rougeau, and they are tag-team champs of the WWF. We recognized each other and began talking."

Walsh estimates that he has wrestled in over 2,000 matches in his career. He has wrestled the top WWF stars, including Shawn Michaels, Psycho Sid, Adam Bomb, Bam Bam Bigelow, the 1-2-3 Kid and Brian Christopher, among others. On the other hand, he has wrestled little-known grapplers in independent promotions all over the world. Of all the styles of wrestling and his opponents, Walsh picks one time in his life as his favorite in the ring. He stated, "I liked the British style better. It was different. I remember that I was lost in my first singles match in England. I was trying to keep up with this little guy, Kid McCoy, who was even smaller than me. I never had the opportunity to wrestle someone smaller than me and was watching this guy doing these rolls, reversals and tip-ups. I said, 'Look at this guy go.'"

With the WWF, Walsh loses to big-name opponents. However, when he wrestles for independent promotions, his television exposure makes him a celebrity, much like being the big fish in a small pond. Despite being thrashed by the superstars of the sport, Walsh has a lifetime winning record in professional wrestling. He said, "There are definitely more wins than losses, but the losses have been seen by everybody."

In 1998, Walsh began to write in-depth columns about professional wrestling. He is eloquent and goes deeper into the sport than many professional wrestling journalists. His experience in the ring helps him write about the little-known facts of professional wrestling. Following are two of his articles[1] which touch upon topical items—injuries and the psychology of "jobbing."

1. © Bryan Walsh. Reproduced by permission of Bryan Walsh.

THE FEAR OF SERIOUS INJURY

Until recently, I had no fear of being severely injured in the ring: injuries have always occurred, but one was never apprehensive about them before a match. Today, however, I've noticed, before the bell rings, even for a three-minute TV match, I wonder if I am going to be leaving the ring under my own power.

Ten years ago, I did not have the same apprehension. I have not changed my style much in taking risky bumps, but I took bumps where I landed on my back, not face-forward bumps where you can separate a shoulder trying to slow the momentum down.

In addition to the normal bumps, I've taken piledrivers and I've had them done to me, but nothing off the top rope, like the one that injured Buff Bagwell recently. I don't fancy the idea of taking one of those either. That's just too much of a risk.

There is a debate about the increase in high-risk maneuvers. Some maintain that the promotions are calling for them, while others state that the wrestlers themselves are at the root of the problem—trying high-risk maneuvers to make themselves more noticed. I must admit, that is an excellent way to get noticed, but your longevity will suffer. You are not going to last long in wrestling doing all those maneuvers.

You can perform all those high-risk moves when you're 18 to 23. Then, one night you're 27 and you slip and break something. Now you're out for at least 12 weeks and you come back with ring rust. You want to prove to the fans that you can still do what you did before you left, so you have to step it up again and get that crowd attention. Then you take even higher-risk maneuvers. It's self-perpetuating.

The promoters are loving it because the fans want it. Sad as it is, as long as you're okay and working, your phone's going to ring. But once you're injured and out of it for a while, your phone's going to ring less and less. That's one of the sad facts of wrestling.

If, however, you are the main moneymaker for an organization, they may work around your injury. Take Stone Cold Steve Austin, for example. He's wrestling at less than 100%, but they put the strap around him. His matches are short to keep the risk factor at a minimum: give the audience three minutes of Stone Cold, which they go nuts for. They only give three minutes because the next day they want him in another town. Another factor behind the WWF putting the belt on a less-than-100% Stone Cold is his ability behind the mike. He's good in the ring and great behind the mike.

There are definitely more injuries in wrestling today than at any other time in my career. There are injuries all the time that you don't even hear about. They're doing moonsaults off the top rope onto the floor. They've stepped up the maneuvers both inside and outside the ring. Another ploy that has become popular since Extreme Championship Wrestling (ECW) came on the scene is real stiff chair shots. You blast somebody the wrong way with a chair and there's a broken nose. If he tries to block it the wrong way, there's a broken finger or a fractured wrist.

It has just totally become a violently saturated form of entertainment to please the audience. I don't like it because I am one of the performers and I know what it's like being in the ring when somebody comes at you with a chair and the crowd is literally screaming for blood.

I prefer the audience of the wrestling I grew up watching. Bruno was champion and the people adored him. Now, if he were champion in today's society, the people would hate him. The fans like all the rebels of society and the audience's fixation with being bad is really kind of scary. It makes you wonder.

Even only 10 years ago, the people loved Hulk Hogan. Now they hate him. Even before he turned heel, the audience was booing him out of buildings.

Today, I walk down the aisle and, being a babyface, I have to smile and wave. I hear people say, "Fuck you! I'll kick your ass." People want to jump over the restraining barrier to fight you. And I'm the good guy! While they're saying, "You suck, you fucking faggot," the camera's right in your face and you have to smile.

It wasn't that way when I started. If they didn't know you, they may have given you a "boo," but nobody would challenge you to fight. They say things that a normal civilized person would not say. I hope, when the ring crews are taking the ring down and all the lights are off and everyone's heading home, they adjust to a better mannerism on their way home and the next day they're back to "normal." I hope they don't live outside of wrestling with that mentality and behavior.

I've been quite lucky in my career with injuries. The worst injury I've had was a broken wrist on my left hand. I did not have medical insurance, so I just wrapped it up and it took forever to heal. It took an entire summer before I could even take an Olympic bar off a weight bench and do one rep.

Despite my not having experienced a career-ending injury, I have had many bumps that come with the trade. For instance, I've wrestled with bruised ribs, sprained ankles and a loose jaw. The loose jaw is common: someone clocks you accidentally in the jaw when you're not looking. It goes real loose and it hurts to chew for a few weeks.

I've had that many times. I'm sure my nose has been broken because I have a blockage of cartilage in my right nostril that I should have fixed so I can breathe properly.

All the time I'm in the ring, I'm out to protect myself, but sometimes you don't do what you are supposed to and an injury occurs. Once, when I was working with Bam Bam Bigelow, he accidentally punched me in the face full-blast because of an error on my part. I was supposed to duck a clothesline and my timing was bad. I caught a big shot right in the nose and the teeth.

I did a good job for him. Everything else went smooth in the match. In the locker room, he asked me if I was okay and then he apologized. However, in reality, it wasn't his fault. It was I who had forgotten to duck a clothesline.

The big guys appreciate someone like myself doing a good job for them. Psycho Sid was the same way. I did a good job for him and he was behind the curtain waiting after the match. He couldn't thank me enough.

The product today is in a quandary. How can you produce the action that the fans have become accustomed to without diluting the product? I don't think that can be done.

It always seems that society calms down after a major war or a major tragedy. In our trade, we have had various tragedies in the last couple of years, but not one big enough to change our craft. Perhaps it will take a major disaster, such as a death in the ring, to pull people together, to be humane with one another.

PSYCHOLOGY OF JOBBING

Professional wrestling jobbers are unique in their trade. In no other sport is one paid to lose and make his opponent look good while doing so. We must approach our trade in a psychological manner that is totally opposite from that of main event wrestling.

For instance, a good jobber should only utilize offensive moves from 10 to 15 percent of the time and he must use a tremendous amount of common sense in respect to when he uses these moves. The jobber has to look at his match through the eyes of the fans. He must actually be involved with the match but also have the ability to step back and watch the match happen as it is going on. I know that sounds three-dimensional, but every move, whether you're giving the move or taking the move, has to be at its absolute best that it can be performed to.

When you're taking a bump, aim high with that bump. When you do the bump for a big star, you have to sell it like it was the most devastating thing that ever happened to you. Every time I took a knockout finish, and I've taken quite a few, I NEVER got up and walked out of the ring. I always had the referee roll me under the ropes and help me back to the locker room.

We jobbers have one task to perform—to get the star over. When the office of a major promotion sees that you're getting the star over, really coming up with some creative moves, combinations and sequences to get the star over, you will always get a phone call the next time they're in town. From a jobber's standpoint, that's very, very important.

I can't tell you how thrilled I always am to hear Howard Finkel's [WWF booker] voice on the other end of the line because I know he's probably calling me to come and do a job. I love the professional wrestling trade and I've always wanted to be a part of it, so, when I receive a call, I look at it as another chance to be part of the business, even if it's only going to be for one or two nights. There's always the slim chance that you might be there when someone did not show up and you get to fill in for him and the office will tell you that you did a great job and they ask you to stay with the promotion on the road until the next *Monday Night Raw* tapings. Then you do just that: behave yourself on the road, do a real good job and you hope they appreciate that.

Being a jobber presents a quandary at times. Many young wrestlers become jobbers and then progress through the ranks toward stardom. However, some have been so good as jobbers that they are stereotyped as lifetime jobbers. Louie Spicolli was one. He began to job for the WWF when he was a teenager and was used over and over at house shows. It became evident that he had the talent to move on, but he had been seen so many times at WWF events as a jobber that he had to work extra hard to break that image. Another jobber who was so good that he had a hard time progressing is a friend of mine, Scott Taylor. Fortunately, he has been given a push as the current tag-team partner of Brian Christopher. They're doing well together. In addition, I've always rated the Hardy Boys highly, yet they're still doing jobs. They are jobbers, but when you take a look at what they're doing in the ring, they're both very talented. They've almost stereotyped themselves as jobbers, but they're both very young and who knows what tomorrow will hold for them. If you step back and forget who the star is and who the jobber is in one of their matches, you can really appreciate the talent they have.

Many hardcore wrestling fans criticize big-name wrestlers for having a deficient amount of talent and only being popular because of their size. At many times in my career, I have had to do jobs for wrestlers who can count the number of moves they can execute on one hand. I accept it because it is part of the game and I am always happy to be there and be a part of it. I must admit, however, that I'm a little resentful if I'm putting somebody over who's got such a long way to go and I'm already at the point, skillwise, where I should be in my career. I don't resent doing the job, but I resent myself for not being 6'6" tall and weighing 250 pounds with the talent that I have. Not that my talent is superior or I'm above anybody else, but I've been in the ring with guys whom I've felt I had a lot more talent than, yet I had to do the job. I did the job and I'm not complaining. It was work and it was money, however, there is a little bit of me that says, "I wish they'd appreciate, which I'm sure they do, what I've done. Jesus Christ, the next time they need someone for a gimmick, what's stopping them from calling me?"

Part of me does get frustrated after working for a major promotion. After the glamour of Monday and Tuesday night tapings, I go back to my job. I empty out my bag, wash my trunks, put them in a drawer, and know they're not going to be used again for maybe another month. I fold my boots almost inside out and let the leather dry, knowing that they're going to sit there and collect dust until the next time comes.

There is a little resentment. If I told you that jobbers who have worked for years didn't have any, I would be telling an untruth. I want to be on the road. I want to be on TV. I train just as hard as anyone else.

I have recently obtained a new job and I'm not afraid or ashamed to admit that I'm going back to a minimum wage job just so I can work around my wrestling schedule.

I'm working this job with a guarantee that I have any two nights a week off that I desire should a show come up. I am doing this job to pay my bills and with the hopes that I will make it in the wrestling business someday. I still have my hopes to comfort me that I will make it.

I know I can wrestle full time. As long as I can maintain a level of performance that will keep the audience pleased and interested, I could do that on a nightly basis. There is a part of me that resents going home after *Monday Night Raw* tapings. I get up early the next morning to arrive at work at six o'clock while everybody else is going to Colorado, or California, or Canada, or wherever they're going the next night to continue with the never-ending show of professional wrestling.

Some people maintain that jobbers are always being offered a carrot and they get enough to keep false hopes of stardom alive. I don't know if they're giving us a carrot or if we are creating a carrot. There is always that chance that we magnify that little carrot dangling in front of us to the point where it becomes larger than it really is. It is nothing more than a job, but we're all starry-eyed and we want it. This is what we have waited for—to be under the bright lights of the WWF, to be a part of that team.

After wrestling for years as a jobber and knowing the business as well as I do, even I misinterpret some things about going in and doing a job. Every time Howard Finkel calls, although deep down in my heart I know that I've been in the business for 15 years and I know I'm supposed to do a job, I hope against hope that some situation has developed where they would need me on a more permanent basis: "Okay, look Walsh, can you go on the road with us? So-and-so needs a tag-team partner. Joe Soaks just got stuck in a snowstorm and he's buried in

Denver for a week." We are all hoping something like that will happen.

For my entire career, my size has been against me in terms of becoming a main event wrestler. I had the finest training in the world under Killer Kowalski, and I have wrestled in thousands of matches. I consider myself a skilled craftsman, yet my size, or lack of it, still looms in the background as a deterrent to my progressing to the next rung on the ladder; however, I am more inspired about my future than I was 10 years ago.

Steroids are being used less today and the "bigger is better" attitude of the '80s and early '90s, although still there, has become diminished in importance. When I was in my early 20s, I attended a WWF event in Providence, Rhode Island. I had every dream of making it and was filled with confidence. Hulk Hogan was champion at that time and the Ultimate Warrior was the Intercontinental champion. When I entered the locker room, I knew I had been misleading myself. Steroids were running rampant then. You had a team of guys who were 6'4" tall and 240 pounds when they were dry; however, they went on the gas and went from 240 to 280. Here I was at 5'11" and 185 pounds soaking wet. There was just no way.

I saw that I had been misleading myself, so I got in touch with a promoter and went to Europe where I did all my wrestling against "normal" sized guys. Now that we are in the late '90s, steroids are still being used, but things have changed.

I still have dreams about my future. I have another eight or nine years ahead of me if I continue to work out, train and stay in shape. I would love to offer that to the WWF on a full-time basis. Those are my hopes.

If my dreams are not fully attained, I will still job for the WWF and kick around in the indies for another eight or nine years. At least in the indies my name carries some clout. If you are seen on TV, even if you get the thumbs-down every week, the fans know who you are.

Last year, I wrestled Brian Christopher in Canada. After that match, in which I actually wrestled for about eight minutes and looked good, the fans at indie events came up to me and said, "Wow! I saw you on TV with Brian Christopher." In fact, Christopher was a real nice guy to work with. He helped me look good and I think he will do real well in the business. I wish him luck and hope he can stay healthy for some time and have a good run.

***   ***

Scene II

THOSE $&%!?#' SHEETS

Prior to the 1980s, the only way fans could gain information about professional wrestling was through the various publications and TV shows that featured grappling. Virtually every word in print or on the airwaves was hand-fed to the publications by the wrestling organizations, and the fans only saw what the promotions wanted them to know. The publications themselves went along with the cozy relationship they had with the promoters. Ironically, most of the magazines actually felt they should not "expose the business." In other words, the fans were treated like youngsters and had to read and hear about the angles and wrestlers in an in-character manner.

This Fort Knox-like security about the business of wrestling was supported by most organizations, even if they were enemies in other fields of the business. No fans were aware of steroids, drugs or alcohol abuse. According to the promotions, such adverse parts of society never reached the domain of professional wrestling. In addition, fans did not know that a match which they thought was unique in say, Philadelphia, would be copied move-for-move the next night in Pittsburgh and then again in New York and Boston.

During this period of public relations tranquility for the promotions, many wrestling magazines were available on the newsstands. Some lasted only a few months, while others lasted years. The common denominator for all of them, however, was the fluff they produced which the organizations relished in having the fans read. There were fabulous pictures of all the stars and interviews in which they maintained they were better than their opponents, extolling the virtues of their athletic skills and their win-loss records. The writing was for 12-year-olds, forcing adults to read a fabricated history of wrestling. There was nothing else.

There were a few attempts at developing publications which wrote about wrestling in a realistic manner, mentioning the creative and business side of grappling, as well as the athletic slant, but they did not last long. In the 1980s, things changed drastically.

If you ask 10 people in the current wrestling journalism field who was responsible for the change in the way in which wrestling is reported, you will be given 10 different names, so no attempt will be made here to pick one name to call the "father of real wrestling journalism." One thing is sure, however, the two major professional wrestling groups today, the WWF and WCW, have no love for the new fashion in wrestling reporting.

Since the beginning of the '80s, various people have attempted to publish wrestling newsletters, commonly called "sheets." Some have been, and still are, in the vein of the old magazines which treat wrestling as an aboveboard sport in which the results are not predetermined. The organizations have no problem with these publications and cooperate with them. Others have gained access to real wrestling info and have changed the way in which many fans view wrestling. These are often referred to in the front offices of the major organizations as "shit sheets," "dirt sheets" or "those fucking sheets."

The reasons why the WWF and WCW do not like the sheets are numerous: they tell angles before they happen; they talk about the abuse of drugs in the trade; they give results showing the same opponents wrestling night-after-night with the same outcomes, almost down to the second in the time of the matches; and they "expose the business" in general.

Currently, there are dozens of sheets available either through printed publications, or electronic media, such as the Internet. The sheets vary from publication to publication. Some highlight wrestling's history, while others stick to current angles and results. A substantial "sheet community" among the sheet readers is now in place. Most readers will "fight to the death" advocating their favorite publication, while at the same time, ruthlessly savaging another sheet in the most vile language one could imagine.

The following is an in-depth look at several sheets. These were not selected because they are better than other publications. That is a subjective decision that only a reader can make. These sheets are included because of the diversity of the way in which they portray professional wrestling. A list of sheets and their addresses is included in the appendix. In most instances, the editors are willing to supply readers with a sample of their publications. You should try to obtain a few samples and then subscribe to one or more. Without doubt, the sheets today supply more information about professional wrestling than any other type of media.

WRESTLING OBSERVER

Many refer to this publication as "the king of sheets." Editor Dave Meltzer has built a publication with a readership of thousands. He is one of the most-quoted people in the wrestling business, and the *Observer* is rated highly among readers and those people in the business who do not try to protect the business.

Meltzer is 38 years old. He began watching pro wrestling bouts which originated from the West Coast in 1970, featuring such stars as Pat Patterson, Ray Stevens, Billy Graham and Rocky Johnson.

Meltzer began to write while he attended college. His writing included such subjects as politics, sports and wrestling. At times, he covered the high school sports scene for northern California newspapers.

The *Observer* was not Meltzer's first publication. According to him, "I actually did a newsletter from 1971 to about 1974—*International Wrestling Gazette*. In a lot of ways, it was a lot harder than the *Observer*. It was 40 pages every month and it was a predecessor to the *Observer* in many ways. Eventually, I got tired of it because wrestling on the West Coast just went down and the whole scene was pretty boring."

After a few years, something occurred to rekindle Meltzer's interest in grappling. Cable television was in its formative years in the United States, and Meltzer began receiving and viewing Georgia Championship Wrestling in 1979 via the new outlet. He said, "I started trading tapes with people—a guy in the Carolinas, a guy in Texas, a guy in Japan. All of a sudden, I was one of the first people who saw wrestling from all the different territories. I was getting to see all these guys who you wouldn't have gotten to see in the '70s. I was seeing all the different wrestlers in all the territories, so I knew who was good and who was bad but getting pushed because they were the son-in-law of the promoter and things like that. Just watching the videos from all over the world sparked my interest enough to start the *Observer*."

The first edition of the *Observer* was published in 1982. Its format was different from the current text-only version. Meltzer stated, "I had pictures and things like that. I dropped the pictures in 1985, and, believe it or not, my subscriptions started going up."

By 1982, Meltzer was corresponding with wrestling fans from all over the United States, so he used his existing list of fans to push his new publishing venture. "I just sent the issues out to those people, and they pretty much told their friends. The growth of the *Observer* was mainly word of mouth. For the first two years, there was nothing like it in wrestling. The word just got out real quick to the underground wrestling fandom, and that's where the growth started. I did it monthly, then three weeks, then two weeks and then every week."

As the publication grew, Meltzer began to go more and more inside the business. The readers enjoyed the new inside information, but the wrestling promotions differed in their opinions. According to Meltzer, "I consider that if I'm trying to do the job I'm trying to do and the people in the business like me, then I'm not doing my job because it's a con business. If the con men are happy with how you cover them, then there's something wrong."

Meltzer maintains that his sheet does the same for the wrestling fan that a mainstream newspaper does for the sports fan: it gives them information. He stated, "One of the reasons why the *Observer* got so popular was because professional wrestling was a very popular form of entertainment. The wrestling magazines covered the wrestlers in a way only for children, so there was a total void. People wanted to know what was really going on and that's pretty much the void it fills. The newspapers say, 'It's fake.' I say, if it's selling out, then put it on the entertainment page. I'm not trying to say it's sport. I'm not trying to say wrestling is anything but what it is."

Wrestling Observer Newsletter

PO Box 1228, Campbell, CA 95009–1228 *February 23, 1998*

Late Saturday night, Louie Spicolli was at his home in San Pedro, CA, a beach town suburb of Los Angeles, hanging out with a few friends watching pro wrestling videos. When they started watching his match against Chris Adams from Nitro five nights earlier, his friends started razzing him about this being the start of what appeared to be his biggest career push, and how he had put on so much weight and was looking out of shape. He had stopped going to the gym and he was letting his hair get messy, he explained, because his new WCW character was going to be like Chris Farley. But he told his friends he was worried, because the drug use of some of his co–workers and friends in the company was starting to scare him, and he was no stranger to the pitfalls of drugs. Ultimately, like far too many others in this profession, he was right on. On both accounts.

Spicolli was found dead by his friend John Hannah the next morning at about 8:55 a.m. Hannah, who stayed over at his house that night because they were up late watching tapes and he lived so far away, woke up to a really bad odor. When he opened the door to Spicolli's room, he knew right away what had happened. Spicolli was off his bed laying face first on the floor, there was vomit all over the place, his ankles were swollen and his body was already discolored. He had just turned 27 five days earlier.

Spicolli had taken 26 somas, a prescription sleeping pill/pain killer that is the drug of choice in the wrestling profession today. The drugs are easily obtainable through noted "mark doctors" who want to be friends with celebrities, modern day Zahorians. He combined the pills with drinking a lot of wine, apparently it being the only beverage in the house at the time, while his friends were there. His friends had been worried about his use and actually hid his bottle, but he somehow searched the house and found it and nearly emptied it. While he was noticeably buzzed, they had all seen him in far worse condition in the past as he had built up an incredible tolerance to somas. It was more his normal daily routine to get to sleep and by no means an attempt at suicide. He would take 15 without it even affecting him. He took 25 to 30 somas every night before going to bed which he felt he needed to sleep, a dosage that would easily hospitalize an average person but he had built up such a tolerance for it that he'd wake up fresh the next morning and go to the gym. For recreation he'd take even more, and after a while he'd lose count and once he was buzzed he'd pop them indiscriminately. Friends recalled that it wasn't unusual for them to have to bring him to his room and put him to bed when he'd pass out, but on this night even though he was drinking heavily as well, he was able to get to bed on his own at about 2:30 a.m. Hannah, sleeping in the next room, recalls being momentarily awakened at 4:15 a.m. by Spicolli's heavy snoring, and also recalls the alarm clock going off at 5:10 a.m., and Spicolli reflexively turning it off. Hannah said he never woke up hearing a thud of Spicolli falling off his bed to the floor, or trying to get up and get to the bathroom and collapsing on the floor after vomiting heavily. However, the paramedics were surprised only because the state of the body the next morning indicated he'd been dead a lot longer. Hannah was going to wake Spicolli up to get him ready for an early afternoon flight to Tampa for Nitro the next day. The actual cause of death could not be determined until the full autopsy report came back later in the week, but it was believed to have either been a bad reaction to the combination of alcohol and pills, ironically almost a nightly staple of far too many in the profession despite all the warning signs and deaths in the profession, or choking on his vomit from getting ill from the combination. When the police arrived, they theorized that the wine multiplied the effects of the somas by as much as tenfold. That's a scary bit of math when one considers the percentage of pro wrestlers today who take somas and mix alcohol on a routine basis on the road. Perhaps the tragedy of this, just like the previous tragedy with Brian Pillman, is that it did not shock those who knew him best. While broken up, his parents reaction was that it was something that was eventually going to happen because he hadn't heeded so many warnings and near–misses, and this simply was when it happened. Funeral services were scheduled for 2/20 at 9 a.m. at the Mary, Star of the Sea Catholic Church in San Pedro.

Spicolli, real name Louis Mucciolo, took his ring name from the character of the always stoned surfer played by Sean Penn in the cult movie classic "Fast Times at Ridgemont High." He had been a big wrestling fan from the age of 14. He was enamored with the World Wrestling Federation during its glory days of drawing big houses monthly at the Los Angeles Sports Arena, which he attended religiously from getting interested in wrestling in 1985 during the early days of Hulk Hogan's title reign. There is actually a tape of a teenage Lou Mucciolo at ringside in the crowd on a Saturday Night's Main Event show taped at the Sports Arena in November of 1986. While attending a show at the Sports Arena, he met up with ring announcer Bill Laster (Billy Anderson) and began training with him at a garage in East Los Angeles with the Mexican Luchadores when he was just 16 years old. Mucciolo was a good natural athlete, a standout high school pitcher with a great arm who was actually believed to have had great potential, perhaps even pro potential, in that sport. But he never really cared for baseball, or school, or anything but wrestling and dropped out of high school to follow his dream. His natural athletic ability made him pick up things rather quickly and after just three months of training, just a few days after his 17th birthday, Anderson brought him as a jobber to a WWF television taping in Bethlehem, PA where he had his first match putting over Ron Bass. Over the next several years, he worked as a WWF jobber, highly regarded enough that he was used not only on local tapings, but flown to wherever the tapings were being held and generally considered one of the best jobbers the company had. He continued that for several years on–and–off, until he basically quit because he knew if he continued any longer he'd be typecast as a jobber, and he may have actually stayed a little long in that role, but even in later years would be brought in as an opponent for certain guys such as Lightning Kid (not Syxx) and Latin Fury (now Konnan, who actually started out his career with him working Tijuana and Southern California independent shows) in dark matches at WWF tapings. He also teamed with Anderson and various third members of a trio as Los Mercenarios Americanos, a main event foreign heel trio, working regularly at Auditorio Municipal in Tijuana holding a version of the World Trios championship where he learned to work against Mexican wrestlers.

He had used the name Spicolli for so long since starting in wrestling that virtually all his friends and everyone in the wrestling industry knew him by that name. His friends looked up to him as the one in the group who had made it, who was starting to live out his dream, but also feared for him because his drug use was hardly a well–kept secret.

In early 1996, while working for the WWF as Rad Radford, after taking about 55 somas, he was found face–first in a puddle in the rain in front of a neighbor's house in early 1996 and was rushed to the hospital. He was in life–threatening critical condition for two days. At one point he was actually clinically dead for a few minutes, and talked of smelling the cigar smoke of his deceased grandfather before the doctors got his heart started beating again. While he tried to keep the cause of his collapse secret from the WWF, the company must have figured it out as he was heavy into the somas behind closed doors every night with the boys and at home with his friends. The WWF wanted to get rid of him immediately, eventually after a lot of public haggling back–and–forth, giving him a full release after initially giving him a restricted release that wouldn't have allowed him to wrestle for World Championship Wrestling for the duration of his WWF contract even though they were dropping him.

He had gotten the WWF job after the WWF hierarchy had seen him on the AAA "When Worlds Collide" PPV in November 1994 where, through weights, which he didn't really like doing, and steroids, he bulked

1

The barrier between wrestling "sheet" and wrestling "magazine" is virtually impenetrable. One gives words of information, while the other generally supplies great photos and in-character fluff. Meltzer sees the opportunity for someone to incorporate the sheet style of wrestling journalism with pictures. He stated, "I'm absolutely shocked that no one has attempted to do a magazine along the lines of the *Observer*. It would have worked easily. When all the old magazines died off, you would have thought one would have tried a novel approach."

How does Dave Meltzer categorize wrestling journalists? He explained, "We're part theater critics and part news reporters. It's not sport. We're entertainment writers, not sports writers. It's more real than any Rocky movie because the wrestlers don't get second takes. In a live show, you don't get a second take. It's just professional wrestling; that's what it is. I don't like to categorize it."

The Internet has changed the face of publishing in the United States, and the wrestling sheets are not exempt from either the positive or the negative impacts of the Internet. According to Meltzer, "I think the Internet will reflect society. If newspapers die—a lot of people predict that—or magazines die, then the sheets will die too. They'll be on the Internet. If newspapers can still exist, then the sheets will too. It won't be any different from any aspect of information. It'll go the exact same way. If the sheets die, I'll do a newsletter on the Internet. It's not a big deal."

New sheets appear almost weekly, and others die out at about the same frequency. Meltzer sees room for more sheets of quality. He stated, "If someone is going to do a good sheet, there will always be an audience. I don't know if there's an audience for a real bad one. There never was."

courtesy of Dave Meltzer

Dave Meltzer,
Editor & Publisher, *Wrestling Observer*

Today the *Observer* is a full-time business for Dave Meltzer. His operation has outgrown that of many sheet editors who publish their wares monthly and on a part-time basis. You could call the *Observer* a great success story in the realm of wrestling journalism. Not everybody, however, thought Meltzer was putting his time to good use in the years before his publication began. According to Meltzer, a college professor once told him, "If you spent as much time on doing schoolwork as you do wrestling, you might become a success in life."

WRESTLING THEN & NOW

Most wrestling sheets stick to current events in the ring. In January 1990, however, Evan Ginzburg of New York began a publication that featured the old-time wrestlers. Since then, he has not missed a monthly issue for his readers, recently topping the prestigious 100-issue mark.

Ginzburg began his sheet because of his love of the sport of wrestling. His first impressions of professional wrestling have remained firmly in his mind and did not leave when he gained the status of adulthood.

According to Ginzburg, "I became a wrestling fan in 1972. I was flipping the dial of the TV one day—it was a rainy day. All of a sudden, Chief Jay Strongbow was taking a pounding on TV. He was just being beaten unmercifully. I was 12 years old, and my eyes were popping out of my head. All of a sudden, he's doing this war dance out of nowhere and makes this miraculous comeback. I had discovered wrestling."

Ginzburg was hooked for life, yet he was still a couple of years away from being able to see a live match at wrestling's Mecca, Madison Square Garden. He added, "I watched it on TV for two years simply because at that time, Madison Square Garden, which was our home arena, didn't allow anybody under 14 to come to the shows, and they strictly enforced it."

Ginzburg had thought that watching wrestling on TV was as good as it gets, but he was soon introduced to a whole new world of excitement. He stated, "They had the Valiant Brothers, who were the most colorful tag team ever, against Dean Ho and Tony Garea. It went two-out-of-three falls and was an absolute bloodbath. I was hooked and it wasn't even the main event. That was Fred Blassie and Nikolai Volkoff against Bruno Sammartino and Chief Jay Strongbow. I mean, just to see the legends like that, it was unbelievable. Kowalski was on the card also.

"For a 14-year-old kid, it was like seeing superheroes and supervillains. Of course, at that time, I was a mark and believed everything I was watching. Every blow that the heroes took I felt. It was just incredible. The building vibrated. There were 22,000 people there. I can remember it like it was yesterday. It's almost impossible to believe that it was a quarter of a century ago. I went almost every month until it started to turn into a circus. From 1974 to probably 1986, I MAYBE missed two cards a year, if that much."

A wrestling newsletter was almost a natural for Ginzburg. He was an avid fan of wrestling and had received his Master's degree in English from Queens College. His first job was as an elementary school teacher, then he went into educational publishing as an editor and proofreader of textbooks. A few years later, the publishing firm where he worked laid off 15 percent of its employees, including the future editor of *Wrestling Then & Now*. Ginzburg stated, "*WT&N* came to me right after I was laid off. I was very depressed about it because it was a job I really liked. I said to myself I like to write, I love wrestling and nobody does a history wrestling sheet. Some of the sheets have history features, but it had never really been done. I thought there must be a market for this and it proved to be right, because I'm now in my ninth year."

Shortly after Ginzburg began his newsletter, he obtained a job as an English as a Second Language (ESL) teacher with the City of New York. He still holds this job today.

In January 1990, issue number one of *Wrestling Then & Now* appeared. Ginzburg reminisced, "For issue one, I wrote a piece on the irony of seeing a match between Bruiser Brody and Jose Gonzales, which was a meaningless prelim, and years later Jose Gonzales allegedly stabbed Bruiser Brody to death. How ironic it was to see them in an eight-minute match that nobody even remembers and years later, it was the same two guys who changed wrestling history.

AT WORK . . .

courtesy of Evan Ginzburg

. . . AND AT PLAY

Mike Lano

Evan Ginzburg,
Editor & Publisher, *Wrestling Then & Now*

"I had absolutely no subscribers. Some of my more charitable friends and family members would throw me a couple of dollars and say 'good luck' with it, never realizing that the thing would last and eventually be read all over the world.

"I sent out copies to other fanzines, and several gave it good reviews. By the second issue, I had a handful of paid subscribers. It sort of mushroomed from there."

The newsletter grew at a slow but steady rate. Because of the nature of the subject matter, Ginzburg knew his publication would not expand as quickly as one which featured current wrestling news. He explained, "I've never had more than a cult following, but it's something I'm proud of, regardless. For the most part, the fans who are interested in wrestling history disappeared in disgust after 10 years of hillbillies and ridiculous gimmicks and steroid freaks. The old-time fan is gone, and it's very hard to lure him back to reading the newsletter when he hasn't even watched wrestling in a very long time. It's a tough sell, but the spirit of fanzine publishing is that you do something you love because you want to be creative and express yourself, not to live off it and get rich from it."

Today's wrestling has put fans in opposing corners. Some love it and others hate it. The question arose, "Is some of the allure of modern wrestling detracting from the wrestling or enhancing the entertainment?" Ginzburg answered, "For a while, I was doing play-by-play for a small promotion, Ultimate Championship Wrestling. Believe me, some of those guys were doing moves that the guys from the '70s couldn't even dream about. I mean, the acrobatics, the high risks, the maneuvers off the top rope and things of that nature.

"Speed has definitely increased, but sometimes it's flash just for the sake of flash. I don't need blaring entrance music.

I don't need glaring lights. I don't need wrestlers in the stands with microphones interrupting a good match. I basically want to see a good match with a good story.

"The wrestlers were literally turned into cartoon characters. The WWF has had actual cartoons and comic books. Wrestling in the '60s and '70s, however, was really pretty much like the movies. The theme was revenge. Somebody did something wrong, they were out for blood and they were out for revenge. There was an intensity that isn't there today.

"Hulk Hogan comes out. The guy has a stupid TV show and no matter how much he screams, it's always like, 'nudge, nudge, wink, wink.' When Harley Race, Jack Brisco, Nick Bockwinkel or anybody came out for a title defense back then, people were in awe. It was important. It had meaning."

The sheets sometimes hold a disproportionate amount of importance in the wrestling business—an influence that at times can be far wider ranging than their actual size. Ginzburg explained, "I think the sheets' effect on ratings and sales of tickets is absolutely minuscule. The most successful sheets have either hundreds or thousands of readers, not millions. On Monday night television, around five million people watch wrestling. The sheets do not affect ratings or ticket sales, but where it does have a tremendous effect is that every major sheet gets in the hands of the people in power and the opinions of the hardcores, who are in a sense the experts of the fans, are valued by the promoters.

"For example, guys like Cactus Jack, Sabu and Sean Waltman were making $50 a night in little rinky-dink independents, and once the sheets began hyping them, they became major, major stars."

Do the sheets serve a purpose other than supplying information to their readers? According to Ginzburg, "They serve in a sense that in society wrestling is looked down upon. It's considered imbecilic, and the hardcores love it and respect it. It's a forum for them to express this passion that society doesn't understand. They see big cartoon characters and laugh at it, whereas we can distinguish just like a film critic can between garbage in the ring and art. When a Terry Funk gets in the ring, it's art. When a Hulk Hogan gets in the ring, it's garbage. It's like a film, play, book or any other form of entertainment. The hardcores grasp this, where the casual fan, channel-surfing, does not see this at all. They just see big men in tights throwing phony punches at each other. The average person thinks this is goofy, this is comedy. We understand exactly what it is and enjoy it for that reason."

One of the hottest topics for wrestling sheet editors today is the Internet. Ginzburg is no exception. He thinks the Internet may take away sheet readers who subscribe to news sheets, but he sees little interference from the Internet with *WT&N*. He stated, "I think the Internet is going to have a negative effect on the news sheets, because even if the news sheets are weekly, the Internet is instant. From what I understand, it's having an effect right now on the news sheets; however, it won't affect the history sheets because there are very few history sheets and they (Internet journalists) just don't have the knowledge. I've documented over a thousand pages of wrestling history over the past eight years. They don't have this information, for the most part.

"The Internet is really a news medium; however, a lot of the information they're giving out is absolutely wrong. There have been reports that Sid Vicious died. It was all over the Internet. There were reports that Rick Steiner had died in a car crash."

Ginzburg is well aware of the history and the progression of wrestling newsletters. He stated, "Early on, the sheets were very much like the wrestling business itself. Never expose the business. It was a taboo. It was an absolute taboo. I once wrote an article for a small sheet in the '70s saying how pitiful Ivan Putski was. He was a major headliner in those days. He headlined Madison Square Garden when Bruno was injured. I said how lazy Putski was and the editor was offended that I used the word 'lazy' because it exposed the business, even though it was absolutely true.

"One of the early pioneers of real wrestling journalism was Mike Lano, who actually had wrestlers writing for the sheets. He actually treated it much more mature and adultlike. The wrestlers would never, never give legitimate information to the regular sheets, and Lano changed this. It just got away from, 'I'm gonna get that guy in the ring and beat him up.' It just took it to a different level. Unfortunately, Lano went to dental school and didn't pursue it like he could have. He sort of missed the gold mine.

"After Lano, a few sheets emerged which became much more open and took wrestling reporting to heights that had never been experienced before. And when the more knowledgeable fans discovered these sheets, it was almost like this secret world had been opened up. It was an incredible thing to see it written so openly. I think when the Internet explodes even further and people really want to explore the history of wrestling, these sheets will be the texts because it doesn't exist otherwise.

"The promotions themselves almost make a mockery of their own history. They bring back former champions under different names and turn them into buffoons, like the Iron Sheik. It's criminal. They have no sense of pride in their own history. With the promotions, it's all about money, and it's all about money TODAY. In fact, when major stars die, it's rarely mentioned or acknowledged. That's the money from yesterday. Even though wrestlers like Andre or Big John Studd made them millions and millions of dollars, that's yesterday's news."

Every major sport has its own Hall of Fame. Many athletes do not consider their careers fulfilled unless they are given the accolade of Hall of Fame membership in their respective sports. Wrestling is no exception. The WWF has its own Hall of Fame, but Ginzburg tells us about the travesty of its membership. He concluded, "Baron Scicluna, who was for many years an opening match wrestler, although he was a legitimate tag-team champ at one point, he's in the WWF Hall of Fame. Putski is in the WWF Hall of Fame. Bruno Sammartino, who was their legendary champion for 10 years, but who is on bad terms with the WWF for a variety of reasons, is not in their Hall of Fame. Until they put Bruno in, how can you take the WWF Hall of Fame seriously?"

If you ask Ginzburg why his publication has endured while others have gone the way of the dinosaur, he will give you one answer: "The staff. We have the best writing staff in wrestling sheetdom—published authors, award-winning journalists and many other writers from columnists to feature writers. We differ because of the emotion our writers put in their works. In addition to the factual stories, our writers produce heartfelt and emotional pieces that transcend the subject matter of wrestling."

About a year ago, Ginzburg expanded *WT&N* to 16 pages. With the additional pages came a new look. The newsletter now is produced in a magazine-style format and includes photos. Wrestlers Killer Kowalski and Bryan Walsh write monthly columns, and the legends of the sport are regularly interviewed. At a time when some sheets either have decreased their number of pages or ceased to exist because of the Internet, *WT&N* appears to be ready for the next century in its chronicling of wrestling history.

THEN . . .

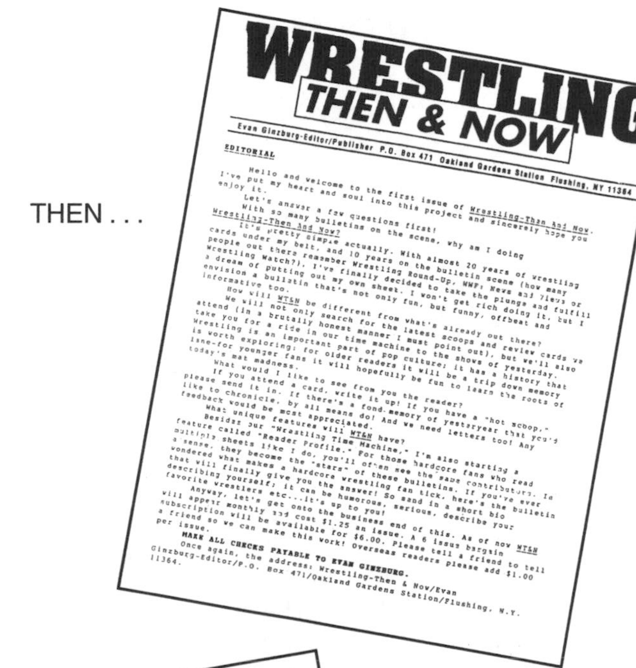

WRESTLING THEN & NOW

Evan Ginzburg-Editor/Publisher P.O. Box 471 Oakland Gardens Station Flushing, NY 11364

EDITORIAL

Hello and welcome to the first issue of Wrestling-Than And Now. I've put my heart and soul into this project and sincerely hope you enjoy it.

Let's answer a few questions first!

With so many bulletins on the scene, why am I doing Wrestling-Then And Now?

It's pretty simple actually. With almost 20 years of wrestling cards under my belt, and 10 years on the bulletin scene (how many people out there remember Wrestling Round-Up, WWF: News and Views or Wrestling Watch?), I've finally decided to take the plunge and fulfill a dream of putting out my own sheet. I won't get rich doing it, but I envision a bulletin that's not only fun, but funny, offbeat and informative too.

How will WT&N be different from what's already out there?

We will not only search for the latest scoops and review cards we attend (in a brutally honest manner I must point out), but we'll also take you for a ride in our time machine to the shows of yesterday. Wrestling is an important part of pop culture; it has a history that is worth exploring: for older readers it will be a trip down memory lane-for younger fans it will hopefully be fun to learn the roots of today's mat madness.

What would I like to see from you the reader?

If you attend a card, write it up! If you have a "hot scoop," please send it in. If there's a fond memory of yesteryear that you'd like to chronicle, by all means do! And we need letters too! Any feedback would be most appreciated.

What unique features will WT&N have?

Besides our "Wrestling Time Machine," I'm also starting a feature called "Reader Profile." For those hardcore fans who read multiple sheets like I do, you'll often see the same contributors. In a sense, they become the "stars" of these bulletins. If you've ever wondered what makes a hardcore wrestling fan tick, here's the bulletin that will finally give you the answer! So send in a short bio describing yourself; it can be humorous, serious, describe your favorite wrestlers etc...it's up to you!

Anyway, let's get onto the business end of this. As of now WT&N will appear monthly and cost $1.25 an issue. A 6 issue bargain subscription will be available for $6.00. Please tell a friend to tell a friend so we can make this work! Overseas readers please add $1.00 per issue.

MAKE ALL CHECKS PAYABLE TO EVAN GINZBURG.

Once again, the address: Wrestling-Then & Now/Evan Ginzburg-Editor/P.O. Box 471/Oakland Gardens Station/Flushing, N.Y. 11364.

. . . & NOW

Wrestling Then & Now

WRESTLING CHATTERBOX

In the words of Monty Python's Flying Circus, "And now for something completely different."

Most sheets report on wrestling's current news while a few feature the history of professional wrestling. The *Wrestling Chatterbox* covers both news and nostalgia, but its specialty is reporting on the human side of the wrestlers themselves. For instance, you can read about a wrestler's birthday or the birth of a wrestler's child as well as other little-known tidbits of personal information about the grapplers.

Georgiann Makropoulos of New York has been the editor of *Wrestling Chatterbox* for almost eight years. Her publication is one of the few sheets that provide inside information for its readers, yet is well-liked by the wrestling promotions as well.

Makropoulos began to admire professional wrestling early in life. After she had a bout with meningitis, her grandfather, a big wrestling fan, treated her to a live wrestling match. She was a teenager at the time. Makropoulos stated, "When I got out of the hospital, my grandfather took me to Sunnyside Gardens. He took me just to get me out somewhere. I don't even remember the card, but it was love at first sight. Being I'm six feet tall, I just fell in love with those big men."

After her introduction to professional wrestling, Makropoulos became insatiable in her pursuit of following the sport. She added, "We had Channel 9. We had Bruno Sammartino, Buddy Rogers, Bill Miller, Hans Mortier, all those guys, Rocca, Miguelito Perez, Ricky Starr. I saw Gorgeous George in person at Sunnyside. I've been a continuous fan. I go to every show at the Garden (Madison Square Garden). I think I've missed, like, five shows since 1960."

Makropoulos began to expand her affinity for professional wrestling in fields other than viewing the sport. She explained, "I always wrote for wrestling magazines. That's how I started. I worked for Lou Sahadi in the late '60s or early '70s. Once you get involved with it, you can't stop.

"Before I met Lou, I had fan clubs for Buddy Rogers, Bruno Sammartino, Bob Orton, Sr. and Bill Zybysko. That's how I really started. I became friends with Lou Sahadi, and he said I had to write for magazines. He said, 'Let's make some money for you.' The fan clubs made no money back then.

"The first magazine I wrote for was *Wrestling World.* Then he got *Wrestling Confidential,* and I started writing three columns. I listed everybody's fan club and started selling pictures. Eventually, I started writing editorials on different wrestlers. We had 'Wrestling After Dark.' It was like who's having a baby, who's married, who's not, that kind of stuff."

After she began writing, Makropoulos discovered that there was a restraint on certain subjects in the wrestling business. She said, "I let the news out. Nobody stopped me, but there was still a closed lid on personal lives, even back then."

After a few years, Makropoulos found herself without publications to write for, yet she was still addicted to reporting on inside wrestling news. She stated, "I wasn't into anything. Lou Sahadi was no longer with wrestling magazines. You miss when you start and then you're not doing anything. A friend of mine brought my first copy machine to my house. We started running a few things off and *Wrestling Chatterbox* was started."

Once issue number one was ready, Makropoulos had to get it into the hands of prospective subscribers. She said, "We handed out free issues when we went to the wrestling matches.

courtesy of Georiann Makropoulos

**Georgiann Makropoulos (center)
with Superstar Billy Graham and Ric Flair**

We started with about 40 subscribers and now have over a thousand. We're quite pleased. We're overseas—England, Belgium, Japan and Australia."

Makropoulos provided a few more details about her fan-friendly sheet. "I always announce birthdays a month in advance so if the fans want to send their favorite wrestlers a card, or whatever, they have the opportunity to do it. We do a lot of personal stuff. Adam Bomb just got married. He's sending us a picture, and he doesn't mind if we use it in the *Chatterbox*. It's something no one else is going to have."

Makropoulos has begun to write more critically of the wrestling business and has come close to the line where the fans and organizations do not like the criticism, but she has not crossed it. She added, "I really try to stay away from the politics of wrestling. We do touch it, however. Lately, I've been doing a lot of bashing, and I'm getting a lot of heat for it because I'm not too happy with the product right now. The people don't want to hear that. They love wrestling if it's bad or horrible or whatever, but they want to hear good stuff. I've begun to tone down my editorials a little bit. But I am really disgusted with the product right now because it's Mickey Mouse."

The

WRESTLING CHATTERBOX

Newsletter

November 1996 Kno Chatterboxer !! *Issue LXXVII*

Hot Rod is back .... and WCW's got him!

Wrestling Chatterbox is published 12 times Per Year
Subscriptions: **USA** - $2.50/month, $25/year **OVERSEAS** - $4/month, $40/year
Make check or money order payable to **Georgiann Makropoulos**
(Not responsible for cash sent through the mail)
Editor: **Georgiann Makropoulos** - 23-44 30th Drive, Astoria, New York 11102-3252
Cover: Drawn by **Pete Theophall**

WWF / courtesy of Georgiann Makropoulos

Currently, *Wrestling Chatterbox* consists of 12 pages. Makropoulos raves about the quality of the publication's covers and the artist responsible for them, Pete Theophall. Every month, she sends a copy to the major wrestling promotions. According to her, "Everybody is pretty positive."

As is the case with most fanzine publications, the best publicity for *Wrestling Chatterbox* is "word of mouth." According to Makropoulos, "If someone writes me a letter because they've heard about it through the grapevine, I always send out a complimentary issue. I feel that if they see the product, it will draw them. I'd say that out of every 10 complimentary issues, we get seven or eight who will subscribe.

The turnaround is good. A sample copy is worth a thousand words. We go to a lot of shows. We hand out newsletters to the audience."

Makropoulos has no intention at this time to expand the size of her publication. She said, "We're doing well at 12 pages, so we'll keep it as it is. We do have a nostalgia page because it's important to remember the history of wrestling, and if we or other sheets don't do it, it's going to be forgotten."

What does Makropoulos see for the future of wrestling in the next decade? She concluded, "That's hard to say because every time I think they're down and out, they sort of pick themselves up by the pants and pull themselves up again. If it goes like it's going, professional wrestling will really do well."

MAT MARKETPLACE

Sheldon Goldberg of Boston produces a sheet which highlights wrestling memorabilia. In his publication, you can find items for sale, or gain the information about how to find wrestling-related memorabilia. Wrestling memorabilia is as varied as that of other sports, including dolls, posters, event programs, autographs, masks and other collectible wrestling items.

Goldberg, like many of those involved with the sheets today, became a professional wrestling fan at an early age. He said, "My first memory of professional wrestling was sitting with my old grandmother in our apartment in front of the Philco black-and-white TV set watching Buddy Rogers and people like that. I was four or five years old. At about the age of seven or eight, I began to comprehend what was going on. Bruno Sammartino was the champion. Sammartino was the man."

As he got older, Goldberg expanded the list of the wrestlers whom he admired. He added, "There are a number of wrestlers I've really liked a lot through the years—Victor Rivera, Tony Marino. I'll never forget while I was in junior high school seeing Karl Gotch and thinking he was the greatest thing I ever saw. He and Rene Goulet were tag team champions. When Gotch came in, he was billed as the man of a thousand holds. You could see that he was really something special just by the way he moved and what he was able to do. He was such a skilled guy. I hate to use a cliche, but 'poetry in motion' applied to Gotch. There is really no other way for me to describe him.

"Another wrestler who was very special was Bruno Sammartino. You just saw Bruno and believed he was the guy for the role. I have this theory about Bruno. A Hollywood studio is looking for a guy to cast in the role of a wrestling champion. You couldn't come up with a better guy than Bruno Sammartino. He was a guy who a lot of working-class people identified with—an Italian immigrant who escaped the Nazis at the end of World War II. He came to the United States as a 98-pound weakling and built himself up into one of the strongest men in sports. It's a real Charles Atlas story."

Goldberg earned a degree in Theater from the University of Massachusetts. He produced plays in Boston, New York and Atlantic City, specializing in musical revues until the economics of the 1980s slowly led him away from engaging in theatrical productions. While he was in the business, however, an event occurred which, unknown to him at the time, would whet Goldberg's appetite for business-related professional wrestling ventures. He said, "Just before I started producing, I did publicity for Broadway shows on tour here in Boston. I met a guy called Joe Perkins, and he was a big deal in terms of local advertising. What I didn't know at the time was that he was the guy who syndicated the local WWF show. He had worked for years for Vince McMahon, Sr. He went all the way back to the '50s with Vince, Sr. When I found this out, I talked to Joe about it. I began to look at professional wrestling in a different way.

"I was in the live event business, so I had a tremendous amount of respect for wrestlers. I had met a number of wrestlers around that time, and having been a theater person, I can tell you that I never met an actor who is worth a damn compared to a professional wrestler. It takes a very special kind of person to have the amount of dedication that one has to have to be a professional wrestler. One takes a tremendous amount of risks just to step out from behind the curtain and step down through the ropes. It takes a special kind of person to be an actor, too, but not to the same degree. When you become an actor or a professional wrestler, you're making a commitment to leading a life that is different from everyone else's life. Being an actor, you're not always putting yourself in physical jeopardy. If you're a professional wrestler, your career could be over in a heartbeat. For a guy who's working with actors, singers and playwrights, people who are artists, I have a built-in appreciation for professional wrestlers that perhaps most people don't have. I simply saw it differently."

After meeting Joe Perkins, Goldberg took a step up from ordinary fandom and began to research wrestling publications. "I began to subscribe to some of the newsletters and followed the business a lot more closely. When the mid-'80s hit and wrestling started to take off, I had this enhanced interest in wrestling."

Goldberg finally put all his pieces of the puzzle together—love of wrestling and knowledge of wrestling memorabilia—and produced his first edition of *Mat Marketplace* in 1991. He said, "I had an idea that I wanted to do something in the wrestling business and, even if it weren't successful, I would at least enjoy the attempt at doing something that rekindled all my memories. Before I came out with my first issue, I started looking for stuff and found there really wasn't a publication out there which catered to collectors. I started doing serious collecting; mostly paper—books, posters and things of that nature. I soon discovered that whenever you start collecting something, you become a resource for other people who are doing the same thing. People would call and say, 'Gee, I just bought this book off you, do you know anybody who has this poster?'

"The whole sports memorabilia field was really beginning to take off at that point, and I came out with a sample two pages. I sent it out free to prospective subscribers and got about 120 subscribers immediately."

Goldberg's initiation into the publishing business was successful, but something occurred after putting his second issue out that he never anticipated. In describing the big break, Goldberg explained, "When I put the second issue out, I was looking for information from people who were professionals in the sports memorabilia field and what they knew about professional wrestling memorabilia. I sent a copy along with a letter to Leland's, which is like the Sotheby's of sports memorabilia. What I did not realize was that this gentleman wrote a column for *Sports Collectors Digest*. He published an article with a story about my publication.

"I went to my mailbox one day and found a note saying that I had a lot of mail to pick up at the main post office. When I arrived, the postman gave me bags of mail. I couldn't believe that I had three or four hundred inquiries from the article that was written about my publication—and a fair number subscribed. That's what really started the ball rolling."

After he had a few newsletters under his belt, he saw that his publication filled a void in memorabilia collecting. "I started serving as more of a personal clearinghouse. When you have a publication like *Mat Marketplace*, you soon realize that you have easy access to information about what the public wants to buy. If you can fill the needs of the readers, then you are serving your subscribers in a valuable way.

"I began dealing in things to sell, but I limited what I would deal in. I dealt with items that I thought were worthy collectors items or worthy merchandise items that were somewhat unusual—things you couldn't get readily anyplace else. I started to import a few things such as toys from Japan and masks and other items from Mexico. Occasionally, I will have a find of something that is vintage, but it's harder and harder to find that stuff.

"The wrestling collectibles market is probably the most undervalued collectors market there is. The reason for that is the lack of real cataloguing or history behind it. It's not a defined market. For example, boxing collectibles are very defined. If I ever have the time, I would love to do a master guide."

In May 1998, the Arts & Entertainment Network presented a documentary on professional wrestling called "The Unreal History of Professional Wrestling." The repercussions of this documentary were immediate. The program attained the second-highest rating of any program that A&E had ever produced, and the mainstream media began to discuss professional wrestling on a level higher than it had previously. One of the experts that A&E interviewed for the special was Sheldon Goldberg. His face was seen by tens of millions of viewers.

The experience gave Goldberg an aura of notoriety for which he was not prepared. He said, "You have no idea of the responses I received because of the special. I must have gotten over 100 e-mails from people, including one from a cousin I hadn't seen in 25 years. The only person I spoke to who really didn't like me on the special was my girlfriend."

Goldberg's newly found fame came unsolicited. According to him, "I got a letter from the producer of the documentary. Apparently, they had gone on the Internet and looked for people with web sites for wrestling. They said, 'Ah, merchandise and memorabilia. Maybe this guy knows something.'"

Goldberg is an expert on wrestling history, yet he fully acknowledges that there are wrestling historians who exceed him in knowledge of the sport's history. He added, "I don't consider myself to be as much of an expert as I've been publicly

portrayed. There are guys out there who are certainly far better as far as historical knowledge of professional wrestling is concerned. I was extremely nervous.

"As much as I enjoyed it, the more you're in the history of it, the more of a stickler you become for accuracy. You have to remember, it's impossible to cover 100 years of anything in two hours. There is no record book in wrestling like in other sports."

For the time being, Goldberg is putting all his energies into increasing his involvement in the wrestling business. He concluded, "I am so fascinated by the professional wrestling business, and I've been very fortunate to have become more involved in the business in the last couple of years. It is incredible show business.

"As I started to put the publication out, I was not only amazed with the response, but also with what people were responding. I literally had lawyers, doctors and accountants; not just little kids who were looking for a Hulk Hogan doll. These were people who were professionals who really loved wrestling, who had memories of it they cherished. The quality of people really impressed me. I've met many wonderful people publishing the newsletter and have made some tremendous friends and tremendous friendships. I have readers in 25 countries. I never cease to learn things from people who write to me. It's been a very rewarding experience emotionally."

THE INTERNET

Every time someone in a professional wrestling organization says, "Those fucking sheets," there is someone in sheetdom saying, "That fucking Internet." In the past year, the amount of information about professional wrestling on the

Internet has increased at an incredible rate and is still expanding almost daily.

This new infusion of information carries a dual message—there is good news and there is bad news. First, let's look at the good news.

Once one logs on-line, there are myriad wrestling sites, including many with sheets themselves. Some sheet editors run an Internet version of their publications while keeping the "hard copy" rendition for their regular subscribers. For some, the Internet is a tool to enhance their publications.

In addition, there are dozens of chat boards which bring instant news to wrestling fans. These boards are updated daily and, in some instances, immediately. An Internet surfer could literally go back and forth on a few bulletin boards and be instantly up-to-date on most wrestling news.

There are many feature sites that combine current news with history. They usually do not present themselves in the same manner as a sheet, but they are loaded with information and often with pictures.

Now for the bad news. The Internet is immediate. Until recently, when a subscriber received his or her weekly newsletter with current news, it was the most up-to-date information available. With the Internet, however, this sheet news is mostly outdated by the time a subscriber receives a sheet. In other words, the immediate information gathered on the Net makes the sheets dated. Because of this access to immediate news, many sheets have suffered drastic decreases in subscribers.

It appears to be a cut-and-dried issue: the Internet has put sheets out of business while increasing the amount of on-line readers. However, there are a couple of glitches in the system.

For one, the Internet sites aren't always accurate. Take the rumors that are constantly bandied about, for example. Last year, the Internet was abuzz with the death of Psycho Sid. Sid never died. He is wrestling regularly today for various independent promotions. Shortly after Sid's fictitious death came the news of Rick Steiner being killed in a car crash. Steiner is still a regular with the WCW today. Unfortunately, there is much more misinformation on the Internet than in the sheets, but it takes the reader a long time to discover the variances.

Now for the worst part of Internet wrestling sites. The sheets use writers of varying degrees of talent. Some are wrestling fans who attempt to write and get their message across. Most of the time, the articles are accurate. There are experienced, published writers who happen to be wrestling fans who write for certain sheets. When a reader digests an article by one of these craftspeople, he or she is reading the finest portrayal of wrestling journalism.

The Internet has spawned hundreds of writers or reporters who call themselves "journalists," but, unfortunately, most have a hard time spelling the word "journalist," let alone being one. Their writing is deplorable, mostly at about a sixth-grade level or less. It is tedious even attempting to make out what they are trying to say. Their work would never be considered, let alone accepted, by a regular sheet.

Wrestling news on the Internet is immediate, but it is not always accurate, sometimes bordering on the absurd. If you admire well-written pieces, do not look for them on the Internet—they don't exist. You will only become frustrated as you scroll down the numerous typographical errors, misspellings, and atrocious uses of the English language.

As in many aspects of information, the wrestling community is attempting to make sense of the Internet. Sheet editors are aspiring to find a way in which they can use the Internet as a tool while keeping their higher-than-Internet standards alive. Because of ever-changing technology, there will be dramatic changes in the manner in which wrestling news is distributed. If sheet editors find a way to combine their reporting with new technologies, we could be at the dawn of a revolution in receiving astute, well-written professional wrestling news.

*** ***

SCENE III

LES ARTISTES

Professional wrestling is highly visual and is a prime subject for artwork of various styles. Other forms of entertainment, such as comic books, science fiction books, cinema and horror magazines have had their own distinct styles for decades, yet professional wrestling has no actual tradition of its own artistic style. This lack of strict mode, however, is possibly an asset for the depiction of wrestling on canvas, because those who have taken pen or brush to hand have had no style restrictions. They have combined the effects of different styles of entertainment art to produce breathtaking and creative effects.

There are wrestling artists who have never stepped into a ring, while others actually were professional grapplers. We will look at three artists who produce work related to wrestling, as well as other subjects. This, by no means, is an entire look at the field of wrestling art. In comparison to participants of other sports, there appears to be a disproportionate number of wrestlers who have become artists after their careers in the ring. Some have produced world-class works, while others merely dabble in art as a hobby.

BILL KUNKEL—CARTOONIST EXTRAORDINAIRE

Eventually, you rip off enough people and you've kind of got a style of your own.

— Bill Kunkel

For years, Bill Kunkel of Las Vegas has been cranking out cartoons relating to professional wrestling. He produces one-liners as well as strips. Kunkel, an avid professional wrestling fan, has never been a wrestler, yet he has been involved with the business for almost three decades.

Kunkel was born in Brooklyn, New York, and for the next 39 years, except for a brief stint in New Orleans, he resided in the New York area. In 1989, he moved to Las Vegas, where he still continues his operation.

For the first eight years of his life, Kunkel was unaware of professional wrestling. On Thanksgiving Day of 1958, that all changed. According to Kunkel, "I was enjoying the fruits of the after-Thanksgiving feast—turkey, sandwiches and all that stuff. The TV was on, as it always was in my house. I'm the prototypical boob-tube baby. We got a set when I was two or three years old, and I can't remember a time when we didn't have a TV. It was always on. Suddenly, I turned around and saw the most incredible thing I had ever seen in my life. They were announcing that this man, Dr. Jerry Graham, had just returned from the Orient. He was wearing a kimono. He had peroxide blond hair and claimed he had just developed the deadliest wrestling hold in the world—the Oriental Sleeper. I saw him wrap up a wrestler like a Cobra swallowing an egg. Then he threw on the sleeper, and I fell in love with professional wrestling. I've been in love ever since."

As Kunkel gained years, his list of admirable wrestlers increased. "As a kid, my favorite wrestlers were the Grahams. I never got to see Eddie and Jerry, but I saw Jerry and Luke (Crazy Luke Graham) who was always a favorite of mine. Later on, the Valiant Brothers were my absolute favorite guys. I got to meet them and interview them a couple of times when I was working in the business. I loved the peroxide blond brother acts that I got to see. I remember Killer Kowalski and Gorilla Monsoon who were my absolutely top-of-the-world favorite heels. I can remember Brute Bernard, Handsome Johnny Barend, Magnificent Maurice and, of course, Bruno."

When Kunkel mentioned "Bruno," his voice changed. He no longer was talking about a mere mortal who was gifted with superb athletic and entertainment skills. He was talking about a person who was above the status of human being—a person who was revered like no other for a time in the 1950s, 1960s and 1970s in the New York area. Kunkel explained, "If you grew up in New York in the '50s and '60s and you were into wrestling, there was only Bruno. Even to the very last days of his prime, his ability to control a crowd, as good as Hogan was and as Hitleresque as Stone Cold Steve Austin is, exceeded that of everyone before him and after him. The power that Bruno could generate, the drama and the body language, were operatic. His feuds were classic. His feuds would play out very methodically and very formulaically. In the first match, he was generally attacked from behind and often beaten rather badly. The villain would run away. In the second match, they would actually come to grips and would fight to a contested conclusion. The third match would be all Bruno. The heel would be beating the crap out of Bruno, and suddenly he would do his version of the Superman comeback, which was not unmotivated like the Hogan one years later. He would build to it and would reach this moment of climax when he would sort of turn to the crowd, asking them with his body language, 'Now I destroy him?' and the crowd would respond, 'Yes, Bruno. Destroy him. Strike him down.' He would go in and do it. It was operatic."

Throughout the years, Kunkel has worked on various projects concerning professional wrestling, from art to magazine publishing to photography to computer software design. Until recently, the professional wrestling organizations mostly worked in a stealth manner in depicting their own results or history. The reason was simple. The promotions did not want the public to know that the same show ran night-after-night in city-after-city. Kunkel was aware of this repetition, and a business venture in the 1980s brought this fact vividly home. According to Kunkel, "In the mid-'80s, Arnie Katz and I convinced a software publisher to go to the WWF, who were just beginning to get big, and buy the license for a computer game. We created a computer game using actual footage from the matches so the customer would have to buy a match disk. Once you owned the game, if you wanted to view Hulk Hogan vs. Rick Rude, you would have to buy that match disk. We included two match disks with each game, and if you wanted other matches, you could just buy the disk.

"Someone with the WWF used to send us tapes so we could pick out the footage that would be the best examples of the different holds and we could digitize the footage. You would see Ted DiBiase vs. Hulk Hogan working in four different towns. I would get to see the match as they worked the whole circuit. It was literally the same match—here's the comeback, ducks under the clothesline. I realized then how closely they were duplicating these matches. Today, all you have to do is read a current sheet and check out the times of the matches in each city. They may give you a break and have two endings now—Do we do ending A tonight, or ending B?"

Kunkel had no formal art training. He attended high school in Queens and after that went to Pace College. He stated, "My uncle was head of security at Pace. My only interest in attending was to avoid the draft. Eventually, my life degenerated sufficiently so I didn't need a college deferment to get out of the draft. I was a total degenerate."

During the 1970s, Kunkel dabbled in rock music as well as wrestling-related ventures. It wasn't until the following decade that he finally began to illustrate the humorous side of wrestling with a pen. He added, "I started drawing in 1981. I was 31 years old. I never thought I could draw. My dad had a little bit of art talent and taught me how to draw a sideways head. That was about the limit. I didn't get it. Then I got into science fiction fandom and saw a lot of cartoonists, guys like Bill Rotsler, who died recently, who did a lot of work in nudie films and stuff, but he was a brilliant cartoonist. He would do these simple little characters who were so eloquent and so expressive. I thought, 'Gee, I think I can do that,' and so I started doing it. I began, like most people do—like I did in music—ripping off other people. Eventually, you rip off enough people and you've kind of got a style of your own.

"For years, when I was doing those cartoons, the wrestling cartoons, I would just start drawing something and would get halfway through and I'd go, 'That kind of looks like Michael Hayes, so I guess I'll do a Michael Hayes cartoon.' That was how I did almost every cartoon."

With experience came enhanced skill for Kunkel. In addition, he saw that there was a great need for good wrestling cartoons. He stated, "I think I started doing wrestling cartoons around the mid-'80s. I come from science fiction fandom where the magazines were festooned with cartoons. I saw that lacking in wrestling publications. There were almost no cartoons, and the cartoons that were there were awful. I knew I could draw that well, so I started doing cartoons and they all got published.

"I got very friendly with Wade Keller and became a columnist for him and was voted the most popular columnist the first two years I was writing for the magazine. I think I helped him get the magazine started, and I did tons of cartoons for him. When he had used them and sent them all back to me, it was like a huge envelope they came in. It is unbelievable when I look back and remember the time it took doing these. There were thousands of wrestling cartoons."

Kunkel's love of cartoons opened up doors for him at the top level of the art—comic books. Ironically, his skills at this level consisted primarily of writing the scripts for various characters for several top-name companies. According to Kunkel, "I wrote *Richie Rich the Little Rich Kid* for Harvey Comics. I was one of the main scripters. As far as comics go, I love writing them, but I'm just not that much into superheroes, although I did work at DC and at Marvel."

The list of credits that Kunkel has amassed in the comic book field is impressive. "I sold my first story to DC in 1971. I did mostly horror stuff for them. I continued working for them until around 1977. For DC, I did Lois Lane stuff, and I did some private life of Clark Kent stories. Mostly, I did horror stuff—*Tales of the Unexpected, House of Mystery.* Then I went over to Marvel. I did a *Daredevil* and a couple of Marvel *Spiderman* team-ups. I did a lot of work for their European line."

"Potshot" cartoons from Bill Kunkel

Despite his success at writing for DC and Marvel, Kunkel still wanted to do something outside the superhero/horror realm. Opportunity showed itself when Harvey Comics intervened. Kunkel said, "I got a chance to go over to Marvel and that was really cool. It wasn't superheroes and it gave me a chance to do funny stuff and adventure. I've always thought in a very visual sense. What I use my drawing ability for professionally is to create story boards. In terms of game design or any kind of project design, I can do the original thumbnails that would then go to a real artist who would transform it. This is what I did with Richie Rich.

"When I was at Harvey, Richie was publishing something like 32 titles a month. That's a lot of titles. Our biggest problem was coming up with new names for the books. They would okay two new books and I'd say, 'Christ, we've got gold, we've got silver, we've got platinum, we've got gems. We've got every possible thing.' We raped the thesaurus for any word we could find."

Currently, Kunkel is working for a company that is involved in producing comics. "They own a lot of European licenses. In Europe, comic books are very different. They are so much more popular. We have comics like *Dillon Dog* in Italy that sell a million copies every issue. They have stuff like *Jeremiah* that was the basic inspiration for *Mad Max.*"

Before Kunkel became involved with comic book companies, he was one of the pioneers of modern wrestling journalism. In the 1970s, most wrestling publications were spokespublications for the promotions. They published what the federations wanted them to, and there was little truth or real insight into professional wrestling. The magazines contained fabulous pictures of bloody wrestlers and interviews that were predictable almost to the word: "I hate [fill in name] and I'll beat him if it takes me the rest of my life. If I have to, I'll go all over the world to hunt him down."

Kunkel added realism and color to the depiction of professional wrestling with his magazine called *Main Event.* He reminisced, "It was basically wrapped around the old WWWF. It really was descriptions of the matches and interviews. The descriptions were detailed match descriptions and were longer and much more detailed than anything out there at the time. Frankly, they were better written than those of any other publication. We were trying to set up as realistically as possible. We tried to patch up holes in continuity.

"In those days, the magazines could basically make up anything they wanted—literally make up the wildest crap you could ever imagine. It was great reading on a level of science fiction, but we were trying to be serious about it. We tried to convey that wrestling was a great sport and it should be written in the same manner as one would write about a dramatic baseball game. That was our attempt."

Back in the 1970s, putting together a magazine similar to *Main Event* was a monumental, as well as expensive, task for a small staff. The typesetting alone took many hours of time, and the following paste-up of the publication was just as tedious. Today, one person with a comprehensive desktop publishing computer program can perform the same duties in a fraction of the time that it took several people to accomplish two decades ago. Kunkel called today's methods of producing a magazine, "one of the wonders of the computer revolution."

The magazine was successful for the time that Kunkel had exclusive rights to ringside photography of WWWF matches. Then Vince McMahon, Sr., the head of the WWWF, became ill and the organization began to change. The new policy did not help Kunkel at all. His product was in danger of becoming outdated before it reached the stands. According to Kunkel, "There was a lot of confusion going on. Vince, Sr. was very sick and Vince, Jr. was becoming the power. There was a lot of paranoia, and weird things were happening. We eventually reached a point where we never knew from month to month when we showed up at the Garden whether we would get in to take the shots or not. In those days, the feuds would run on the circuit through all the other arenas. The Garden was the first stop, and by the time we printed up the magazines, we would hit the other arenas where those same matches were happening. When we were uncertain about taking pictures at the Garden, we no longer could guarantee a quality, timely product.

BILL KUNKEL'S TRIFECTA OF FAVORITE WRESTLING STORIES

Everyone involved with professional wrestling has stories to tell, and Kunkel is not deficient in this area. He has many, but over the years, Kunkel has pared his accounts back to three standard tales which he tells anyone willing to listen. Following are the three classic anecdotes in his own words.

THE WRONG PLACE AT THE WRONG TIME

My first story concerns Spiros Arion and Bruno Sammartino. They were wrestling at Madison Square Garden where, at the time, I had pretty much complete access to the ring apron and backstage, although I couldn't go into the dressing rooms. Once the match had started, the photographers tended to be at ringside for the entire match. We didn't have much reason to go backstage.

It was coming to the end of the third or fourth Madison Square Garden Arion-Bruno match. They even sold out the Felt Forum where they had 3,000 people jammed in there watching on closed circuit TV. I was running out of film as the match was closing, so I ran backstage to find the film.

The finish was Bruno and Arion brawling down the aisle and disappearing through the curtain. As I heard them coming, I realized it was too late for me to go back out. All I could do was stand there like an idiot.

They came brawling down the aisle and kept coming closer and closer. They burst through the curtain, all the time brawling. When they were out of sight of the audience, they collapsed in each other's arms, laughing like hell. They suddenly looked around and saw me standing there. I just wanted to totally disappear. They instantly stiffened up, rigid, and walked away from each other, feigning animosity. I just ran back to the ring and stayed there for the remainder of the card.

THE GOOD SHIT

I was supposed to do an interview with Fred Blassie and Waldo Von Erich after a card one night. Fred and I were looking around for Waldo and couldn't find him. I asked someone, "Where's Waldo?" and he told me, "Check out the dressing room."

I knocked on the door of the heel dressing room and a voice asked, "Who is it?" I answered and was told to come in. When I entered, I saw Baron Scicluna sitting there. This was not the Baron Scicluna one saw in the ring. When he was not in his ring attire, when he was just sitting around in his baggy pants and his old spaghetti strap undershirt and his half-size reading glasses, he looked like your uncle. He was the most ordinary-looking guy in the world.

I asked if Waldo Von Erich was there. Scicluna nodded his head toward the toilet and said, “He’s taking a shit.” Suddenly, we heard a “plop.” The loudest plop you have ever heard in your life followed by this wonderfully self-satisfied grunt. Scicluna turned to me and amended his story with, “He’s taking a GOOOOOD shit.”

BLASSIE’S PHILOSOPHY ON LIFE

I showed up very early one night at Nassau Coliseum. There was nobody there except me, Fred Blassie and the ring crew. The head of the ring crew was a guy named Jon “Pinky” Larson, a tiny guy with a fringe of blond hair who was the eternal jobber. This guy never won a match ever. If two or three guys no-showed on a card, he might have to do two or three jobs a night. It was not uncommon.

Blassie was backstage and bored, so he was going to pull a rib on somebody. Larson was one of his favorite targets. He spotted Larson and asked me, “Got any film in that camera?” I said, “No, Fred. Want me to put some in?” He answered, “No, no. Keep it like it is. Just hold on to it.”

He then called Larson over. The jobber immediately asked, “What do you want Fred? Can I get you something?” Blassie countered, “Listen, your days of getting stuff are over. I’m here to give Bill Kunkel and *Main Event* a scoop. You are the next WWWF world champeen [sic], and I'm going to manage you." Pinky was dying at this point. "Look Fred, you wanna Coke? I can get you a Coke. There's Coke back there now." Blassie bellowed, "You're the champeen. You don't get Cokes for nobody, you pencil-necked geek." The harder he's selling this, the more Pinky is dying because he knows there's a sting waiting. Eventually, he broke and ran saying, "I'll get you that Coke, Fred."

Blassie was heartbroken. His rib had been ruined. He turned to me in disgust and said, "You can't make bullets out of shit."

WAYNE St. WAYNE—PORTRAYING WORLDS WITHIN WORLDS

A friend of mine wiped his program in Crusher's blood. Can you imagine what a collector's item that would be now?

– Wayne St. Wayne

Wayne St. Wayne approached the sport of wrestling in a no-holds-barred frenzy when he was in the ring. Today he approaches art in much the same manner. He is a prolific artist who specializes in wrestling art as well as cityscapes.

St. Wayne was born in St. Louis, Missouri, in 1954. He lived there until he went on the road on May 1, 1976. When his wrestling career began to wane, he again chose the city known as the Gateway to the West as his domicile.

Today, the 5'9" artist weighs 180 pounds. During his mat career, his weight would occasionally rise to about 225 pounds. According to St. Wayne, "I had to work hard to get my weight up, and it fluctuated a lot. Sometimes I would work hard in the ring, and sometimes I'd just say, 'Aaah,' and concentrate on partying and my weight would drop."

At the age of 13, St. Wayne acquired his first taste of professional wrestling on television. He took an instant liking to grappling and began a quest to find out as much information as possible about his new passion. He stated, "Later on, I would go downtown to the library and look up old newspaper clippings on microfilm and get all kinds of wrestling results. It was still several months before I went to my first live match. I remember not only the date, but the entire card. It was a double main event on May 17, 1968, at the Kiel Auditorium in St. Louis. In the first main event, Wilbur Snider took on The Crusher in a *Texas Death Match*. It was hard to tell them apart because they both had black trunks and were beefy with suntans. Both had blond flattops.

"I remember Crusher being thrown out of the ring, and he threw a chair up into the ring from the floor. By the time he got back in the ring, Snider had caught the chair and bashed Crusher over the head. We had a bit of color, which I realized later was kind of a rarity here in St. Louis. They always were pretty conservative as far as the use of blood, run-ins and interference. Later, I appreciated this restraint because when you do it less frequently, it means more when you do it.

"Afterwards we went down to ringside, and there were gobs of saliva and stuff on the mat. Also, there was some of Crusher's blood. A friend of mine wiped his program in Crusher's blood. Can you imagine what a collector's item that would be now?

"The other main event was a tag handicap with Dick the Bruiser against Bulldog Brower and Pat O'Connor. Bruiser won that one. And then the other matches were Edward Carpentier against Danny Miller; then there was Cowboy Bill Watts against The Spoiler. He unmasked The Spoiler, and it was Dale Lewis. It's still real vivid in my mind."

St. Wayne's attendance at his first live match whetted his appetite for more knowledge about professional wrestling. His passion was beginning to take on a comprehensive form. According to St. Wayne, "I was pretty obsessed with wrestling. I had penpals from around the country and up in Canada. When I went to the matches, I wouldn't buy just one program. I'd buy about 20 and send them to people, and they started taking snapshots, so I always had lots of fun stuff coming in the mail. I knew who was wrestling around the country because of the magazines and the programs. Any time a new guy came to St. Louis, I already knew about him."

After he graduated from high school, St. Wayne gained employment at the downtown YMCA in St. Louis. His job opened the door to his eventually becoming a professional wrestler. "I used the weights and gradually learned how to do them the right way, more or less. I just picked up different things from people I met in the gym. I met a guy named Joe Millich, and he kind of took a liking to me and trained me up in the mat room. There was no ring, just a mat. It took a couple of years for me to be skilled enough to actually go on the road and wrestle. He got me booked in Amarillo, Texas, in May of 1976."

St. Wayne's career began in 1976. For the next 17 years, he wrestled all over the United States and Canada. According to him, "The first few years, it was full time. In the early '80s, sometimes I would drop out for a few months. Other times, I would drop out for a year or more."

Like most wrestlers, St. Wayne can recall the best workers in the trade with whom he has performed. "I worked with Buddy Rogers in 1979 in Tampa. I had a short TV match with him, and it was just a thrill to be in there working with somebody like that. I worked with O'Connor a bunch of times."

The roster of opponents whom St. Wayne has faced is formidable. In addition to Rogers and O'Connor, it includes: Harley Race, both Briscos, Nick Bockwinkel, Dusty Rhodes, Paul Orndorff, Rufus R. Jones, Gene Kiniski, Dick Murdoch, Reggie Parks, Tully Blanchard, Buzz Sawyer, Ox Baker, Ray Stevens, Angelo Poffo, Rip Hawk, Swede Hanson, Loch Ness (Giant Haystacks of England), Dynamite Kid, Davey Boy Smith, Bret Hart and Jimmy Valiant.

Throughout his career, St. Wayne wrestled under various monikers. They include: Mike Hammer, Michelle Hammer, Buddy Frankenstein, Juice Elliot and Dr. Blood. Fans around the St. Louis area are familiar with St. Wayne as Dr. Blood, with some of his matches still making the rounds on local public access TV stations.

St. Wayne hung up his trunks in 1993. He said, "The last I worked was in 1993 for the local independent here in St. Louis. By then, I was only doing it once a month. I don't think I'm in ring shape today."

Wrestling has been an important aspect of St. Wayne's life since he was 13 years old. Art, his other passion, began to intrigue him at a much earlier stage in life. According to St. Wayne, "I have memories from when I was just a few years old. I have visual memories of being a baby in a crib. I recall being fascinated by the color funnies in the newspaper. Later on, when I was six or seven, I started getting into comics heavily. In the early '60s, I was fascinated by the DC superheroes. The colors of the costumes plus the personalities of the characters and all the monsters and the mad scientists

courtesy of Wayne St. Wayne

Wayne St. Wayne with Ox Baker

and the laboratories and all that stuff just completely captivated me. Pre-superhero Marvel comics were a huge influence on me.

"I can remember going into Wildy's Drug Store. It was one of those neat corner drug stores, and I can still smell the soda fountain and the smell of the new magazines and comics. I can actually remember covers of comics that I've had in vivid detail. There was an utter thrill of going into the drug store on Tuesdays and Thursdays because those were the days when new comics arrived. There would be an instant sort of magnetic fusion between my brain and the covers. Superman would be hovering in midair, overlooking some scene of potential disaster, and they'd have a thought balloon with a big paragraph where Superman would describe the entire situation."

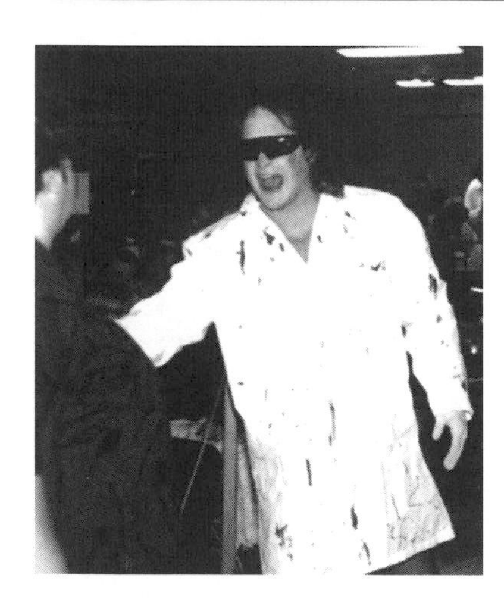

DR. BLOOD

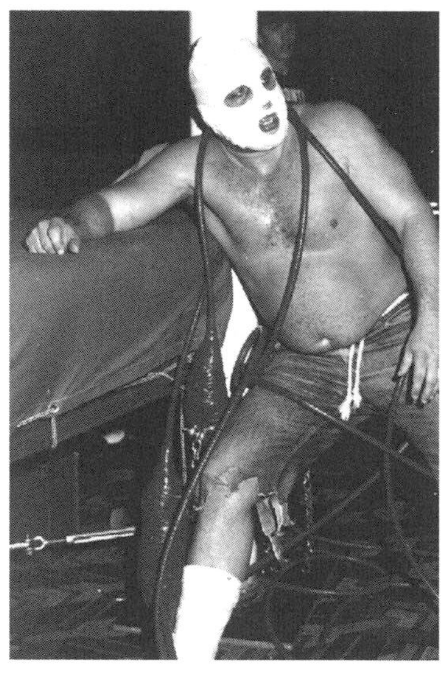

BUDDY FRANKENSTEIN

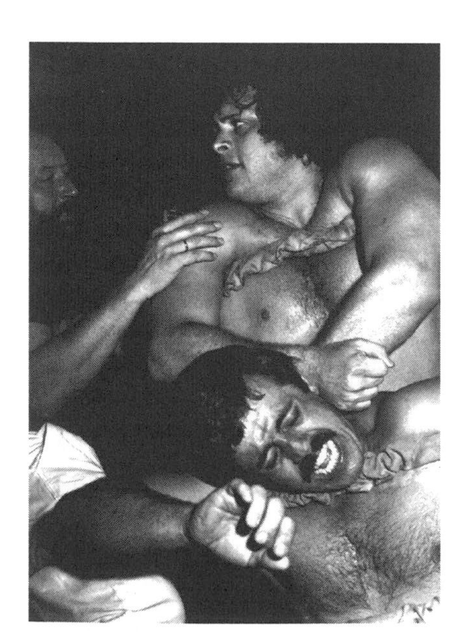

MICHELLE HAMMER
(vs. Keith Hart)

Some Faces of Wayne St. Wayne

Comic books have been an American institution for decades. Very few males in this country grew up without reading comics, whether it be superheroes or Disney-like characters. When one reaches the early teenage years, interests change, and the comic book days are over for many. The impression that comics made on St. Wayne, however, has lasted for his entire life after becoming introduced to the art form. "Intellectually, I knew it was just a piece of paper and imagination, but the suspension of disbelief came into play, and I had so much fun getting into the stories and different worlds. The other thing was *Mad Magazine*. In the '50s and early '60s, it was pure genius."

The same medium that introduced St. Wayne to wrestling, television, also played a part in his future artistic endeavors. He stated, "In second grade, I'd come home for lunch every day, and Channel 11 had its afternoon movie. In the early '60s, it was always a black-and-white movie from the '30s and '40s. I remember coming home for lunch, and I suddenly became ill and wasn't able to go back to school, and wouldn't you know it, by some weird coincidence, *House of Frankenstein* was on." In addition to the horror movies, *Famous Monsters* and other monster magazines, as well as movie poster art, were a huge influence on me."

Attending the cinema in the 1960s was a far different experience from that of today. St. Wayne reminisced, "There were still neighborhood theaters then. Right near home, there were three or four within walking distance. Most of them are long gone, unfortunately. I remember scenes in movies where they would show somebody walking toward something, and the camera would switch to what that person was looking at and it would be coming closer and closer. I recall that same effect when I'd be approaching the theater and the marquee would get closer and closer. It was like worlds within worlds. My favorite way was to go by myself, and when you got closer to the theater, you were getting closer to a different world. Then you would go in the lobby and smell all the popcorn. In the old neighborhood theaters, there would be the weird characters hanging out smoking in the lobby. That's one step further. Then you went into the auditorium and you're just a little bit deeper. When the show on the screen started, you stepped into a whole different world."

When St. Wayne began to draw, he would copy the cutout masks that used to be part of the packaging of Kellogg's cereals. Then he graduated to copying monsters from the magazines and the old films. He stated, "My whole life revolved around TV, movies, comics and magazines."

In the eighth grade, St. Wayne diversified his artistic endeavors by incorporating wrestlers into his routine. He said, "I remember that one of the girls in my class was kind of stocky, and I would do caricatures of her along the lines of Bulldog Brower. I'd have her lifting about 20 wrestlers. I was pretty well known for doing not-altogether complimentary caricatures of teachers and students. I started doing wrestling drawings about that time."

A turning point came in St. Wayne's life that pushed him to expand his art career. "In 1985, up in Edmonton, I was kind of dabbling at wrestling art. In the ring, I worked for Stampede and a couple of short-lived would-be independents. I was doing it on a very infrequent basis. The Harts would call me if someone got hurt or they needed somebody quick. Then I might be out for three months. It just hit me that I wasn't going to be wrestling forever, and I didn't want to make a life of normal employment either, so I kind of began staying up all night and drawing all the time. Before then, it might have been months where I wouldn't do anything."

When St. Wayne returned to St. Louis, he knew that art would be his future. For a short time, he worked a "normal" job in a restaurant. He was putting in many hours every day and night in honing his skills, but he was still not sure of what direction to take. “I wanted to make a living at art somehow, someday, and the most important thing was to keep putting the time in to sharpen the skills.

“Then several things happened close together that changed my life. I was in a neighborhood bar and the bartender was a painter. He had some of his canvases up in the bar and a couple of other places. He mentioned that paintings were a lot better attention-getters than drawings because of the size and the color and the fact that you could hang them in different places. I thought about that and one of the customers at the restaurant where I worked asked me if I would do him a painting sometime.

“I still hadn’t started painting yet and kind of gave him the ‘one of these days, maybe,’ sort of thing. Within a week or two, I got a small package in the mail. My sister was living in Germany and sent me a set of acrylic paints. I thought, ‘Maybe it’s time to start.’ I loved it right away.”

When St. Wayne began painting, he worked on one canvas at a time and then progressed to painting several works simultaneously. After a while, he became comfortable with painting and took his next step towards becoming a full-time artist. “It got to where it coincided with a lot of interconnected things. I quit that job, for better or worse, to strike out in the art thing. I was still doing the local monthly wrestling here as Dr. Blood and managed to fuse the art and the wrestling in a way that got a lot of publicity. I got the attention of a couple of the local media people and was lucky enough to have a few different newspaper articles written about me—the ‘Wrestling Artist’ theme.”

Wrestling had taught him the assets of promotion. He began to incorporate angles to promote his artwork that were quite unorthodox in the world of art. According to St. Wayne,

"Just before I quit work in '91, I started doing open-mike stuff at the Venice Cafe. It gave me a lot of notoriety. I was Dr. Blood, and my manager was a big chubby guy named Big Daddy. I did a thing where Big Daddy hit my forehead at open-mike, and I gigged myself. I got some really good color, like a real good flow. There was a full-house that night because I had really publicized the event, not saying what I was going to do. What a mixture of reactions I got from the audience. Some people enjoyed it, while others were in tears. I guess certain friends of mine, who were into the inner child and unhealed wounds, had their own interpretation of why I would do something like that. Others realized it was a kind of promo. There were a lot of different reactions."

Wayne St. Wayne

Elvis in Purgatory by Wayne St. Wayne

Wayne St. Wayne

Grandopolis 4 by Wayne St. Wayne

The notoriety that St. Wayne was gaining began paying off in his art career. He started to bring his work wherever he went. "I began to bring paintings to the wrestling matches. Any time I would go out, I would combine my painting with going out. The only exception may be going to the dollar movies with my kids. Any time I would go out by myself, whether it was a party or to some bar to listen to blues, I would bring stuff along and paint on the spot."

Wrestling and monster characters were the impetus for Wayne St. Wayne's art career. However, for the past few years, he has embraced a new subject matter for his paintings—cityscapes. His affinity for city scenes had its roots over two decades ago. "I went to many movies before the malls were popular. There were still movie houses downtown. I soaked up a lot of the architecture and all those old buildings by roaming

Shana Ermatinger

Wayne St. Wayne, undertaking a monumental work: "The History of the World"

around downtown. A lot of scenes from old Hitchcock movies of the '50s and '60s would take place in areas similar to those. I always loved that stuff."

One home-away-from-home for St. Wayne is the Mangia Italiano Restaurant in St. Louis. "I have people coming down there looking to commission me for something based on what they saw at another restaurant. They'll ask the owner, and he will tell them to go down to Mangia on South Grand. I'm associated with the old neighborhood. It's real mixed ethnically. There's a six- or eight-block restaurant row with ethnic restaurants—Croatian, Nicaraguan, Thai, Vietnamese, Italian and others."

What is the future for Wayne St. Wayne and his art? He concluded, "I want to get more of my work out. I don't really have the money obsession. The main thing is to have stuff up in restaurants, cafes, bars, coffeehouses and bookstores all over the world. I want to know people in all those cities so that someday I can just bum around and stay in different places for different periods of time."

TED LEWIN—WORLD CLASS WRESTLER, ARTIST & ILLUSTRATOR

For a while, Ted Lewin was regarded as one of professional wrestling's best young performers. With his brothers Mark and Donn, the Lewins appeared to be creating a family dynasty. Almost suddenly and without fanfare, Ted Lewin disappeared from the wrestling scene.

A few years later, he was again visible, this time, however, as a world-class illustrator. Among his literary and artistic achievements is a book, *"I Was a Teenage Professional Wrestler,"* which was originally published in 1993 as a Richard Jackson Book, and later reprinted as part of the Hyperion Paperbacks for Children series.

I Was a Teenage Professional Wrestler,
by Ted Lewin

Ted Lewin

Haystack Calhoun,
from *I Was a Teenage Professional Wrestler*

Ted Lewin

Haystack Calhoun,
as interpreted in paint by Ted Lewin

In 1997, Evan Ginzburg and Robin Young of New York radio station WBAI-FM interviewed Lewin[1] about his mixing of two careers.

RY: He's one of the country's foremost authors and illustrators of children's books with over 100 books to his credit as an illustrator alone. These include such titles as *Sacred River, Birdwatch, Tiger Trick, When Rivers Go Home, Paper Boy, The Reindeer People, Amazon Boy, Cowboy Country* and *Peppe the Lamplighter*, which has the distinction of being a Caldecott honor book. Also, an extraordinary volume called *I Was a Teenage Professional Wrestler* which recounts the 15 years that Mr. Lewin spent as a wrestler to finance his studies and early years as an artist. If his name sounds familiar to grappling fans out there, it should. Mr. Lewin is one of the legendary Lewin brothers, the others being Donn and Maniac Mark Lewin. Ted, thank you for joining us tonight.

TL: It's a pleasure to be here. You made me tired thinking about all those books.

RY: Tell us how your love for art began and how you decided to be an artist initially.

TL: Well, ever since I was a kid, a really little kid, I've had a pencil in my hand, so it was really out of my control. I was kind of stuck with it, and my parents thought it was a wonderful, wonderful thing, unlike a lot of parents who say, "Be a doctor. Don't be an artist." For me, it was just being born with a gift, as my parents called it, and their encouragement, and encouragement all the way through grammar and high school. My high school teachers especially encouraged me to go to Pratt Institute and further. From early on and with all this great encouragement, I was very, very lucky.

1. This interview, originally broadcast on WBAI-FM, and has been transcribed by kind permission of Evan Ginzburg and Ted Lewin.

RY: That's a very important element, the encouragement. You had the momentum from the beginning. What was the first book that you illustrated?

TL: Let's see. The first picture book, which is what my main focus is now, was called *Faithful Elephants*, a true story of animals in war. It's a true story of the animals in the Tokyo Zoo during World War II that were ordered poisoned by the Japanese military. Three performing elephants at the zoo wouldn't eat the poisoned food and were ordered to be starved to death. It's a very, very tragic story. When I read it, I thought if there's ever a strong anti-war statement to make, it's this book. They had gone through over 50 printings in Japan. It was the first time it had been illustrated in color. It was my first book that got me interested in telling stories sequentially with sequential pictures, which is what picture books do. It's been in print for eight years and is still going strong. I'm kind of gratified that the message got out. Teachers and libraries around the country tell me that it's a very thought-provoking classroom discussion book.

RY: This seems to be a common theme in your books. From the several that I've seen, they're more than children's' books, Ted. They're really for everybody.

TL: They're kind of called crossover books. I never talk down to kids when I write and illustrate my own books. I figure that kids are intelligent. A lot of my books involve the natural world. Kids know more about the natural world; they're extremely well-informed.

I just talked to some third-graders in Ohio, kind of visiting my earliest roots in wrestling, about my travels—tiger trek and watching elephants and traveling to India. They knew where India was. Everybody knew that tigers are endangered. They are terrifically bright about that. These books can be enjoyed by adult armchair travelers or kids who are fascinated by the natural world.

RY: It's really a new form of book almost, isn't it; the crossover book?

TL: Kind of. Somebody once called it coffee table books for kids. In a way, they're kind of like that because I try to make the art as beautiful as I can and try to recreate the places I've been and seen. I try to give the reader a sense that they, too, are visiting there and a kind of sense of magic and awe that I feel about these places. If some may cross over to adults, I'm not surprised.

RY: Well, they really should. Adults should be made aware of these books. They're wonderful, they're beautiful, they're evocative—beautifully illustrated.

TL: I'm amazed by how many adults collect children's books. I think it's probably a holdover from their own childhood of being read to and loving their picture books and holding on to them. I've talked to lots of adults at conferences and different places, not only libraries and teachers, but just people who have a great fondness for children's books and really see the worth in them, especially picture books and how they can reach the audience in a way unlike any other kind of book.

RY: There's a purity and a simplicity to them, and that's what's so attractive, I think, to everybody.

TL: You know, I've had adult authors who have written novels and all sorts of things. They try their hand at writing picture books where the text may be only one or two double-spaced typewritten pages, there's very little text in some of them, and they say it's the hardest thing they've ever done.

RY: I believe it. You have to pare so much down.

TL: It's just the essence of what you're trying to do.

EG: As an educator, I've taught kids. I was wondering just how much leeway the publishers give you with children's books.

TL: That's a really good question. If nobody asks me that, I bring it up myself. I've been in all facets of illustration throughout my almost-40-year career now, the last 10 specifically doing picture books. I must tell you, I've never had as much fun as I'm having right now. I'm given much freedom. If you illustrate someone else's manuscript, which I do part of the time, you're given a manuscript by the publishers and told to fly with it. The only restrictions you have are on the length of the book and editorial correctness. If it's supposed to be nighttime in the text and you don't make it nighttime, you're not doing your homework. Other than being editorially correct and having a certain number of pages, you have complete freedom. You just have to go in a bookstore and thumb through them and you see that there's nothing, no style, nothing that a person can think of from computer art to photography to collage to cut paper. I mean, any kind of style you can think of, any kind of format or approach is just wide open. The possibilities are just wonderful. More and more illustrators are coming to it and trying their hand at it because they hear about this. They know that this is a wonderful thing for self-expression. There is very little constraint on you, other than editorial.

EG: It seems to me that based on that alone, Ted, the kids today have quite a few advantages that we didn't have in the realm of education. I'm kind of envious right now.

TL: There's that and also the technical aspect of it. They're able to produce books now that are so beautiful that they couldn't do, even 20 years ago. They weren't able to produce a beautiful book like this one on beautiful paper and still sell it for any kind of reasonable price. They're making these books reachable and at the same time, very, very beautiful. I think kids are lucky today, really. I don't remember picture books looking like that when I was a kid.

EG: Give us a rundown on any future projects you may be excited about.

TL: Well, I've got about six or seven books of my own under contract. These are books that I've written and illustrated from our travels.

I'll give you an idea where these stories came from. One day, we passed a little boy fishing in a dugout canoe—the people who live in that part of the rain forest. As we were passing him, he was spearing a fish with his bow and arrow, and he caught one, and he held it up to show us and he smiled, and the words "Amazon boy" popped into my mind. I thought, there he was, there's the little kid. Now, what am I going to have him doing? Here he is out in the middle of nowhere. I thought maybe he ought to go for the first time to the big city, which was at the mouth of the Amazon. It has a wonderful market in it. I thought, what if he goes there and he sees the real treasures that the Amazon gives him, what will he see and how will it affect him? We spent five days photographing the incredible old market there.

The story began to evolve just from the experiences we were having. We saw a man carrying a seven-foot-long fish. It took four men to lift it up and get it up on his head. He carried it on a pad he put on his head and carried it into the big fish market where they cut it up into steaks. I thought maybe my little character should be this guy carrying this enormous fish. Then his father could tell him how the fish used to be bigger, but they're getting smaller all the time. Then I could get my ecological message in there.

The stories kind of evolve out of our trips. Sometimes, I make them a fiction story, and sometimes I'm reproducing an experience. In *Sacred River*, I watched literally millions of pilgrims come to the Ganges to purify their souls each morning at sunrise, as they have each morning for thousands of years. It was an extremely moving, overwhelming experience. It took me five or six years to figure out how I would present that—how I was going to make the reader feel this experience. I thought the best way would be to put him in a creaky old rowboat, which is what I was in when I saw this, and take them with me down the river and as the sun came up, let the drama unfold as it unfolded for me.

To get back to your original question, *The Tortoise* is a story about a little boy based on our experiences climbing a volcano in the Galapagos—one of only two places in the Galapagos where the giant tortoise runs free. They haven't been rounded up and kept as pets. They're allowed to run free there. We had a wonderful, incredible experience seeing them there. I decided to see this through the eyes of a little boy momentarily marooned on the island. He gets inadvertently left there by his father who lost an anchor and the boat drifts away. These are experiences that have happened to us.

I have books about the bushmen of Botswana coming up. We've made six trips to Botswana over the years. We spent lots of time with the bushmen there. I wanted to do a book about them. I also have a book about the wildlife there coming up—*Guarding the Giants*—kind of a search for an elusive herd of elephants.

It was a very interesting experience for me. As the delta area begins to flood, there is less and less land. We couldn't find elephants. Each day we drove out, and there would be no place to drive any more. Pretty soon you would have to do everything by boat. It was kind of this race-against-time before everything was under water to find this enormous herd of elephants. That's another one.

RY: Tell us about the books that are brand new.

TL: *Paper Boy* is just out. The book is set in Cincinnati, and it was kind of fun for me to do because it was set on the eve of the Dempsey-Tunney fight in 1929.

RY: I read it.

TL: It was interesting because it was the first time there had ever been a big radio hookup to broadcast a prize fight to a huge audience. It was kind of interesting for me to do that. I tried to recreate the feeling of listening to the fight on the radio. Kids now are used to looking at things, looking at a television. All the images you were hearing on the radio, you made pictures of in your mind. I've kind of put a fuzzy black-and-white backdrop behind the whole family as they were sitting and listening to the fight. That was a lot of fun.

I have a new project called *Sea Watch*. It's a followup book to *Bird Watch*. It's about sea creatures. *Bird Watch* was about common backyard birds. I just finished the third in that (series). It's going to be kind of a trilogy because the third one, which is in production now, is going to be called *The Originals*. It's a story about the original breeds of farm animals that we know today are bred from. Around this country and in Europe, you can see those kinds of animals, like four-horned Hebridean sheep or the many, many breeds of heavy horses. They're all, for me, very wild things to paint. For Jane Yolen, who writes wonderful, magical, mystical poetry, a lot of these animals have these origins in Viking legends and a lot of them came from Scandinavia thousands of years ago into England. She gave it that kind of slant in her poetry.

We have all kinds of fascinating projects. I'm doing one now called *Ali, Son of the Desert* by Jonathan London. He spent some time with the Berber people of Morocco several years back and wrote this fictional account of a little boy lost in a sandstorm.

A couple of years ago in my book *Market*, there was a little oasis market in a town called Rasani in Morocco on the Algerian border. I went to that town specifically to research *Ali, Son of the Desert*. I got to this town and said, "This is the oasis market I want to use in my own book." It is just absolutely wild. I shot all the locales there. The great 13th-century gate that is the entrance to the town, all the surrounding dunes, all of these locales, even sunsets and sunrises, will be the raw material for what I'm working on.

I brought back costumes and I even brought back an antique musket because in the story, the little boy uses a musket so that his father can find him. He fires it all day long, and he's finally rescued in the end. His father finds him.

All those props I brought back, plus all that photography, I'm in the process of piecing it all together. Kids reading that book, believe me, will know just what it's like to be trapped in the desert and finally walk through that 13th-century gate.

I love getting the research exactly right so that I, myself, know that it's perfect. I don't have to guess. I don't have to look through reference files or books. I've been there myself, and I know the way it feels and the way it looks. You can rest assured that those things are exactly right when they finally appear in the book.

EG: Ted, hearing the excitement in your voice, you're a walking testament to following your muse.

TL: I'll tell you. I've got to be the luckiest man in the world. Every morning I get up, and I can't wait to get to work. I know that's not the way most people live their lives.

I'll tell you about things coming up. We made a trip to Australia a few years back and spent some time in the Northern Territories. It's Crocodile Dundee country up there with 20-foot big saltwater crocodiles. I'm doing a book about spending time in a little skiff traveling around during the wet season. It's one of the most beautiful places on Earth and has that incredible wildlife, including these big saltwater crocs.

I've got another one signed. All of these are up to the year 2002, so I'm pretty busy. I wish I could have been that far booked when I was wrestling. I could have used a few more bookings to pay my way through school.

RY: When did you actually start?

TL: Wrestling?

RY: Yeah.

TL: I was 17 years old and just getting ready to enter art school at Pratt. My brother Donn was already three years in the business and was wrestling in Columbus and was really a main-eventer there, having some terrific matches with Nature Boy Buddy Rogers. So he was over like crazy there.

He called and said, "You're going to need a job for the summer, so why don't you come down here and be my tag partner for a while and break into wrestling?" I should tell you that my kid brother and myself would go to the matches when we were younger. We'd come home and go through all those holds; the takedowns and the body slams. We had a little 4x6 mat in our sun-porch backroom in our house in Buffalo.

By the time I was 17 years old, we were very good workers. I didn't really need to be taught that much. The only thing that I'd never done when I was 17 years old and stepping into the ring for the first time, literally, I had never stepped into a ring with ropes. All the wrestling we had done was on mats and just practicing. We never actually had gotten into a ring and used the ropes. That's the part we had to learn. We had to learn flying tackles off the ropes and how to use the ropes and all the things that are done.

I spent that summer with my brother Donn, sometimes as his partner and sometimes on the road alone. Then I got a letter from the promoter in Columbus to the promoter in New York saying that I was going to school, and it would be appreciated if they could book me a few nights a week.

Kola Kwariani was the booker then. I think I was a special favorite of his because I was an artist.

RY: Let's talk about him for a little bit. He was quite a character.

TL: He was formerly known as the "Russian Bear." He wrestled for years and years, but when I met him, he was kind of at the end of his wrestling career. He was doing office work, and he would travel around and do the shows. He was a monster of a man and was in the movie *The Killing*, with Sterling Hayden.

RY: A classic film, Ted. A wonderful film.

TL: It is a great film. Stanley Kubric's first or second film. Nobody ever heard of Stanley Kubric then.

I remember when Kola was heading out to California. He said he was going to make a movie for a kid named Stanley Kubric. He said, "He's going to be great. You watch and see." I said, "Okay."

He said there's a scene in a chess parlor, and they're trying to recruit an old retired Russian wrestler who loves to play chess. They were trying to recruit him to be part of a gang that robs a race track. He said that he knew Stanley Kubric and that Stanley Kubric wrote the part around him.

Here he was, a giant old retired Russian professional wrestler who spent all his time at 42nd Street in a Greek chess club playing by the hour. Stanley Kubric simply lifted his character from life and used him in that movie. Of course, he was wonderful in that movie.

He was only out there two or three days, and he came back. He said that the scene he did with Sterling Hayden in the chess parlor, everyone on the set applauded him. He wasn't an actor, but he was such a natural. He didn't have to act. All he had to do was be himself. He was just wonderful.

Whenever I could, I would jump in the car and travel to towns with him because we would sit and talk about art constantly. He loved to talk about art.

I used to do sketches in the dressing room of the guys waiting to go on. I would do portraits and tear them out of my sketch book and give them to them. I once made a whole bunch of sketches of Kola, and then I made some sketches of the midget wrestlers—Sky Low Low and Fuzzy Cupid—and those sketches became the basis for a little pastel drawing that I did, no more than 8x10. One day, I took it up to give it to him in his hotel room, and he was deeply moved by that.

RY: You had encouragement from everybody.

TL: Oh yeah, I really did. Nobody ever told me I should be doing something else.

EG: Ted, could you tell us a little about your brother, Mark. He's a legendary figure.

TL: As I've said, I've kind of lost touch. As kids, we were extremely close. He went on the road when he was 16 years old. My brother-in-law, Danny McShain, was wrestling in California and was really quite a big name out there. He gave a box of Dutch Masters panatellas to the right person, and they gave my kid brother a license at 16 out there. He took the name Skippy Jackson. Where he got that from, I have no idea.

He traveled all over. He was supposed to come back and go to high school. He promised my parents, and he never did that. From the time he was 16, he's been on the road. He'd pop home once in a while at Christmas. He'd be coming from Texas, and he'd be talking about Rito Romero and El Medico, and he'd go on and on and on.

He'd disappear for a while, and then he was in Australia and then Japan. He was all over the place. He'd call in the middle of the night. I'd get a call from the damndest places—usually collect—Bali or Singapore or New Zealand or some place or other.

Then he was around New York for a while. We all were as a matter of fact. We had some three-man tag matches in Washington. For two or three years, they were around. We lived in the neighborhood, right near the Pratt art school. They moved over here. For a while, there were more wrestlers around here than there were art students. Wrestlers kind of flock together—got a good place to stay; it's cheap; I'll come over. We spent a lot of time together then. He was, for a while, tag partner with Don Curtis. They were United States Heavyweight Tag Team champs for a while.

EG: They were legendary, selling out the Garden many, many times.

TL: People still talk about the matches they had with the Graham brothers. We again got very close when he was around here, then he kind of went on the road again. I've seen him once or twice in the past 10 years. I saw him once passing through Honolulu on my way to Australia. He lived in Honolulu for a while. I saw him passing through there, and that's kind of the last time I laid eyes on him. I've lost touch with him. He doesn't call me, and if he doesn't call me, I don't know where he is, so I can't call him. I'm hoping he gives me a call one of these days and checks in because I'm worried about him. He's two years younger than me, and I haven't talked to him in a long time.

EG: We'll try to get the message to him.
Combining art and wrestling, you had the distinction of probably being the only wrestler to have a self-portrait painting smashed over his head by the original Sheik.

TL: Well, my brother Mark was in Chicago with the Sheik, and he wanted to know if I could come out for a few matches. I said okay. This was long after art school, and I was already freelancing and working a few nights a week around New York, wrestling to kind of make ends meet until I could get my feet wet in the illustration business. Freelancing is tough in this town. There are a lot of people doing it.

I went out there, and they wanted to have an interview and asked if I could bring some of my paintings along. Lord Leighton was doing the pre-match interview. He was about 6' 7" and looked like he should have been king of England. He was a really wonderful character.

When I was 15 or 16 years old, I designed a robe for him back in Buffalo, and he was wrestling around there. He asked me, "Will you design a robe with ermine tails?" He wanted it kind of based on the King of England gowns and all that stuff. He had it for the longest time. He got it made from the sketches that I did.

Anyway, he was conducting this interview. He asked me where I went to school and what I studied. It was a very cerebral kind of interview. All of a sudden, he said, "Would you show the TV audience the painting you brought along?"

I held it up, and it was a life-size sort of bust, from the waist up, self-portrait that I did. I was kind of holding a pallet in my hand and a brush—typical self-portrait of the artist. As we were showing this to the TV audience, the Sheik came flying out of the dressing room, and he ran up to me, threw fire at the both of us out of his hand, picked the painting up, and smashed it over my head and ran back to the dressing room.

We stood there rubbing our eyes from the fire and, where my painted head had been, my real head was sticking through. The audience went right off their rocker. The painting was expendable, as you can see.

EG: That should be on film.

TL: I should have saved it. I should have had somebody tape it or I should have had a picture of the painting.

EG: Don't you feel also that the wrestlers were better subjects in those days? They had more interesting faces, and they were just more interesting to draw.

TL: It's funny. Wrestlers in those days, as you know, it's now called the Golden Age of Wrestling, which seems to be a funny thing having been part of it. To be part of a Golden Age makes you feel ancient.

In a way it was the Golden Age, and everyone who was there then, fans and wrestlers both, and anyone who was involved in it, feel that way. There was a kind of purity, a kind of sincerity about it. It's different now. It's for the '90s now.

Kola Kwariani was a real person. Kola Kwariani the Russian Bear was Kola Kwariani the Russian Bear, not somebody pretending to be Kola Kwariani the Russian Bear.

All these characters, every single one was legitimate. Their personas were their characters, and they lived them. I think that seems to be gone.

EG: There was personal integrity in those days.

TL: That seems to be much, much different now. Getting together with the Cauliflower Alley Club, which is a club for old-time wrestlers who get together from time to time, I did that for the first time recently.

To see these old characters again, some are in their 90s. Abie Coleman, the Hebrew Hercules, 91 years old, he was Abie Coleman, the Hebrew Hercules. He was nobody else. He's still Abie Coleman, the Hebrew Hercules. He's no different. It was kind of a period that came and went. I think it's the basis for what goes on now, but it was a much different feeling.

RY: Speaking of that night, that's actually where we met, where we all met. Did you notice that there were some of the younger workers there and that they paled by comparison to people old enough to be their grandfathers? Just on the charisma level.

TL: They did. They seemed to almost be in awe. These people were all legends. Look at them, they're still legends. They haven't changed one bit. Fred Blassie is as much of a wild man today at his advanced age as he was when he was 25 or 30. These are just amazing characters. The longevity that they had as well is another thing that was amazing. These guys were in the business for years, 30 years or more.

RY: Look at Thesz. Look at the shape he's still in at 80. He looks like he could beat any of the young punks.

TL: Yeah, he really does.

RY: Is it true that Bull Curry was considered pretty much to be the toughest brawler in the sport?

TL: He sort of had a reputation for that, and he sure looked the part. He just died not too long ago, which I was sorry to hear about. He was a very sweet man, I must tell you. Apparently, from what I understood from articles and things I read about him at his death, he was kind of a philanthropist and a real citizen. He was just a terrific guy, but a tough guy. He was one of those, not a super-heavyweight character, neither was I, but one of those raw-boned tough characters.

RY: He's not a bodybuilder.

TL: He's not a bodybuilder, but he was tough, and he looked tough. He convinced people. He had one eyebrow that grew from the side of his head to the other with no indentation. Like a Fuller brush. He was quite a character. They all were. He was Bull Curry.

RY: You said Kola was a giant of a man. How big was he?

TL: Oh, he was probably about 260. Remember, these guys weren't bodybuilders. They were just big men. He was about 260 and around 6' or 6'1". He wasn't real tall, but he had a barrel chest, and his head, he had this massive bald gleaming head with huge cauliflower ears, a big beetle brow and a big strong jaw. He was a wonderful subject. I made many, many drawings of him.

Guys came along like Bruno, again, a big huge man, but he was a bodybuilder—different. These guys were just monsters. So was Killer Kowalski. But, again, lean and mean. He looked like a southern preacher. Tough as nails, but he convinced everybody. And again, Killer Kowalski, he was nobody but Killer Kowalski. There's never been another one.

RY: What are your memories of Buddy Rogers, one of the all-time legends of the sport?

TL: Oh, Buddy Rogers was a real smoothie, a great worker, and he looked fantastic. He invented a lot of things that were legendary. People emulated him, especially the strut, although that was supposedly invented by my brother-in-law, Danny McShain, according to Danny McShain. Either he or Gorgeous George invented it, and Buddy Rogers carried it to the ultimate. He actually did it everywhere he went. He strutted on the street. He also was one of the great characters with his big cigar and the pulled-up corner of his mouth. He could talk and talk and talk. Like magic. Wonderful character.

EG: Ted, we have to wrap it up shortly. Is there anything else you'd like to say to our audience?

TL: I'd like to tell the kids in the audience to read, and, of course, to read my books.

RY: How about the motto of yours: "Follow your dreams."

TL: Absolutely. Follow your dreams. I don't know anybody who has more fun than I do in my life, and that's exactly what I did. I dreamed about being an illustrator. The wrestling helped pay for that, and it got me established and made it possible to continue until I could freelance and devote full time to it. Now I'm doing books, which is a dream I wouldn't even have imagined. And writing and illustrating my books is the ultimate thing.

I've been very, very fortunate in my life, and a lot of it has been encouragement. If I'm going to tell anything to the audience, I'd tell all those parents out there to encourage your kids to do the same as my parents encouraged me. Tell them to follow their dreams.

*** ***

Scene IV

THE SCRIBES

Over the years, professional wrestling has had the luxury of being described by many astute writers. As stated earlier, though, there are also people who write about wrestling and call themselves "journalists" or "reporters," in spite of their lack of talent. Those in the latter group have taken to the Internet in droves and actually give the coverage of the sport a bad name.

In this chapter, we will only deal with those superb writers or journalists who have spent many hours putting the emotions and facts of wrestling into words. Some writers, like artists in the previous scene, were wrestlers themselves, while others have never entered a ring but hold a lifetime admiration for the sport. When describing their talents and works, the word "eclectic" is an accurate moniker to use.

BILL McCORMACK

I was introduced to Bill McCormack's writing in 1997. While I was perusing a group of articles, I saw one titled "Didn't It Rain, Children?" and pulled it aside. The words flowed like silk off the pages, and I could feel the rain in Roosevelt Stadium. Right then, I knew Bill McCormack has a special skill with words that transcends competence alone.

Bill McCormack lived in New Jersey his entire life until July 1998, when he moved to Florida. He attended Seton Hall Prep School and went to Montclair State University to pursue his Bachelor's degree. After attaining that goal, he received his Master's degree at Farleigh Dickinson and went on to gain his Doctor's degree in Education at Seton Hall University. According to McCormack, "I wanted to teach and I wanted to coach. I was a social studies/history major and a phys. ed. minor. I wanted to do both."

McCormack's background also includes athletics. He played and coached amateur baseball, a game he still has as much passion for today as he did in his childhood. His other love was history, so McCormack took a job as a teacher in south New Jersey for a year until the school closed down.

He next worked in Milburn, New Jersey. "The first 13 years I was in Milburn, I was in a junior high school, but I coached on a high school level. I coached track, baseball, football, wrestling and cross-country during my career there. I was there for 33 years. I just moved up the street and went to the high school."

During his teaching career, McCormack began to write. In addition to working in the classroom and on the various athletic fields, he began to work for the *Milburn Item* as a reporter/columnist. He covered high school sports and had his own column called "Bill McCormack's Items in Sports." In

courtesy of Bill McCormack

Bill McCormack

1973, McCormack won the New Jersey Press Association's award for "Best Sports Columnist for a Weekly Newspaper." He stated, "That kind of made me feel proud. I have a very nice plaque on my wall in the den on that one."

Despite his love for many sports, McCormack's passion is professional wrestling. He has been a fan for about five decades. According to him, "It goes back before I owned a television. I used to go to my uncle's. They used to put the chairs up in rows. They turned all the lights off. It was like a movie theater. They had an old Dumont television with a green dial. The matches were coming out of Marigold in Chicago. Jack

Burkhouse was doing the announcing, and there was Gypsy Joe and Karl Schmidt and gosh knows who else on those cards. I was a little boy, and I couldn't wait for Sunday nights to go down and watch the wrestling. If I was good all week, I was allowed to watch."

Among the wrestlers McCormack has admired over the years, a few come to the forefront. "Marvin Mercer was my first hero. He epitomized everything to me that I thought wrestling meant."

Who were McCormack's favorite workers? The master scribe said, "The first without a doubt was Buddy Rogers. I went to every match he wrestled in and booed him and booed him. Next was Killer Kowalski. He came into the old Garden and talked to us. He couldn't have been a better gentleman."

About his least favorite grapplers, McCormack confided, "If you talk about people I have no feelings for because I think they broke out of mental institutions, I would say Brute Bernard and Skull Murphy. Both of them were off-the-wall."

McCormack writes for *Wrestling Then & Now*. With the proliferation of professional wrestling information on the Internet, some have predicted doom for the sheets. McCormack differs with these critics, however. "In five years, even with the Internet, I think there will be a good readership in the sheet (newsletter) world."

My words alone cannot do justice to Bill McCormack's writing about professional wrestling, so I have included two of his columns[1] and you can decide for yourselves what adjectives to use in describing his works.

1. © Bill McCormack. Reproduced by kind permission of Bill McCormack.

KISS ME MAMA!

It's hot! So damn hot you wonder why you came. But, this is Bruno's shot at the "Nature Boy," and pre-sheets that related who burped on the commuter flight from Toronto. The Garden house was a tin of sizzling fat waiting for Rogers' fry to drop.

This was my third year driving the truck for John Lubato and his hometown market. It paid for college with tips and John wasn't a daily despot. Best of all, in the family trades of my era, you know who wasn't paying enough.

John's mother-in-law was the mark of marks. If she wasn't in fear of needles, she would have had "Hatpin Mary" emblazoned in her corpulent upper arm. On the night of the great Bruno emergence, she, along with my boss, his wife Concetta, his cousin Paolo the Produce King, and this no-mind were row three ringside.

I had seen Buddy do his magic so often as U.S. Champion and NWA kingpin that this night offered no clue to what McMahon, Sr./Johnson had in store for the Garden gullibles. I had been sure Cowboy Bob Ellis, once he discovered how to reverse the dreaded figure-four, would reign as lord of goodness. He failed—twice. I paid to be there; resident rube.

Our presence at the Rogers-Sammartino meeting was only a gesture of job retention by this victuals jockey, because John knew I understood how to get tickets and tuition was coming due.

The undercard brought no surprises. Joe Scarpa, now an Indian, did his thing, and Miguel Perez unzipped his sweat-discolored Puerto Rican Star-sequined jacket to slip by Crazy Luke Graham. The beers were warm, the dogs cold, and I still didn't spot the one-fall change in the Buddy-Bruno format.

When the hour arrived for the ultimate test of good versus evil, Anna Bututta, my boss' mother-in-law, was throttle open. Bruno's entry was enormous. My ears hurt with the screams, especially Anna's through my left ear. "Heeza gonna kick heeza butt!" was the best I could excerpt from her litany of Bruno blessings. I observed Buddy's belt. The old U.S. strap with his face in the center of a 48-state tribute to dominance was about his waist. Something was wrong! Where was the NWA bellybutton buckle?

"John," I yelled, but he paid me no heed. The clang of the bell came faster than lightning, and before you could check your program, the Italian Muscle Man had the blond bully in a death-grip bear hug.

Arms skyward, the Nature Boy declared "no more." Noise never experienced before or since shook my being. Sammartino was king. My mouth could have caught softballs in its gape.

As the eruption continued and Buddy slipped out under the lower velvet rope near the timer's table, the ring began to fill with Bruno people. Not the kind that start riots after Polish groin shots, but squat, gray-haired ladies in dark dresses with black stockings and low-heeled tie-front shoes.

John hit my arm. "Where's Mama? Where's Mama?" Laughter was appropriate as I pointed ringward. There, between the hairy arms of the new WWWF champion, was Anna, lips suctioned to his chest cavity. The alpha and omega of her Chedonian life had come to be.

In time, Mama returned to the seat assigned to her and the anti-climatic tag-team match calmed the house until curfew. Buddy was a memory. The NWA would never be the same. *Wrestling Review* would note a new ring league and I would graduate and leave John and the truck behind. But over the years, I'll always envision Mamma Bututta's sweaty forehead on the ride home to New Jersey. Her Bruno "waza king." It was a kinder, gentler America.

NOW YOU SEE IT . . . NOW YOU DON'T

Reviewing the moments of genuine excitement in life can produce wispy feelings. When your birth certificate indicated you were 16, and you were melding with sounds of Little Richard, Clyde McPhatter, or Screaming Jay Hawkins at an Allen Freed bash, the goose bumps were instinctive. In present modality, with hair gray, lines of time engraved upon your face, and people calling you Grandpa, the rekindling of those vibes can be a stretch.

The same may be said for the joys of ring wars past when contrasted with the monotonous blind referee, outside interference, and "screw job" scripting of today's offerings. It's like the movie *Groundhog Day*. You see it over and over and feel as if your mind has deserted you for expending precious life time upon packaged trash.

There was an era, however, when not only were there more creative mat monsters, but endings of confrontations which, to this day, make a body wonder whether it was genius or a referee with too many bottles of Blatz before the opening bell sounded. Willie Gilzenberg/Babe Cullen events offered such mysteries.

In my favorite wrestling slum, the Newark Armory, major titles seldom, if ever, changed hands. There were great draws with time-limit closings, and quick four-count disqualifications. But, when it came to an NWA championship transfer, one could have bet on the Roller Derby with greater assurance of an honest close.

With this awareness as a given, I went to almost every show. I fathered two sons which interfered with my addiction. Therefore, when paying for a Bobo Brazil versus Buddy Rogers main event, the best this dreamer could hope for was a close loss by the Michigan giant, or even better, a one-fall-per-warrior conclusion.

Enter Tom Gellhauser, a man in white shirt with clip-on bow tie, and history could be distorted beyond any booker's dreams.

All calls were contingent upon "T.G.'s" pre-match stops at local good times gatherings. On one occasion, this writer witnessed an irate cheap seat resident chuck a Mighty Like a Rose empty at the incompetent authority of ring decency, only to crown the timekeeper on the skull and have the state-paid slug toted out on a stretcher. He bled like a major Dusty Rhodes blade job, but didn't get to be promised a return match.

Thus it was that the Buddy Rogers/Bobo Brazil feature, although a great draw, even to this prayer for miracles, was not projected as anything but a 35-minute or so night of action. The Nature Boy would keep the strap. Bobo would score a fall. Time would expire or one of the gladiators would be disqualified. But it didn't end in any of the above-noted fashions.

True to form, Rogers won the opening fall, after being thrashed by the Bobo-man, with a cheap shot, trunk-pull and three-count.

Ten minutes or so into segment two, Brazil brought the mob to its feet with his dynamic "coco-butt," which had been said to fracture skulls or at least produce instant concussions. The ring physician declared the champion fit for the crucial and deciding fall.

Buddy Rogers could kneel cross-legged as no one before or since. With arms outstretched, he cried for forgiveness better than Jimmy Swaggart when exposed after an afternoon with a bimbo. Big Bobo would have none of it. He scooped the bleached blond baddy, held him shoulder height and smashed him to the mat. His cover was predictable; loose enough to allow an escape at the two count. Everyone who loved the production knew it. Everyone except the man who counted three and shocked the potatoes out of both wrestlers.

The Nature Boy gazed at Brazil in total disbelief. The victor forced a smile as he was proclaimed NWA champion. Rogers exited rapidly; no strut, no fan-disrupting cuss words, and disappeared into the dressing area. Bobo held the belt aloft and then strapped it to his waist to the approval of the amazed congregation at casa Gilzenberg. He then left with equal quickness as the house lights came on.

To this day, I have not the definitive answer as to whether it was a "wrecked ref" or a temporary bone thrown to loyal Willie for being a McMahon, Sr. associate. Regardless, on the next Capitol Arena telecast, Bobo Brazil gave back the coveted strap and the voice of Ray Morgan told the viewers that there was a question upon film review as to whether Rogers' left leg was over the restraining rope when the fall was scored. As a man of honor, Bobo Brazil would not accept the NWA title under tainted circumstances.

If you were in the Armory, you knew the mystery pin was called in damn near center ring. To the best of my knowledge, the talented Brazil never again was proclaimed "King for a Week."

And yet, in the words of Walter Cronkite from his contemporary TV series on historical happenings, "It was a night to brighten and illuminate our times, and you were there."

And I was.

ROYAL DUNCAN

If you want to know information about baseball, you can purchase an *Encyclopedia of Baseball,* and you will be inundated with historical information as well as the entire records of every player who has played at least one inning in the major leagues since 1876. Major League Baseball Incorporated keeps accurate records and encourages readers to know the history of the sport as well as the records of everybody who ever played the sport at its top level.

If you want to know information about professional wrestling, however, do not depend on the major promotions to supply the information. They rewrite their own history on a weekly basis, and there is absolutely no accuracy in their accounts.

There are those in wrestling fandom who are virtually obsessed by wrestling history and records, and it has been left to them to record the history of the sport. If it weren't for these individuals, there would be no recorded history, but they struggle on pursuing their labors of love.

Royal Duncan of Illinois is one such individual who decided to take on the unrelenting task of compiling title histories as well as a roster of wrestlers' real names. He has had two books published in this field—*Wrestling Title Histories* and *Wrestling Real Names and Aliases*. The former was coedited by Gary Will, and the latter received the help of Gary Will and Dominic Macika.

Duncan, like most people who have indulged in the wrestling business, has been a fan of grappling since his childhood. He said, "It was in about 1962 or 1963 that I became a wrestling fan. I started to become interested in boxing, and I would buy those magazines that were half boxing and half wrestling. My stepfather was interested in wrestling, and that's

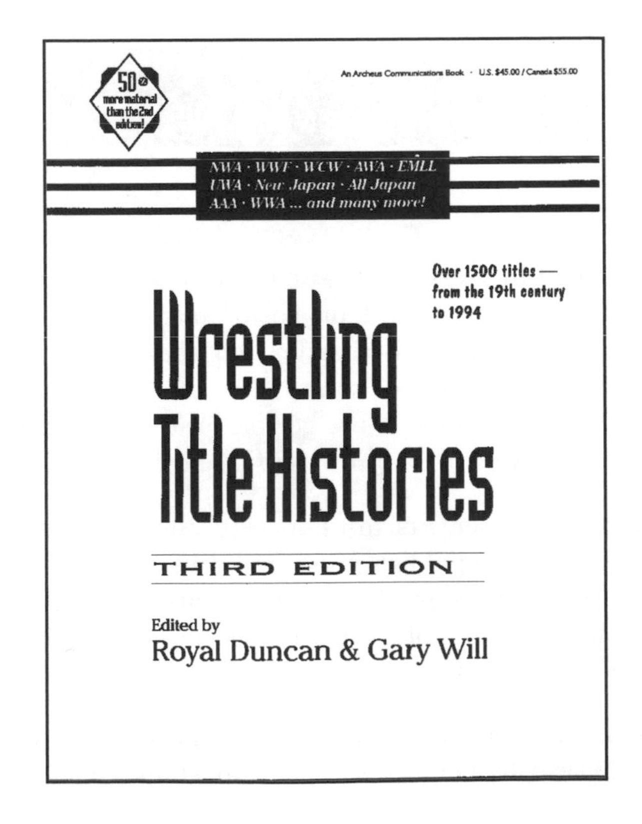

how I became interested. I went to my first show in Miami Beach when my family was on vacation in 1964. I saw Lou Thesz and Gene Kiniski wrestle, and that's how I started becoming a fan, although I was pretty much hooked before I saw my first live match. I just got off on the theatrics of the whole thing. It was like a grown-up Disneyland."

Duncan carried his fandom into adulthood where he eventually began to publish program books for a living. "I put together program books for high schools and colleges and sports. Auto racing, motorcycle racing, any sport that really needs an event program, that's what we do."

With publishing skills already in hand, Duncan needed a catalyst to start him on his quest to publish his comprehensive works on wrestling. That ingredient was already there—he was an avid collector of autographs. According to Duncan, "I collect autographs, including wrestling autographs, and I was trying to find where there was a list of wrestling champions so I could check them off—you know, to see what champs I had to fill in. It's kind of like baseball cards. Of course, these lists did not exist. There were partial lists here and there, so I thought it would be great if you could put them all into a book; have a book with all the titles that would be in one spot. I don't do anything by halves, so I started contacting people in the wrestling world.

"There are guys who are historians, so I started networking and got quite a network going throughout the U.S., Canada, Japan, Australia, New Zealand and other places. Gradually, guys contributed. Guys would look through their collections of programs. I got in contact with promoters and got their title histories. It was just a compilation of magazines and programs and newsletters and posters."

When *Wrestling Title Histories* was finished, it included over 300 pages. The monumental task took its toll on Duncan. "It cost me two relationships. It took the better part of five years. When you're about three-quarters of the way through, you just ask, 'Why did I ever do this?' Then you finish it and you're happy."

His next tome, *Wrestling Real Names and Aliases*, was not as large as his first work. The final product had a total of 127 pages. His research and approach to this book differed from his first endeavor. According to Duncan, "I didn't rely on the network as much as for the other book because the alias book all evolved out of Ed Garea, who was the first one to have lists of these. Again, it all goes back to my autographs. I was trying to match up the autographs with who they might have been if they were under a hood or if they were using different names.

Ed Garea started off by sending this list to me, and it just kind of grew from there."

Garea moved and in the process lost material on the aliases. When the dust had cleared, he told Duncan, "Here, you take this. You do what you want with it. If you want to sell it, it's your baby." Duncan stated, "I took it."

Other people came on board to assist Duncan in finishing the project. When the book was finished, it gained immediate notoriety in the world of professional wrestling. Duncan said there will be changes in the next printing which will add cross-references with real names and aliases.

Are more books on the horizon for Duncan? "No, that's probably going to be it. I just don't have the time anymore. We'll keep fine-tuning these books. These will just become future editions with more research and more spots filled in."

Duncan encapsulated his experience by saying, "The only roadblock is that it was so time-consuming. You have to go to areas where people either have this information or know someone who has the information. It's busted down geographically. A guy in Canada isn't going to have Tennessee information. A guy in Florida isn't going to have Texas information. It was just a lot of phone calls, a lot of digging up dirt and finding guys. But there are enough wrestling nuts out there, and you can find guys who kept track of this stuff. It's kind of unbelievable, but that's how it was."

With the proliferation of the Internet, Royal Duncan has not been spared in having his years'-long research literally robbed and put on the Internet for anyone to view free of charge. There are dozens of web sites which offer wrestler's real names and/or title histories. A recent letter sent to the editor of a wrestling newsletter asked the question, "Why pay for a book when you can get the same information on the

courtesy of Royal Duncan

Royal Duncan

Internet free?" The reasons for paying are numerous, such as giving the author what is due him, but one important factor still stands out when discussing wrestling information on the Internet—accuracy. The Internet is laden with professional wrestling sites, but many are woefully inaccurate. If someone wants the real, reliable information on title histories or wrestlers' real names and aliases, Royal Duncan's books are still the primary source.

MIKE MOONEYHAM

Mike Mooneyham differs from most writers of professional wrestling in that he is a "legitimate" journalist who writes for the *Charleston (SC) Post & Courier*, a daily newspaper with a circulation that exceeds 100,000. He was and is instrumental in having professional wrestling articles appear in the mainstream press on a regular basis. Many newspapers relegate professional wrestling to their entertainment pages and write about the sport about once a year, giving wrestling the appearance of a non-legitimate form of fringe entertainment. Mooneyham describes wrestling as an athletic art form that is a part of the fabric of American society.

Mike Mooneyham was born in Charleston, South Carolina, in 1954. He attended his first live match in 1963. According to Mooneyham, "I still remember it vividly. It was a three-bout card at the old County Hall here in Charleston. That's a building where wrestling was held for almost 40 years. I can still tell you the lineup—Tim Woods against Pedro Godoy in the opener; midget tag with Fritz and Hans Hermann against Lord Littlebrook and Chief Littlehawk; the main event was Johnny Weaver and Haystack Calhoun against the Masked Bolos, who later became the Assassins.

"I was just a young kid at the time, but I was pretty much hooked from that time on. It's funny, I was just talking to Tim Woods a few weeks ago about seeing him in that first match. It wasn't too long after he broke into the business when I first saw him."

Before he attended his first live match, Mooneyham, like most lifelong professional wrestling fans, had been introduced to grappling on television. He stated, "I just happened to see it by accident one day. I was outside playing football with a bunch of friends who were big sports fans. We just happened to go inside and flip the TV on. There were these weird-looking guys. One guy weighed 600 pounds—Haystack Calhoun. There was just a bunch of crazy stuff. We had to check this thing out."

Today Mooneyham is in the major leagues of serious writing. In addition to his producing professional wrestling articles, he is a newswriter. Long before he ever wrote his first news article, however, Mooneyham had jumped into the wrestling journalism field. In the mid-1960s, he wrote for various wrestling publications, including, *Wrestling Review, Boxing Illustrated* and *Wrestling News*. The latter was arguably the biggest wrestling magazine of its day, being labeled by Mooneyham, "the real heavyweight of that period."

When Mooneyham began writing for the magazines, he was only in his early teens. A writer did not have to send a photo with his articles, so the publications did not know how old he was. According to Mooneyham, "I don't think the magazines knew I was as young as I was. I got a pretty good exposure to the business and writing."

After his introduction to wrestling journalism, Mooneyham decided to create his own publication. "In the late '60s, I started my own fan club publication. Back then, we called them bulletins. It was sort of an introduction to the current-day newsletters. It was called *Championship Wrestling Fan Club,* and I had correspondents from all over the country, some of whom are still involved in the wrestling business—guys like Mike Tenay and Scott Teal.

"I got to cover matches all over, places like Charlotte, Savannah, Augusta, Atlanta, Orlando and Miami Beach. Friends or family would take me to the venues because I was too young to drive. I got to see a lot of great wrestling. That was sort of the Golden Age of professional wrestling."

When Mooneyham began to attend college, he put some of his wrestling interests on the back burner. "I took more of a passive approach to wrestling when I went to college and began working for newspapers. I was studying law at the College of Charleston. I wanted to get into the legal field, but I always loved writing and had experience in writing, so one thing led to another and I began working at the *Post & Courier* part-time while I was going to school. I had veered away from the wrestling business as I went on to other things, such as a profession and a family."

Mooneyham began to work in advertising at the Charleston daily, and then opportunity knocked. Another daily paper offered him an editor's job, and he accepted. He worked there for two years and then returned to his familiar surroundings at the *Post & Courier*. "I really got a lot of good basic background there, so when I came back here to Charleston, I was able to handle a lot of stuff. I worked here in various capacities—sports reporter, sports editor, news editor."

Mooneyham cited his love of sports and added, "My kids play sports. I've coached sports. I was a big sports fanatic, but as you get older, your priorities change. I got into news and that's where I am now—a news editor."

How did Mike Mooneyham convince the publisher of a daily newspaper to run a column on professional wrestling on the sports pages? "Back in 1988 or '89, we had a change in management here at the newspaper. It was a much more aggressive and open-minded management that was listening to a lot of new ideas. I had always thought that a wrestling column would be a great thing to run in a newspaper, but before, the management was not receptive to such an idea. When I made that suggestion to the new executive editor, he really went for the idea. Not only did we do it on a weekly basis on every Sunday when our biggest readership is there, but we did it in the sports section—not the TV section, but the sports section. The column took off and the rest, as they say, is history.

"It was difficult at first to determine how many readers the column actually had, but now, through the Internet, we can gauge who reads what. The wrestling column is normally the first or second most-read thing in the paper every week."

Mooneyham is an astute student and writer of wrestling. He has seen many changes in the business over the past three decades—some good, some not so good. He said, "I have a very special feeling for the wrestlers of yesteryear. There are many fans who are still interested in the old days. I feel that history is a very important part of what we're enjoying today as fans. Since I was around for that other era of wrestling, that part of history will never die."

Professional wrestling has undergone revolutionary changes in the past 10 years, and Mooneyham has addressed them. "Ten years ago, you would have neither organization (WWF/WCW) acknowledging that the other existed. Competition, newsletters and the rapid dissemination of news have caused the business to change."

What about professional wrestling's future? Mooneyham pondered, "Just look at the statistics. Wrestling is as hot as it's ever been. Demographics show that there are about 20 million wrestling fans. It's the number one and the number two rated cable show on television with *Monday Night Raw* and *Monday Nitro*.

"You have to wonder when the bubble is going to burst. Wrestling is a sport that's always gone through cycles. I think certainly that wrestling will continue to have a lot of success and there probably will be a couple of downturns. There always are, but I think wrestling is a sport that will always be there and, during certain periods, it will thrive."

Today's wrestling has little in common with the sport which Mooneyham was introduced to in the early 1960s. The WWF, in particular, has changed wrestling's image and marketing strategies. The Stamford, Connecticut, organization began putting outrageous costumes on wrestlers in the 1980s and 1990s and, to some, killed the sport. However, for every fan who lost interest, the new-style promotion gained many new followers.

How does Mooneyham feel about the new direction taken by the WWF and, in a more toned-down version, by WCW? "The WWF has gotten away from the clowns and what I call

courtesy of Mike Mooneyham

Mike Mooneyham

the real silly characters, and they've gone to a more bizarre approach—certainly a more contemporary adult approach. Personally, I don't like it, but apparently a lot of people do because they're getting bigger ratings than they had before."

Despite his disdain for some of the current angles used in professional wrestling, Mooneyham does admit that gimmicks are necessary for the sport to exist and progress. He concluded, "Something has to attract you. Back in 1963, if I hadn't tuned in on a television and seen a 600-pound guy and two guys wearing masks and a guy with a cane, I wouldn't have thought twice about it. I wouldn't be a fan today."

DALE PIERCE

Dale Pierce is an individual whose careers could have fit in various chapters in this book. He is a published author, a professional wrestler and an accomplished businessman. Pierce's passions include bullfighting and wild west characters as well as wrestling.

Pierce was born in Akron, Ohio, in 1958. His father worked for Goodyear Aerospace as a designer and was shuttled from place-to-place across America. He was assigned to Boeing in Seattle and McDonnell Douglas in St. Louis. Finally, in 1969, Pierce's father was transferred to Phoenix, Arizona, where he stayed until he died.

According to Pierce, "My father had been a wrestling fan at the old Akron Armory in Ohio. He used to delight in irritating the other fans down there because he would cheer for people like Rogers and Hans Schmidt."

The regular changing of homes helped introduce Pierce to wrestling in various parts of the United States. "I grew up seeing matches all over the USA, and it was mainly because of my father's profession. In Seattle, I saw Dutch Savage, Haystack Calhoun and the Tolos Brothers. In St. Louis, I saw Thesz, Kiniski and Dory Funk, Jr. Then, finally, we moved to Arizona."

Pierce's Arizona childhood played heavily in his future endeavors. Unlike most kids, however, he dreamed of being a wrestling manager, not a professional grappler. According to Pierce, "When I was a kid, I used to play manager with G.I. Joe dolls. I'd put a sheet on the bed for a ring. The black doll was Abdullah the Butcher, and I managed him and we'd beat the white doll. I always liked Abdullah the Butcher, so the black guy became Abdullah, and the white guy would become Bob Backlund or another white babyface. I'm white, too, but I always liked Abdullah.

"Now, I see the G.I. Joe dolls and realize that some of them are worth hundreds of dollars, and I wished I would have saved them instead of slammed them through tables. From playing with G.I. Joe dolls and designing feuds and such, I already had an interest in working with the pros without even realizing it."

Pierce moved his recreational pursuits from his house to the arena soon after. He was intrigued with professional wrestling and wanted to become a part of the business, but not necessarily as a wrestler. "During the 1970s, I would take pictures in Phoenix at the matches, and from there I started doing the programs at the weekly shows. I had access to a carbon copy machine so we would carbon copy a whole bunch of programs and sell them at the matches.

"Phoenix was an indie circuit that ran weekly during the '70s. We had an occasional top name from California or Texas come in, but they were mainly locals back then.

"Selling programs was my way of getting in. I got to know the wrestlers. They realized that I was all right, not a real flake. Gradually, I built up the trust of the wrestlers.

"Back then, it was a lot more closed-door than it is now. It was like being in the Mafia. To get in, you had to know somebody who was in already who would vouch for you: 'This guy's okay, let's let him in. We'll give him a trial by error and see how he does. If not, we'll kick his ass out.' I got in by selling programs."

Pierce used his programs to get his foot in the managerial door. "A couple of the local guys gave me some basic training on how to manage and started me working in 1979. I made my debut in Phoenix, and that's how it started. I've never really considered myself much of a wrestler, but as a manager, I think I am one of the best around, especially on the independent circuit. As a wrestler, I've always considered myself mediocre."

There are many young talented wrestlers today who may never get a shot at ever appearing on a card, even in the smallest independent organization, yet Pierce, who prefers not to wrestle, has been in over 200 professional matches. In addition to the indie circuit, he has appeared on TV for the WWF. About this quandary, he explained, "My first match was a spur-of-the-moment thing. They needed a body on a card in Phoenix in 1980. After the match, I knew I still preferred managing. I do the occasional shot in the ring today, but only if they need a body for a card or if a promoter insists that I wrestle.

"I had four WWF matches in 1981, and it was the biggest mistake of my life. I wrestled Buddy Rose, Bob Orton, Jr., Tony Garea and Tony Atlas, which was a joke in itself because he's like twice my size. It was a good experience, but it was also a good wakeup call to realize my limitations and that I should stick to managing if I wanted to be active in this sport."

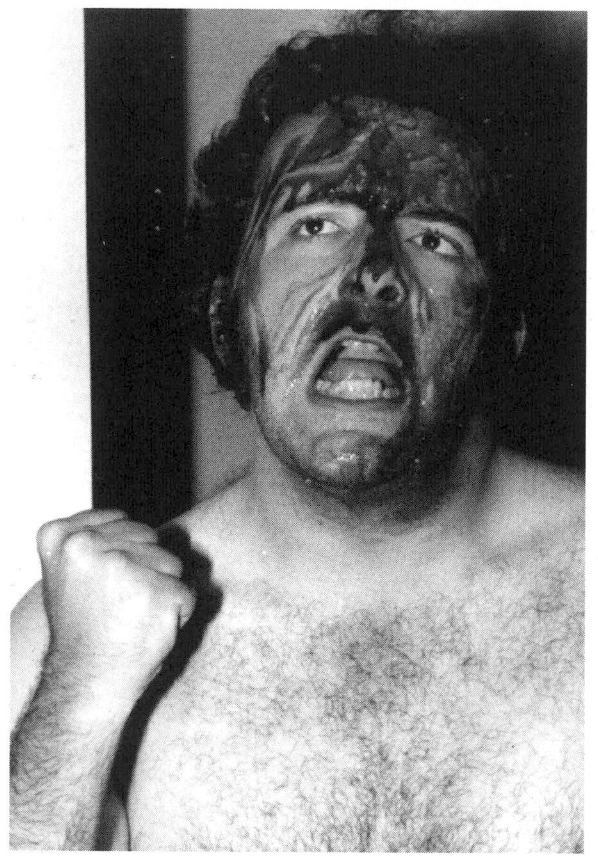

courtesy of Dale Pierce

Pierce as "Marcial Bovee" early in his career

Over the years, Pierce has written hundreds of pieces on wrestling for publications all over the world. He is also a published author of books that do not relate to wrestling. His passions for subjects include bullfighting, wild west characters and stories of the horror genre. Pierce has a Bachelor's degree in English and a teacher's certificate. Long before he gained his higher education, however, he was already an accomplished published author. According to Pierce, "I sold my first magazine story when I was 14 years old. I had an interest in writing before I actually started taking courses for it. The story was on bullfighting, which I covered extensively on the U.S./ Mexican border.

"In 1977, just out of high school, I sold a book called *The Wind Blows Death*, a western/horror novel. A San Diego publisher picked it up and it did okay. *Play Me the Song of Death* has been my best work. It is a horror story which has had four reprints and has been published in Spanish and French. In 1990, Golden West Publishing of Phoenix produced a historical book, *Wild West Characters*, which is still on the market. *Bullring*, another horror story, was published in 1991."

Pierce has written many articles about bullfighting which have appeared in various publications worldwide. He gained his affinity for the sport as a youngster shortly after he moved to Phoenix. "My father went down to Nogales on the U.S./ Mexican border and filmed a bullfight. I grew up watching this film and always wanted to see a bullfight. As a teenager, I had the opportunity to see quite a few of them."

Many bullfighting fans are content to watch the sport from the stands, but Pierce has actually attempted to get a firsthand look at the sport by participating. "I fought small calves at festivals in Spain and basically, with the small animals, I realized the same limitations as a bullfighter that I had with wrestling. You get a new appreciation of what is actually being done down there when you're down there yourself. A little calf was able to knock me over its head with such impact that it knocked my shoes off my feet."

Pierce recently married his longtime fiancée and fellow manager, Rainbow (Denise). They relocated to Ohio from Arizona in 1998. He has plans for doing some shows together in the Midwest once they settle in their new surroundings.

Traditionalists come in all shapes, sizes and ages. Pierce calls himself a traditionalist in his writing because he uses a typewriter instead of a computer. He has been successful in wrestling, wrestling managing and writing, yet he's intimidated by a computer screen. According to Pierce, "My wife just bought a word processor, and she's trying to get me to use it, but it scares the living hell out of me. It took me 10 years to go from a manual to an electric typewriter. That's been one of my problems in wrestling and everything else—I'm too much of a traditionalist."

Most people involved in the wrestling business have humorous stories to tell. Pierce includes two classic tales in his repertoire. The following is an account of them in his own words:

> I was working in Phoenix in the early 1980s, as manager Marcial Bovee, and I also ran the concession table where I sold photos, magazines and programs. We were the only show in town, and we were there every week. The fans loved and hated our guys like they're nuts about the WWF guys today.
>
> There was one fan down there who just hated me with a passion. He hated me so much that every week he would buy a photo of me and tear it up in front of me. I'd get mad, holler and scream at him and call him names. He'd walk off smirking, thinking, "I fixed that bastard. I got his goat." The same scene was repeated every week. It was like the Coyote and the Roadrunner.
>
> One time, he got three photos and thought that he would triply upset me. I hollered and screamed again. What he didn't know was that in the back of my mind, I was thinking, "Tear some more up." I was running the photos, and every photo he tore up was one dollar in my pocket.

The next incident occurred in the same arena. The dressing room was close to the ring. It was a compact building.

There was this little guy who was always giving me crap every week. I got on the microphone one time and said, "Look, Grandpa, I'm worried about you. You're getting too carried away. If you don't calm down, you're going to have a heart attack and die right here in front of me and I'm going to have to blame myself for it and I'll have to leave wrestling and quit. Grandpa, sit down and shut your mouth. Take a tranquilizer, watch the matches like a zombie and don't say anything." Everybody applauded.

courtesy of Dale Pierce

Pierce with matador Armando Moreno

courtesy of Dale Pierce

Dale Pierce and "Rainbow" at a TV taping

Mike Lano

The "Time Traveller" and "Rainbow" at a memorabilia show

I went back to the locker room. Ten minutes later, there were sirens. Then there were paramedics working on the old guy. He had a heart attack. I looked at this other wrestler and said, "In 24 years of living, God answers one prayer for me, and this is it?"

The guy didn't die. Six weeks later, he was back at the matches, screaming and hollering again.

*** ***

Scene V

UNSUNG HEROES

There are those in the wrestling world who have contributed greatly to the sport in one way or another, yet remain behind the scenes more than other participants. In the case of referees, they are both visible and invisible at the same time. Fans would have a hard time describing the referee of a match they had seen the previous day. Most modern wrestlers have had to undergo extensive training before they become stars, yet the trainers are seldom mentioned. Wrestling photographers chronicle the visual history of wrestling, but most people who see the dynamic photos would not even think to inquire about the photographer. This scene deals with some of those individuals without whom there would be no professional wrestling as we know it.

MIKE LANO— PHOTOGRAPHER OF THE STARS

". . . in early 1991, Bull Nakano and Chris Benoit dove, and accidentally broke three of my ribs. Benoit kids me about it to this day."

— Mike Lano

Mike Lano of Oakland, California, has worn many hats over the years in his participation in the professional wrestling business, but he is best known for his relentless photographing of the trade.

Lano was born in 1956, and it was not long after that he saw his first wrestling match. According to Lano, "It was about 1963. I was about six or seven years old."

A few years after being introduced to the squared circle, Lano acquired his first photography commission. "I got tapped to start shooting at the Olympic Auditorium for the LeBell Promotions. I was a young teen. Each area had its own unique photographer. We were all proteges of Tony Lanza, the ultimate, ultimate wrestling photographer."

The introduction to wrestling photography whetted Lano's appetite, and he expanded his newly found passion. "I was sports editor for my high school and college (USC) newspapers with the transition from wrestling photo-journalism. Wrestling photography paid my way through USC.

"I was at USC for three and a half years, but by that time I was national because from about 1971 on, I was flying all around the country hitting all the territories. At one point, around 1975, before I started college, I hitchhiked to New York and took pictures in a lot of the territories—Texas, Oklahoma, Kansas, the AWA and the WWWF.

"One of my first road trips was in 1968 to San Francisco to shoot their battle royal. That was my first road trip. 1972 was the first time I went to Madison Square Garden to shoot."

As Lano began to shoot more and more photos, he gained entry to many legendary sports arenas worldwide. His early favorites were "the Tampa Sportatorium, the Atlantic City Auditorium and the Checkerdome in St. Louis. Keil Auditorium in St. Louis was my favorite of them all."

It did not take long for Lano to expand his scope and travel overseas. Before he was 20 years old, he had visited Japan. "The first time I went to Japan, I didn't think it was much. I only shot about 160 rolls. That was in '74 or '75."

Years later, however, Lano had built up a taste for Japanese wrestling and looked forward to his trips to the Orient. According to him, "In Japan in early 1991, Bull Nakano and Chris Benoit dove, and accidentally broke three of my ribs. Benoit kids me about it to this day."

As mentioned before, Lano performs a diversity of functions in the wrestling business. In addition to his photography, he is instrumental in helping to organize various events. The Cauliflower Alley Club is an organization consisting of retired wrestlers and members of the general public. Lano has worked with them as well as his own promotions honoring wrestlers of the past. According to him, "Wrestling is still enjoyable and fun. I try to put a lot of my energy into helping the Cauliflower Alley Club. I was a board member for a number of years.

"I had been trying for a couple of years to try to get some Japanese stars honored. It caused a lot of heartaches, but I was able to get Inoki and quite a few of the Japanese to come, with the help of others, to the March 1996 meeting. It was probably one of the biggest Cauliflower Alley meetings ever. There were a lot of big names, including, Ted DiBiase and Stan Hansen.

"I had met a lot of these guys at my own convention in 1993. It was sort of one of the first outreaches of the Cauliflower Alley Club. We threw a convention right in St. Louis honoring Sam Muchnick. It was a three-day weekend, and some veteran observers of wrestling conventions said it was the best fan convention they had ever attended.

"We weren't charging people for anything. It was 'come and have a good time.' I had 54 top-name wrestlers—54 legends. And that didn't include young wrestlers who are big names now—like Sabu and Al Snow and Lanny Poffo and people like that.

"I had Lou Thesz and Red Bastien. Ernie Ladd was one of my MC's. The names went on and on. Al Costello of the Kangaroos was there as well as Ivan Koloff and Pepper Martin. Killer Kowalski gave a memorable speech where he broke down and cried talking about his friendship with black wrestlers. We were a little overambitious. We tried to honor women wrestlers, midget wrestlers, black wrestlers, and the families of the late Bruiser Brody and Pat O'Connor. We tried to do all of it in one day. Jimmy Snuka's wife talked about the troubles and hardships of a wrestling wife."

Mike Lano's story may appear to be similar to those of others who have become involved in the wrestling business over the years, but he is distinctly different from his peers in one respect. Mike Lano is actually Dr. Mike Lano the dentist. In 1982, he graduated from dental school and began his practice. According to Lano, "I became a dentist, and right away I offered free dentistry for wrestlers and their families. I've treated a number of wrestlers like The Sheik, Abdullah the Butcher and Cactus Jack to name a few."

courtesy of Mike Lano

Mike Lano with Lou Thesz, 1974

Today Lano practices more of his love of wrestling than he does dentistry. Over the years, he has developed back problems which have forced him to curtail his hands-on involvement in the dental trade. "Right now, I have major back disabilities, so I have some people run my practice for me."

Photography is only a portion of Lano's contribution to the wrestling business over the years. He has been involved with writing, publishing and radio/TV production, as well as organizing events and the occasional stint as a wrestling manager. According to Lano, "Back in the late '60s, I started the *Tolos Brothers Fan Club Bulletin*. I did it along with Richard Dawson's son, who was a childhood friend of mine, Art Dawson. Richard Dawson was an actor on *Hogan's Heroes* and *Laugh In*. We (Art Dawson and I) were fairly close to the LeBells, and we'd go back and forth every Wednesday and every other Friday to the Olympic with Gene LeBell and his son Dave. I even jobbed a few times in 1976, probably the reason for my bad back."

After a year, Lano's bulletin was successful, and he wanted to take the next step forward in publishing. "I decided I wanted to do my own newsletter. Within a year of starting it, it won awards from the WFIA (Wrestling Fans International Association), at the time the most prestigious organization for wrestling people.

"The most important thing was that, for the first time, a newsletter discussed inside things such as blading, going over matches and international things. I had page after page that covered every single territory and had sections on European wrestling as well as wrestling in Mexico and Japan. The Japanese column had legendary photographers who would send photos and ticket stubs. We would copy those and put them in the bulletin. No one had ever seen that stuff before."

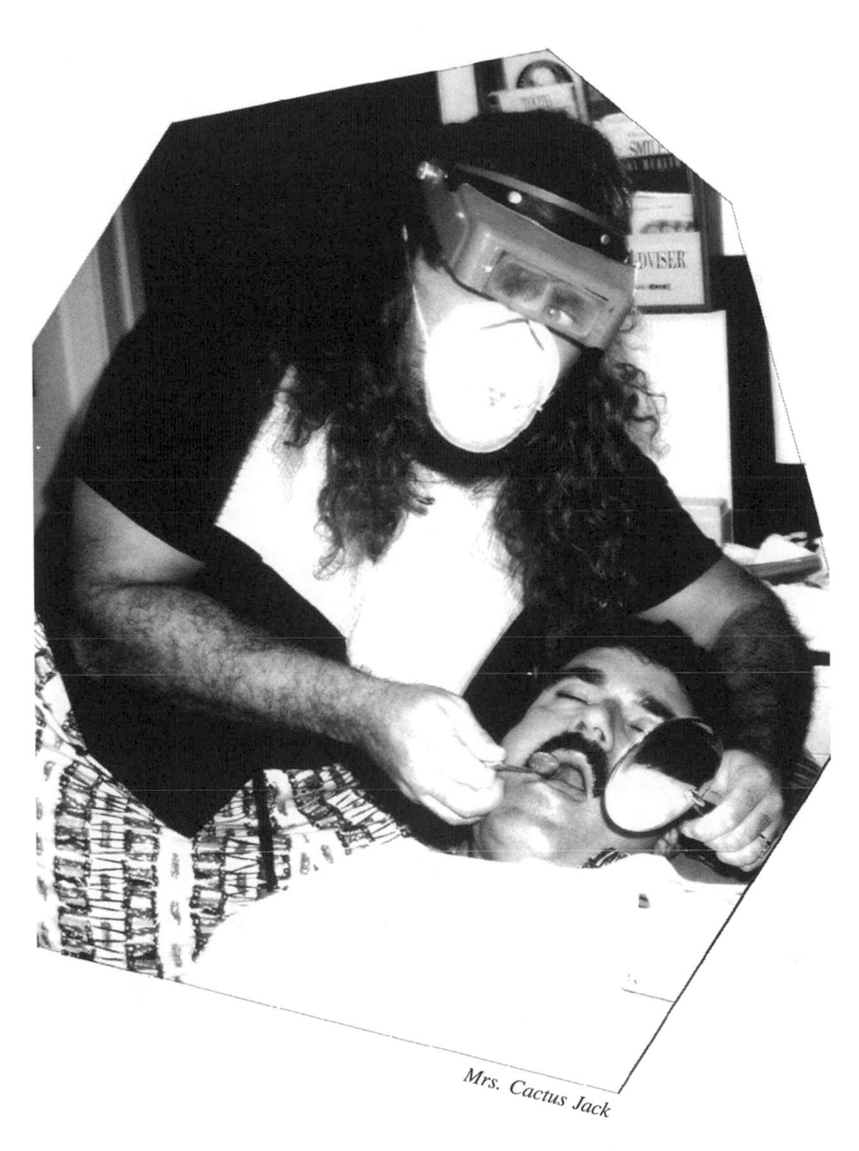

Mrs. Cactus Jack

Role reversal –
Cactus Jack examines Dr. Lano's teeth

The bulletin ran until Lano left for dental school in 1979. At the time, he was also vice president of the Fred Blassie Fan Club, a group that won accolades as the best fan club of the year.

After graduating from dental school and starting his own practice, Lano still was involved with the wrestling business, always keeping several projects alive simultaneously. In 1993, he began a venture for which many know him today. He published the inaugural edition of *Wrestling WReality*. According to Lano, "*Wrestling WReality* began when I saw other publications getting lazy and not checking on results or stories. I started my own newsletter out of that because I thought I could check results and do my own thing and try to do things that I criticized others for."

Before Lano introduced *Wrestling WReality*, he had already ventured into the realm of television production. "I started a TV show in September 1990 called *Canvas Cavity*. It's a show that's broadcast every week on Public Access stations in 36 states. I was the Japanese columnist for *The Torch* from 1990 to 1991, and the name of my column was "Canvas Cavity," so I transformed that into a TV show and have been doing it ever since. A lot of it is real interviews with wrestlers. We tape in Alameda, California."

By the time Lano had begun *Wrestling WReality*, much to the chagrin of the major wrestling promotions, newsletters had become a part of the professional wrestling scene. The new breed of sheets had begun to unravel the secrecy about professional wrestling that the organizations would have preferred kept in the closet. Within this frank atmosphere, Lano maintains that his publication went even further than the existing newsletters. "It is different. We have completely differing views even from other newsletters. We have a lot of contacts, and a lot of these people are friends. I don't simply call them whenever I want a story from them. A lot of the people are friends. Take Sabu, I have been friends with him for over 15 years.

"I think I tend to put out a newsletter that is different. I have wrestlers who actually do their own columns. This is different from any other newsletter around.

"I take my own photos and have a wealth of photos. I try to put out a little nostalgia stuff, but also I'm one of the few who knows what's going on in Mexico or Japan. I purposely try to make each issue as hardcore as it can be. A lot of people don't know what I'm talking about, so they have to be about as hardcore in wrestling knowledge as possible. It's primarily for people in the business.

courtesy of Mike Lano

Mike Lano with Madusa

"Right now, the newsletter is a two or three times a year thing. I just have fun with it and haven't turned it into the business that these guys who do weeklies have."

In addition to the traditional media, Lano uses the Internet in his quest to relay information to the public. His opinions are mixed on how the Internet is being used. According to Lano, "Internet discussion groups and bulletin boards are quickly replacing newsletters. You can get up-to-date information, real information, not worked information, at little or no cost, and get it immediately.

"On the other hand, there are a lot of things, rumors and stuff, that's garbage on the Internet—things like reports of deaths and stuff by people who are not reporters. Kids may hear a rumor and they throw it up."

After being involved in the wrestling business for years, many people before Lano gave up because of burnout. There is no possibility of that happening with Mike Lano. "Zealot" is a word which would offend many human beings when discussing their admiration of a certain subject, but in the case of Mike Lano, it is accurate and at the same time complimentary. About his future, Lano concluded, "The things I can see myself doing in the future include setting up more wrestling Web sites, taking more trips to Japan and Mexico, and helping Cauliflower Alley Club in any way that I possibly can. I would love to see an ongoing wrestling museum. I have quite a collection of stuff going back to the early 1900s that I would like to share with people in a museum or Hall of Fame. Pro wrestling still doesn't have a proper Hall of Fame, and I think everyone would benefit."

BILL ANDERSON— THE SCHOOL OF HARD KNOCKS

"The problem with wrestling is that if you stick with it too long, it gets to be all you know."

— Bill Anderson

If one wants to be a lawyer, he or she must attend law school. Similarly, a teacher must acquire credentials from a university to be qualified to educate the children of our society. Professional wrestling today is almost like many other trades in that an aspiring wrestler almost has to attend an institution of "higher learning."

A few decades ago, personal trainers would work, formally or informally, with youngsters wanting to enter professional wrestling. If a young aspirant was fortunate, an established wrestler may have taken him aside and worked with him. In any case, a young wrestler was accorded the luxury of being able to "learn the trade" in the ring. Because there was little television with the undercards in those days, a young wrestler could improve with ring time. Today, however, television plays such a major part of professional wrestling, from the WWF and WCW right down to small independent promotions, a wrestler must be ready when he gets his first pro match. There is no breathing room for young wrestlers.

By requiring young wrestlers to be astute in their trade almost immediately, the wrestling school has come to the forefront of training rookies. It is virtually the "university" of the trade.

Bill Anderson currently runs one of the most popular and effective schools in the country—The School of Hard Knocks. He was, and still occasionally is, a professional wrestler who took his knowledge to another level and has succeeded in training many wrestlers who have made it into the business.

Anderson was born in 1956 in Detroit. He went to elementary school in the Michigan city before moving to Phoenix, Arizona, where he attended high school. He began college studies in Los Angeles, but stopped to continue his wrestling career. "The WWF started using me a lot out here, and I thought maybe I would stick with the wrestling a little longer. The problem with wrestling is that if you stick with it too long, it gets to be all you know. When I did go to college, it shocked me because I was doing so well. I was just an average student in high school since I did not apply myself because wrestling was all that was on my mind. Going to college, I found that it wasn't really that hard, and I really enjoyed it."

The quest for a wrestling career stemmed from Anderson's fandom of the sport. "I was about 13 years old when I became a wrestling fan. I guess I started kind of old compared to a lot of fans.

"I went to the Olympic Auditorium to see one of my first matches in 1971 and saw John Tolos, Freddie Blassie and Mil Mascaras. Later, I got to wrestle Mascaras many, many times.

"It was really something as a kid growing up and seeing a lot of these great stars wrestling. Watching Dick Lane as a TV announcer and Jimmy Lennon as a ring announcer impressed me by the way they showed the wrestlers off.

"I moved to Phoenix in 1971 and started going to an independent promotion there. I just knew that's what I wanted to do. It captivated my whole heart and soul as a kid. Running our school is so easy because I feel for those kids who want to get into wrestling because I know exactly where they're coming from. I was the same way at their age. We get these 16- to 20-year-olds and they come in here and say, 'Wrestling is my lifetime dream.' I know where they're coming from, and that's why we want to give them an opportunity. It's not to make a lot of money. We don't make tons of money off people. We're very honest with them, and we don't rip anybody off. We train them like we want them to be trained and how we were trained when we were growing up."

When he was 16 years old, Anderson received a break when a local promoter started his own wrestling school in Phoenix. He elaborated, "The local promoter in Phoenix and Tucson in 1973 was a guy named Kurt Von Steiger, the brother of Karl Von Steiger, who wrestled for the Crocketts in Charlotte in the late '60s and early '70s. Kurt started a wrestling school. I helped him set up his ring and worked his concession stand. These tasks were all a part of my training because I didn't have a lot of money. I was just a kid, and my parents weren't that well-off to help me that much.

"In return for training, I did the odd jobs. We have guys doing the same for us right now in our shows. I continue the same learning process for them in setting up the ring and learning this trade from the bottom up.

"I trained for about six months with Kurt in 1973 and early 1974, then I moved to Portland, Oregon. That was my training. It wasn't as good as it is today when we give these guys excellent tutoring. We spend countless hours with these guys. Because of better training, guys today can get into the business a little easier. It's a lot different world now than it was in 1973 or '74."

Anderson's stay in Portland was short-lived. He returned to Phoenix in June 1974 and quickly received an offer for his first match. "Another local promoter started up. Actually, he was one of the guys in my class, and he called up and asked me if I was willing to work for him. I said, 'Certainly.'

"I began my independent wrestling career on June 16, 1974. It was in Tucson against a guy named Buddy Rose, not Playboy Buddy Rose. It was a 20-minute draw.

"It's so funny how you always remember your first match. I know everybody always says that, but it's true. I don't remember all the matches I had that year, but that one match always sticks out. I have one picture of me that night. I was 6'1" and about 170 pounds in that picture. I kind of looked like the 1-2-3 Kid.

"It was funny how skinny I was then. I made a joke and I still do to this day about how I used to wear a loose wrestling top to cover how thin I was. Then as it got later in my career, I wore it because I was too heavy. There was only a slight time period in between when I didn't have to wear it.

"I've had about 3,000 matches. During my career, I used several names, mainly under a mask. Without a mask, I've always been Bill Anderson, with one exception; I was Bill Colt in Tennessee in 1975."

Anderson was in the midst of his wrestling career when an incident occurred that changed his act from one of wrestler to that of instructor/mentor. "It was totally by accident. In 1985, I was going through a divorce and Red Bastien was living out here in southern California. He was a friend I met through the WWF. I needed a place to stay, and he told me I could stay with him, but he added, 'I need a favor from you. I'm going to be starting a training camp. I have artificial hips and I can't get in the ring and do the stuff, but I have an opportunity to make a lot of money, and I need some help. I'd like to have your skill in the ring to take the bumps for these guys.' I said, 'Okay.'

"The school ended up being with Sting, the Ultimate Warrior, the Angel of Death and Steve DeSalvo from Canada.

These four guys were in the class that Red was training. Red couldn't physically do anything because of his hips. I basically became the trainer, and he became the money man. That was one of my first experiences in training people. It was brutally hard on my body."

Professional wrestling is a crap shoot for the participants when they begin their quest for stardom. The chances are slim that a newcomer to a wrestling school will ever make in into the "big leagues" of wrestling, but Anderson trained several who eventually made it to the top of their chosen profession. He elaborated, "Little did anybody know that Sting and Warrior would become the characters they became. You just never know.

"When guys today come in and ask if they have potential, I tell them, 'I need to see a lot of you in the ring before I can actually judge.' Obviously, if someone can't even do a forward roll, I can tell something about his ability.

"It takes a while to determine somebody's skill level. Sting and Warrior weren't that impressive when they first started out training. They were just average bodybuilding looking guys. Look what they became. It's hard to judge success at the beginning stages."

Eventually, Bastien opted out of the training school, leaving Anderson with training experience, but nowhere to go. "I started looking back over the years and started thinking. I had guys, kids and adults coming up to me and saying, 'I heard you trained Sting and Warrior. Can you help me get into the business?'

"I started thinking, 'Why should I deny somebody else the same right that I wanted and needed when I was a teenager?' I didn't want anybody to be ripped off. I had heard about guys who trained people and took them for two or three thousand dollars. They would work with them a few times and literally just stop taking their phone calls after that. I thought that was so ridiculous and insulting because it gave our business a bad name.

"Today, with my partner Jesse Hernandez, we have one of the best schools because we are honest, and we don't rip anybody off. There are a lot of credible people out there, but there are those who rip people off, and some have never been in the business. There are guys running schools who have never had a pro match.

"My partner Jesse started out as a referee in the late '70s and early '80s. He was trained by the Great Goliath in the early '80s as a wrestler. In the late '80s, Goliath did the same thing with Jesse that Red Bastien did with me. He stopped wrestling to train people and asked Jesse, who was a very good wrestler in the Lucha Libre style, to become his head trainer.

"Eventually, Goliath got bored with the business and dropped out of the whole picture. Jesse started his own school and, meanwhile, I was running a school. We thought, 'Why should we work against each other?' We had some students who wanted to go to both our schools because they had become friends of ours. It just became more economically feasible to work together instead of against each other. I had known him since 1982, and we became partners in 1988."

Hernandez and Anderson's school is located in San Bernardino, California, and is called "The School of Hard Knocks." The building which houses the academy was once a TV repair shop, but it's big enough to house a ring. Anderson added, "It's a pretty decent place. We have about 40 students and some come once a month, while others come three times a week. Then again, you have some who only show up every six months. We have veteran guys like Ludwig Borge and Papa

Shango (currently The Godfather Kama in the WWF) who come out on a regular basis to train and practice against our students."

Anderson is proud not only of the big names he has trained over the years but also of the number of his wrestlers that the WWF uses for its preliminary TV matches when it comes to southern California. "I supplied 17 guys for one show in San Diego recently. Our school really shined that night."

Many wrestling people become one dimensional after a few years in the business. Anderson stated earlier in this profile that "if you stick with it too long, it gets to be all you know." Bill Anderson is not myopic about the business and has evaded the pitfalls of becoming trapped in a wrestling-only world. According to him, "I have a few projects. Like a million other people in Los Angeles, I'm a struggling part-time actor. I've worked in a couple of Roddy Piper projects. I wrestled him in *Body Slam* in a tag-team match.

"I did the ring announcing for a show called *Tag Team* with Jesse Ventura. It was a pilot for a TV show. I have my Screen Actors Guild card, and I've done a few other movies with nonwrestling-related themes."

In addition to the allure of Hollywood, Anderson has undertaken emcee work with an international circus. "About 10 years ago, I started doing ring announcing for the WWF in Los Angeles, and I did it in Denver and Seattle. I started thinking that this direction may be okay because I would save my body from a lot of abuse.

"I met this promoter who does circus events all over the world. He books the Peking Circus, an acrobatic troupe from China, and they did shows in Fresno and Reno. I began to emcee for them.

Lynne Gutshall, courtesy of Lanny Poffo

Jesse "The Body" Ventura
(elected Governor of Minnesota in 1998)

"This year, we did 43 shows in Reno, and they called me back again to be the ringmaster, doing emcee work. We're supposed to go to Europe next. I've always wanted to go there and have somebody else pay for it. I've never been to Europe. I've been to the Orient, Canada, South America and Mexico."

Anyone involved in sports wants to see his or her sport expand and become more popular. Anderson is no exception, but even he is amazed at the current wave of popularity that professional wrestling is undergoing. "It's really interesting nowadays. It's amazing what pay-per-views and TV do to people. I'm amazed at the success it's having right now. WCW has made the greatest turnaround of any promotion I've ever seen. However, Vince McMahon will always come back from anything that overshadows him. He's a genius in his own way."

THE BEST SEAT IN THE HOUSE

The only advantage I have over everyone else is that I have the best seat in the house, and I'm being paid for it.

— Ron Barrier

Professional wrestling fans cheer and boo the combatants in the ring. For some, every move of their favorite grappler is held in reverence while his opponent's moves are looked at with disdain. One person in the ring, however, receives virtually no heat (good or bad) until he is involved in a major screwup. That person wears a black-and-white striped shirt and is called the referee.

"Reckless" Ron Barrier is a 49-year-old ref from New York who has lived all his life in the metropolitan New York/New

Jersey area. He attended college for two years and then plunged into the rock 'n' roll music scene. Barrier played bass guitar with various bands although, according to him, "no one famous." The closest occasion Barrier had to attaining fame was a short period in which he played with Billy Idol when the British rocker first came to the United States. His rock 'n' roll career was almost at an end when Idol came stateside and Barrier stated, "It was right after that I decided to retire." After his rock 'n' roll stint, Barrier obtained a real job—an export manager for an international export company.

Unlike many participants in the squared circle, Barrier was not involved in playing sports during his youth. "I really didn't play many sports. I played softball in municipal leagues for a number of years, but other than that, I was not sports inclined."

Barrier may not have been a prolific participant in sports, yet he became a fan of pro wrestling at an early age. "I have been a wrestling fan since I was eight years old. I watched it on TV and went to wrestling shows with a friend of mine and his father. My father didn't particularly care for it, but my friend's father would take us both, and we would go to the Jersey City Armory, which was one of the satellite arenas for Madison Square Garden."

How does one who is not a sports fan and never officiated a sport in his life become a professional wrestling referee? According to Barrier, "My whole venture into refereeing was quite by accident. I happened to have two friends whom I went to a convention with. One was a wrestling promoter and the other was an editor of *Wrestling Eye Magazine*, when that was around.

"At the convention there was a wrestling school run by a former wrestler, Pretty Boy Larry Sharpe. He had his students at a ring up at the convention giving an exhibition. He was signing up possible hopefuls who wanted to try and make it in the field of wrestling either as manager, referee, wrestler or what have you.

"I was with my two friends, and they suggested that because I had been friends with them for quite a while and knew the business, that maybe I should try out as a manager

courtesy of Ron Barrier

"Reckless" Ron Barrier

or referee. That was in June 1990. One of my friends called Larry Sharpe, and he then called me."

Barrier began his referee training at the Monster Factory in New Jersey. It quickly became evident that he had the natural talent and mental attitude for being an arbitrator in the squared circle. Barrier stated, "The course was scheduled to be four months, but he licensed me within two months because, after my first tryout, Larry Sharpe honestly thought that I was already better than 75% of the referees in the business, and he felt I could handle it rather quickly. We cut it down to about eight weeks, and I was out refereeing."

At first, Barrier worked with Sharpe. The mentor gave the student about half of his own promotion's shows to work, but Barrier knew he had to obtain new clients if he were to advance in his new profession. "I marketed myself to other promoters. Basically, what I used to do was contact the Athletic Commissions in New Jersey and get the schedule for upcoming wrestling shows. I would pack my bags and just show up an hour and a half early and just walk in. I'd say I was with the Commission, and they wouldn't question me. Then I got to know a couple of other promoters. That's how I started expanding in New Jersey."

It did not take long for Barrier to gain more clients. Currently, his schedule has him committed to refereeing about 35 weekends a year. "I work with every promotion that promotes in New York. The WWF is obviously in the main arenas, such as the Garden. With the indies, I usually work in other places, such as college gymnasiums, high school gyms and high school auditoriums."

Many performers make a distinction between the "big time" and the bush leagues. Barrier, however, approaches both with the same attitude. "I see no difference whatsoever. In fact, it's much easier in the WWF because there just simply is a lot less for a referee to do. That's a reflection on the talent that these guys have to maintain a flow of a match without any interference or assistance from a referee."

Despite his lack of differentiation in the application of his job among differing levels, Barrier admits that he must work harder at matches for independent promotions. "At the lower levels, the referee is much more important in keeping a smooth flow to the match, helping to point out errors to newcomers, keeping them abreast of the time, and also the fact that it's a bit more unpredictable since some of these guys really don't know what they're doing. They don't understand the psychology of the sport, and that's where a referee's role is much more important in the minor leagues, so to speak."

The WWF and the WCW use plots which involve unorthodox angles, but Barrier maintains that the indies, at times, exceed the major groups in theatrics. "There's a lot more that goes on in the minor leagues. The WWF works with a much stricter regimen. They don't really involve their referees that much. They don't go out into the crowd that much or over into the ringside railing. It's a bit more controlled. In the minor leagues, however, they're a little wild. They want to impress, and they're willing to take a lot more chances in order to get noticed."

Everybody knows that professional wrestlers must be in great shape to perform admirably. Most fans never think about the physical shape of the referees, but Barrier is well aware of this aspect of his trade. He told us, "I'm in pretty good shape. I keep exercise equipment in the house. We do have to pass a physical every year. For the most part, the refs you see on TV are in good shape, but a lot of those in the independent areas where I work are not."

Most of the time, a professional wrestling referee fits into the woodwork, and the fan rarely notices him unless he is part of an angle for the match finish. In 1997, however, the WCW made one of its refs a part of the show. Nick Patrick turned heel ref and joined the NWO. Every match in which he officiated was fixed for an NWO victory. Patrick actually knocked down and hit NWO opponents. Barrier thought the Nick Patrick angle was excellent for the sport and also to give referees a little credit when they normally are invisible to the fans. He said, "I liked the Nick Patrick angle. It's good that they work in referees occasionally. The referee's job is the most thankless job in the business. He's a nonentity who is essentially vital to a match. You cannot have a match between two wrestlers without that third man in the ring to give it an air of legitimacy and sport. We're very, very important, but the referees really never get recognized."

The referee-wrestler relationship is one which is rarely mentioned, but Barrier places much importance on a cordial association with the workers. "I'll tell you, the majority of them are real nice. The Bushwhackers in particular are super nice. Psycho Sid is nice . . . I've worked with him. Nikolai Volkoff is a gentleman and also a gourmet chef. Kowalski is a gentleman, and so is Bruno Sammartino. These are all people I've met or worked with. I've even had the pleasure of working with Kowalski. At this late day and age, it was a real pleasure."

Barrier is well aware of the pecking order for wrestlers who graduate from a wrestling school and their difficult task of making it to the big time. He says that there is a lot of talent in the indies, and it is fulfilling to watch the young wrestlers eventually make it to the "show." Barrier added, "One of the current guys who has progressed is Chris Candido (formerly Skip of the Bodydonnas, in the WWF). We started out at Larry Sharpe's wrestling school at the same time. His talent was apparent then. It's really nice in fact that we've gone the whole route together, and I have refereed for him at Madison Square Garden.

"As far as people coming up, there's the Giant of the WCW. He is also a product of the Monster Factory. I did one of his first matches when he was very, very green. "That school has a number of people. Bam Bam Bigelow came from there. Chris Chavis (Tatanka) came from there.

"As far as future talent in the indies, there's a tag team—I don't know if they're still wrestling under that name, but they're called the Spiders. It's Glen Ruth, who used to be a jobber for the WWF, and Chuck Warrington. Two very fine wrestlers. Very nice tag team. I don't know where they are right now, but I always thought they had a lot of talent."

Recent surveys have shown that approximately 85% of Americans are working in a job that they dislike. Barrier is in a position which emits envy from most inhabitants of this country—he is working in a job he loves. "I would do it for nothing. Let me put it this way: it's one of those rare treats where you're actually making money doing something you would do for nothing.

"I'm still a fan. The only advantage I have over everyone else is that I have the best seat in the house, and I'm getting paid for it."

LARRY SHARPE— THE MONSTER FACTORY

"There are things in amateur wrestling that create bad habits for professional wrestling. Plus, they have rules."

— Larry Sharpe

Most sports require a participant to have played the sport at an amateur level before attaining professional status.

Professional wrestling, however, has little similarity to its amateur cousin, therefore, most pro grapplers have not been amateur wrestlers. Larry Sharpe is one who actually did have an extensive amateur career which included high school and college championship accolades.

Sharpe was born in 1950 in New Jersey, where he has spent his whole life, with the exception of the times he was wrestling on the road for extended periods. He was an early recruit to the ranks of wrestling aficionados. According to Sharpe, "I went to my first matches when I was about five years old at the Camden Convention Hall. Buddy Rogers was the one who flipped the switch.

"My father was a big fan. In fact, it was hard to watch matches on TV because my dad and I would wrestle on the floor as the matches were occurring. By the time I was eight years old, I knew I wanted to become a wrestler. I knew that's what I wanted to do.

"I told my dad that I was going to be a wrestler when I got big and he said, 'Okay. Let's see what we can do.' Then, one night on the way home from the matches, my dad stopped for a cup of coffee and to get me a Coke and Wild Red Berry was in the same restaurant. I had just seen him earlier that evening at the Camden Convention Hall and I went up to him and asked, 'What do I have to do to be a wrestler?' He answered, 'Well, son, you need 10 years of amateur experience.'"

Fortune was on Sharpe's side. He resided in a small town, Gibbstown, which bordered the town of Paulsboro. The two were considered sister communities. "Paulsboro was one of the most famous wrestling communities in the country. They had one of the greatest amateur wrestling teams in the country year after year. It was also the hub where all the WWWF wrestlers stayed at the time. In that town, there were Haystack

Calhoun, Luke Miller, Crazy Luke Graham, Baron Scicluna and Wild Red Berry, all at the same time. They all lived right there because it was a 15-minute trip to Philadelphia, and it was equal distance to New York and Washington. Most of the boys stayed there who were passing through the territory."

Berry's advice to Sharpe did not fall on inattentive ears. He began to wrestle in the Midget League program while he was in the seventh and eighth grades. At Paulsboro High School, Sharpe was an outstanding wrestler, and his performance did not go unnoticed. He received scholarship offers to several colleges, but opted for a two-year institution, Gloucester County College in New Jersey. "I was the first undefeated wrestler in the college's history. I was ranked fourth in the nation by the NCAA. From there, I got some more scholarships and transferred to Trenton State where I wrestled for two years. I ended up with my 10 years amateur experience."

Sharpe was so involved with amateur wrestling that he put his pro career aspirations aside. "Plus, my big hero was Buddy Rogers, and once he retired, I had no interest in the business. I was really involved with amateur wrestling, and I studied criminal justice in college and was going to pursue it as a career."

After his initial meeting with Wild Red Berry, the young Sharpe had developed a relationship with the grappler and had written to him over the years as well as visited him. "I used to go visit Wild Red Berry in Kansas in the summers. Before I got out of college, he sent me a letter asking if I was still interested in turning pro. He said he would introduce me to the people I needed to know. He said he would be coming to New York in a couple of weeks and would give me a call when he arrived. I was all excited, and then I never heard anything more from him."

Red Berry died about a week after he sent the letter to Sharpe, who had no way of knowing the sad news. Without the knowledge of Berry's death, Sharpe did pursue his once childhood dream. He went to a show in which Gorilla Monsoon was wrestling. Red Berry had taken Monsoon to Paulsboro High to watch Sharpe wrestle years earlier. Sharpe called Monsoon's attendance "an exhilarating thing for a kid, to have Gorilla Monsoon come to watch you wrestle."

Sharpe sent a message to the locker room after Monsoon's bout stating that a friend of Red Berry was outside and wanted to see him. According to Sharpe, "He came right out. Four or five years had gone by, and I reintroduced myself and told him about the letter Red Berry sent to me.

"I told Monsoon that I wanted to wrestle. He got me a tryout with Zybysko on Trenton. We had a little workout, and he said to give him a call and he would let me know. I called him up, and he told me that I had the ability, but not great size and speed, and that it was a hard business to get into. He suggested I try something else. He then said if I still wanted to stick with it, he would see what he could do."

Zybysko's less-than-enthusiastic assessment of Sharpe's future did not deter him from attempting to get in the ring with the pros. Sharpe stated, "In the meantime, the boys were still living in Paulsboro, but it was now the era of Fuji, Tanaka, Volkoff and guys like that. I bumped into Volkoff, and he introduced me to Fuji and told Fuji that I wanted to wrestle. I had a couple of meetings with Fuji, and he agreed to train me.

"Monsoon, in the meantime, was still giving me a couple of workouts here and there, but there was no place to go and train regularly. The whole key back then was to find someone who would take you under his wing."

After talking to Fuji a few times, Sharpe had found his mentor. "I would pick Fuji up at seven or eight o'clock in the morning and drive from Philadelphia to North Attleboro in Massachusetts to Jack Witchi's Sports Arena. I would drive Fuji up there, and he would spend three or four hours in the ring with me, then he would work that night and I would drive back home. If he was in Harrisburg the next night, I would drive him to Harrisburg. When the ring got put up, he would work with me in the ring. If he was in Baltimore the next night, we would do the same."

Fuji did an astute job in training Sharpe, and eventually he was ready to step into the squared circle. His first match was in Convention Hall in Wildwood in 1974. Sharpe reminisced, "I wasn't really that worried. You kind of know if you're going to do good or not. One thing about having an amateur background was that I wasn't afraid to get in there and if things went awry, I could take care of myself. I wasn't going to get abused. They put me in the ring against Tony Altimore."

From that point until 1983, Larry Sharpe was a full-time professional wrestler. He was billed as Larry Sharpe for a few years, and then Vince McMahon, Sr. gave him the moniker "Pretty Boy" Larry Sharpe. He wrestled against many big name performers, including Tanaka, Ivan Putski, Andre the Giant, Ken Patera, Wahoo McDaniel and Jack Brisco, among others. This period in the pro wrestling saga was the generation following the "Golden Age" of wrestling.

During his career, Sharpe was injured at various times. Injuries come with the territory of being a professional wrestler, and his list of maladies is neither longer nor shorter than that of most wrestlers. "I broke my collarbone twice. I had a torn pancreas, and I broke my ankle. Those were probably the worst."

With his wrestling career in full bloom, an incident in 1983 broadened Sharpe's participation in the business. "I came back in 1983 from Puerto Rico and was looking for a territory. Buddy Rogers called me and asked if I would like to go into partnership with him in a wrestling school. That knocked me off my feet because he was the guy who got me started in the business. He wanted to break his son, David, into the business, but he was too old to get in the ring and do it. He liked my style of wrestling, so he wanted me to teach his son the style while he taught him the crowd psychology of the ring. We started out as "Champions Choice."

"We were Champions Choice for about seven or eight months, then we became 'The Monster Factory.' By then, I had already trained a couple of guys who had become big stars. I trained Tony Atlas before the Monster Factory and, when I was in Texas, I trained Kevin Von Erich. Having an amateur background has its benefits, but there are things in amateur wrestling that create bad habits for professional wrestling. Plus, they have rules. The NWA back in those days wanted guys who could be tough guys. Today the wrestlers don't know many holds."

Eventually, Rogers took a back seat in the school, which was gradually progressing. Sharpe said, "The school slowly grew. We picked up Bam Bam Bigelow and Virgil in the mid-to-late 1980s. I guess the next guy would be Raven.

"I had trained King Kong Bundy before I opened up the Monster Factory. I wrestled his brother in college, and he asked me later if I could help his brother break into the business. Bundy just went out and rented a ring and a building and paid me to go there and train him. It was like private instruction.

"I capitalized on Bundy's name a bit. I had Atlas, and he told people I trained him. Then I went to Papa Shango, the Headbangers and Tatanka."

After a while, Sharpe had trained many wrestlers who made it to the "big time." After a few successes, people began to look up Sharpe first, instead of an alternative, to fulfill their ring aspirations. The Giant of WCW is one of Sharpe's former students. According to Sharpe, "He was just a bouncer from Chicago, but he had real good ability. I think WCW wants to low-key that I trained the Giant because they have their own school, the Power Plant.

"I trained Chris Candido and the new 7'4" guy from Brazil that the WWF is now using. I sent four guys to the WWF a couple of months ago, and I know they're better talent than what they're putting out in the ring. I can't figure out why they're not being used. Of course, there have been questions like that which have been puzzling me ever since I got in the business"

The Monster Factory is popular among young wrestlers looking to fulfill their ambitions. The roster of students is so large that Sharpe rarely takes a hands-on training approach any more. "Actually, right now the Monster Factory is so busy that I have a couple of trainers, and I rarely do any training with any of the students."

For Larry Sharpe, everything is in place for his future. "I will do this as long as I can. It's something that I enjoy doing."

Attending a wrestling school and acquiring skills is no insurance that a young wrestler will actually get work. Sharpe knows this and conveys the message to his students. He added, "It is a rocky road unless he comes across someone who likes him right away and then it's smooth sailing. They have to go to school. There are no regional territories for someone to break in. Vince and all the other people who had territories could raid territories or trade talent. Now there are no more territories. There are the big two running the whole country, and a guy has to make his name out of a wrestling school."

The "big two" that Sharpe alluded to are, of course, WWF and WCW. When asked about the similarities of the two major promotions, Sharpe uttered, "Greed." When queried about the differences, he stated, "They're really not all that different. When one has something that's working, you can see it beginning to surface in the other organization."

Critics of professional wrestling bring up the fact that many a popular wrestler had little talent, while others with great talent never rose above mid-card status. Sharpe agreed and elaborated, "Wrestlers are a dime a dozen, but if you understand what you're getting into, you are a little better prepared.

"I wish the talent was determined a little more on actual ability. To be a football player, you've got to bench-press so much weight so many times in 60 seconds, or you've got to run a 40-yard sprint so fast for your weight and your size. You can have no talent whatsoever and become one of the greatest professional wrestlers of all time. I don't think that's fair to the people who have talent."

Despite his honest appraisal of the wrestling business, mentioning its warts as well as its apparent glamour, Sharpe appears to be settled in the trade for life. "It's not the most pleasant business to be in, but at times it can be the most fun business to be in."

*** ***

ACT III
NOTABLE CAREERS

Now we take an in-depth look at the careers of several professional wrestlers who are well known to wrestling fandom. This section is not intended to represent the "best" wrestlers of all time.

The wrestlers highlighted in Act III represent time periods from the "Golden Age" of wrestling to the present. All were champions at one time or another for various promotions. Their careers, as well as their personal lives, vary considerably.

You will see how wrestling has changed from the 1950s to today as well as how certain aspects of the sport have remained virtually the same. Contrasts will be apparent. Kowalski is arguably the best storyteller the sport has ever known and embellishes his tales with outrageous humor. Farris, former high school teacher, who later won acclaim as the Honky Tonk Man, gives us an in-depth look at the business and political side of grappling. Poffo, who was an officially registered "Genius," shows his creative side through his poetry. And Backlund? What more could be said? He raised himself from the depths of the "All American boy" image while being WWF champion for six years, to the pinnacle of being labeled "the most hated man in wrestling," while he ran around arenas threatening everybody with his painful cross-face chicken-wing hold, all the time proclaiming that he wanted "to be God again."

Don't look for fluff in the stories of these wrestlers (well, maybe a little bit in the Backlund scene), as these accounts carry much information that either was little known or unknown to the public previously. In reading Act III, you will have a better understanding of the adversity of being a professional wrestler as well as the benefits of taking up this career.

SCENE I

FROM THE CLASSROOM TO THE SQUARED CIRCLE

In our business, logic is an abstract way of thinking.
— Wayne Farris

When the WWF actually tries to convey its history to the public without changing what has already happened, it calls the Honky Tonk Man "the greatest Intercontinental Champ of all time." This is in reference to the 15 straight months in which Wayne Farris held the strap—the longest stint for any Intercontinental Champion in the annals of the WWF.

Wayne Farris has had a lengthy career in the squared circle that transcends cultures, languages and wrestling styles. Long before he was the Honky Tonk Man, Farris toiled in the deep South, Puerto Rico and Canada.

Ironically, the portrayal of Farris as a southern wrestler in his WWF role is accurate. He was born in Memphis, Tennessee, in 1953 and attended school in the city known for its eminent blues music.

Atypical of most wrestlers, however, is Farris' educational background and his first profession. Ask the average wrestling fan what he or she thinks the Honky Tonk Man did before wrestling and you will receive a wide array of responses—truck driver, singer, impersonator, entertainer and so on. Actually, he was a high school teacher in Memphis, specializing in the subjects of civics, economics and geography.

When asked about his background compared to that of other wrestlers, Farris stated, "Some of the wrestlers are educated today as opposed to when I started in 1976. There were not too many guys around other than crooks or criminals in those days."

As a youngster, Farris was an avid athlete, playing baseball and football. His skills on the gridiron enabled him to play on the Memphis State football team.

Despite his athletic ability, Farris did not give serious thought to a pro wrestling career until after he had graduated from Memphis State and was a teacher. Why did he like professional wrestling? According to Farris, "I always say it's an extension of my childhood."

After landing a teaching job and thinking it may be his lifelong career, Farris was asked by family members to try wrestling. "I had three cousins who were tinkering around with professional wrestling in 1974 or '75, and since I was the athlete of the family—they weren't—they invited me to come and work out with them on a Sunday night. This old-time wrestler, Herb Welch, was training guys in his barn. I went and started working out. One thing led to another, and nine months later I was in the ring wrestling. That was in 1976."

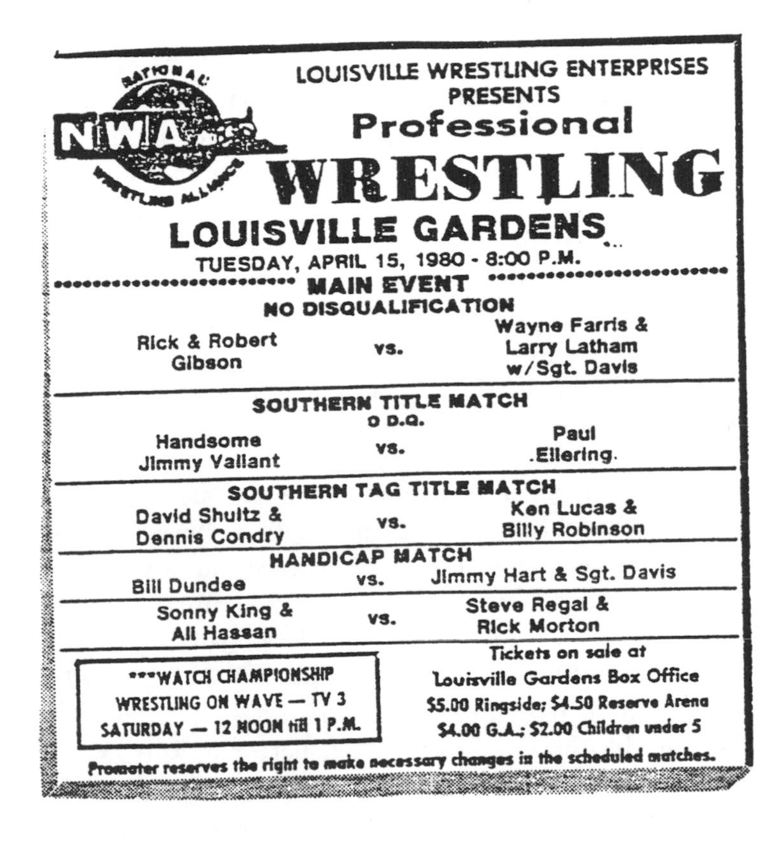
LOUISVILLE WRESTLING ENTERPRISES
PRESENTS
Professional
WRESTLING
LOUISVILLE GARDENS
TUESDAY, APRIL 15, 1980 - 8:00 P.M.

MAIN EVENT
NO DISQUALIFICATION
Rick & Robert Gibson vs. Wayne Farris & Larry Latham w/Sgt. Davis

SOUTHERN TITLE MATCH
O D.Q.
Handsome Jimmy Valiant vs. Paul Ellering

SOUTHERN TAG TITLE MATCH
David Shultz & Dennis Condry vs. Ken Lucas & Billy Robinson

HANDICAP MATCH
Bill Dundee vs. Jimmy Hart & Sgt. Davis

Sonny King & Ali Hassan vs. Steve Regal & Rick Morton

***WATCH CHAMPIONSHIP WRESTLING ON WAVE — TV 3 SATURDAY — 12 NOON till 1 P.M.

Tickets on sale at Louisville Gardens Box Office
$5.00 Ringside; $4.50 Reserve Arena
$4.00 G.A.; $2.00 Children under 5

Promoter reserves the right to make necessary changes in the scheduled matches.

Every professional wrestler can tell you who or what his influences were in determining his choice of career. Farris' choices are a bit unorthodox compared to those of other wrestlers. According to him, "I had been a fan of professional sports and slapstick comedy routines, you know, the Three Stooges and people like that. The Honeymooners, I love that kind of stuff.

"I knew when I was in grade six that I was going to be in some form of entertainment, whether it be radio, TV, sports or something like that. It just happened to fall into wrestling."

When he began wrestling, the Honky Tonk Man grappled under his own name. It was to be years until he would gain international notoriety as an Elvis imitator.

Today many hardcore wrestling fans hold wrestling in the South in the 1970s in a deep reverence. Farris was right in the middle of the mystique. "I began wrestling for organizations which were called 'outlaw' groups back then—small-town promotions who would run a town on a Saturday night somewhere. There was one in particular that most of the guys in the South either worked for or started with. His name was Henry Rogers. There's tons of guys around who remember him, but the new guys coming in wouldn't remember him at all. He ran in Malden, Missouri, in that southeast Missouri area of the country."

For virtually all of his career, Farris has been a heel. Once or twice, he had brief stints as a babyface. "For my first or second time in the ring, I was a babyface, but I was trained more on the heel side, so I never picked up the good-guy babyface moves and things like that. I immediately became a heel, very much like what happened in the WWF when I first went there as a babyface. It didn't pan out. I guess it's a personal projection. I project myself better as this arrogant, cocky heel that everybody wants to beat the daylights out of. It was something that that particular persona was easy for me to project."

With the exception of a tour of Puerto Rico and a few short journeys to Calgary, Alberta, Canada, from 1977 until 1984, Farris wrestled exclusively in the South. He stated, "I had spent my whole career south of the Mason-Dixon."

Southern wrestling definitely differed from its northern counterpart in the 1970s. Farris explained its allure by stating, "It was more colorful and raw. It brought out the best of our creative abilities because we were in these towns on a weekly basis. Every week we went to the same towns. It wasn't like on the East Coast where you went to Madison Square Garden once a month, or Chicago once a month, so your creative juices had to flow on a weekly basis, and you had to be very creative. You couldn't be repetitious in the things that you did. They wanted to see something other than what you did the last Thursday night with a guy.

"When you were wrestling someone on an ongoing basis, night after night, town after town, and you go back to these towns each time, you really had to do something different to create fan interest."

Farris listed some of the fabled venues in the South in the 1970s: Tupelo, Mississippi; Jonesboro, Arkansas; and Mobile, Alabama. "These are really legendary towns. The fans were ready for raw meat and weren't satisfied until they got some raw meat."

Farris says the fans in the South two decades ago were extremely animated. Many thought the results of the matches were on the up-and-up. He went on to explain, "The only comparison I can make is like the tent-revival people or snake handlers. The snake handlers react very much like the southern wrestling crowd did 20 years ago. It has changed, and the southern fan today tends to be more educated.

"In those days, there was always the threat of fans—the tire slashing of your car and the windows broken on your car, and of course, the fights with the fans inside the arena where someone might jump in to try to save some good guy from the dastardly deeds of the bad guy. Ultimately, he would end up getting stomped and beat on himself. There was always a

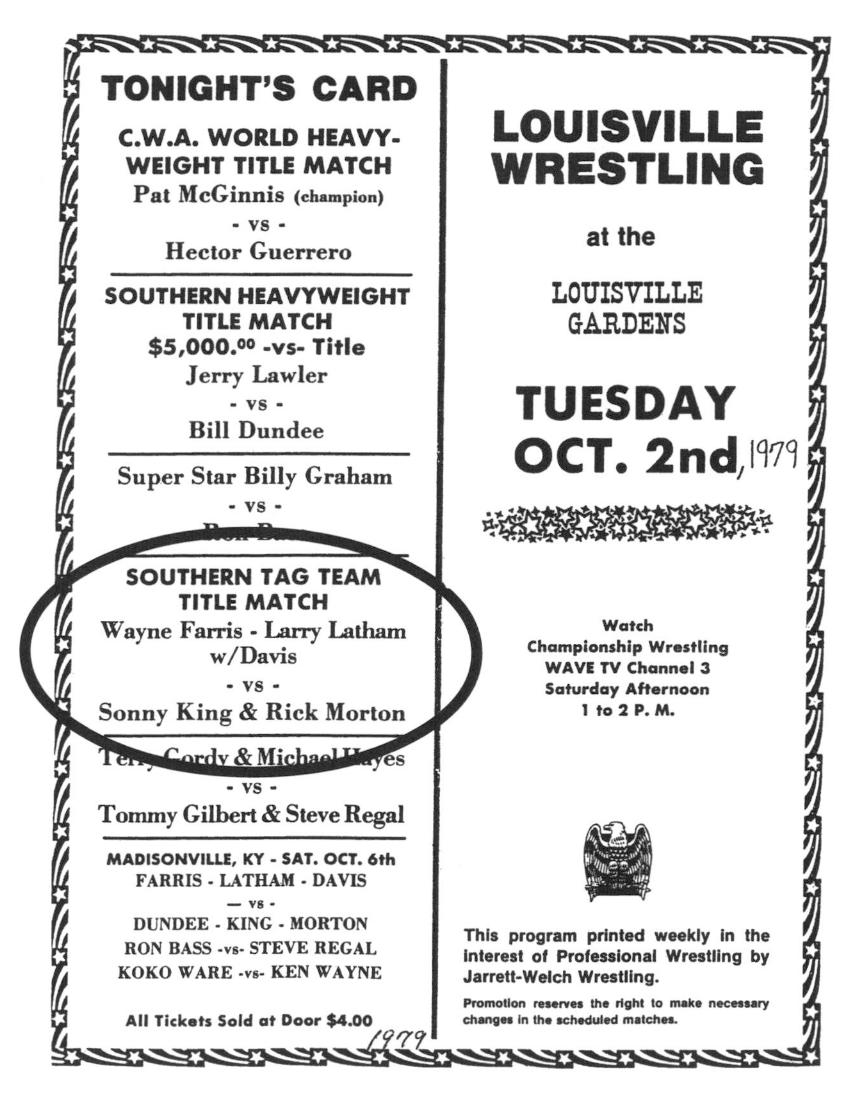

TONIGHT'S CARD

C.W.A. WORLD HEAVY-WEIGHT TITLE MATCH
Pat McGinnis (champion)
- vs -
Hector Guerrero

SOUTHERN HEAVYWEIGHT TITLE MATCH
$5,000.00 -vs- Title
Jerry Lawler
- vs -
Bill Dundee

Super Star Billy Graham
- vs -
Ron B[illegible]

SOUTHERN TAG TEAM TITLE MATCH
Wayne Farris - Larry Latham w/Davis
- vs -
Sonny King & Rick Morton

Te[illegible] Gordy & Michael [illegible]ayes
- vs -
Tommy Gilbert & Steve Regal

MADISONVILLE, KY - SAT. OCT. 6th
FARRIS - LATHAM - DAVIS
— vs -
DUNDEE - KING - MORTON
RON BASS -vs- STEVE REGAL
KOKO WARE -vs- KEN WAYNE

All Tickets Sold at Door $4.00 1979

LOUISVILLE WRESTLING

at the

LOUISVILLE GARDENS

TUESDAY OCT. 2nd, 1979

Watch
Championship Wrestling
WAVE TV Channel 3
Saturday Afternoon
1 to 2 P. M.

This program printed weekly in the interest of Professional Wrestling by Jarrett-Welch Wrestling.

Promotion reserves the right to make necessary changes in the scheduled matches.

chance that if one person came, there would be another and then another. Pretty soon, you had somewhat of a riot.

"Those were the things that were very difficult to deal with, but back then, when we were doing it, we were young and having fun. We didn't know how dangerous it could have been.

"I see a little of that in the fans today where we have the young 18 to 30-year-old fans who break all the rules. If they're not careful, we could have problems."

Many of today's fans have begun throwing items in the ring to show their displeasure at one or more of the performers. According to Farris, this is a recycled action of his formative years in professional wrestling. "Throwing stuff in the ring goes back to the late '60s and early '70s when it was very common for the ring to be filled up with trash by people throwing stuff. It wasn't until later on in the '80s that there was a ring announcement made every night cautioning against such actions. During the '80s in the WWF, we never had anything thrown at us. You might get a beer splashed in your face as you walked the aisle, but as far as the trash and all the garbage being thrown in now, it's a complete look at the way history does repeat itself. In the late '60s and early '70s, that's the way it was. That's why a lot of places stopped selling beer and drinks in bottles or cans.

"I worked for the wrestling promoter Nick Gulas, who was probably known as the worst payoff man in the history of professional wrestling. It was nothing for him to give a guy $15 or $20 for a wrestling match when the place was sold out. All the guys would say, 'Nick, I can't make it. This is a $20 payoff. I can't live on this.' He would say, 'Son, it's not what you make, it's what you save.' It's funny now, looking back." Over the years, Farris has found himself incorporating Gulas' statement into his own repertoire.

Hatpin Mary has a well-deserved reputation for harassing wrestlers. The legendary fan would stick wrestlers with hatpins when they made their way to the ring in the old Madison Square Garden. The fans of wrestling in the South in the 1970s had their own homegrown version of the New York icon. According to Farris, "I was in the ring with these two boys named the Bounty Hunters, a big name back then in the South.

A little old lady, there's always one at every wrestling match, was sitting in the front row. We were in a tag match. One guy was waiting outside on a tag from his partner. She dropped a hot lit cigarette down in his boot. They wore cowboy boots. We didn't know what was going on. All of a sudden you see this guy dancing and jumping up and down on the apron, and you don't know what the heck is going on or why."

How did Wayne Farris, wrestler for independent groups in the South become the Honky Tonk Man of the WWF? "During 1984-85-86, McMahon was coming through, and we call it 'raiding,' where he would just come in and raid a territory and take the best workers. From Minneapolis and from Charlotte and from Florida. He took the top guys from Calgary in 1985 when he took Bret Hart, Neidhardt, Dynamite and Davey Boy. And then in 1986, he came back through, and I came along with Bad News Allen out of that group in Calgary at the time."

In 1981, Farris began to use the Honky Tonk Man character in the South. It started in the Pensacola, Florida, and Mobile, Alabama, areas with Southeastern Wrestling, at the time promoted by Ron and Robert Fuller.

By the time McMahon saw Farris in Canada as the Honky Tonk Man, he was sold on the gimmick. Farris added, "I really came into the WWF with an immediate push because Vince liked this particular gimmick and wanted to push it as a babyface. He envisioned little kids with jumpsuits on, me throwing scarves out to the fans and music and all these things. He saw the merchandising end of it.

"In the beginning, I told him I did not think it would work simply because it was one of those things that people hated. No one wanted to see an Elvis imitator, especially in professional wrestling. Most of our crowd we cater to in wrestling, they're not Harvard graduates.

"There's the people who believe Elvis Presley never took any narcotics. Some maintain he's still alive. They don't want to see someone out there acting as if they're some cheap imitation of Elvis Presley."

When a wrestler receives an initial push, there are pitfalls involved. Farris was aware of this at the time he joined the WWF. "The big push can really make or break you. If the thing when they switched me to a heel had not worked out, then of course I would have just been a dead piece of fruit on a vine. I would have been back down in Mobile or somewhere. It's a matter of supply and demand, and he wouldn't have kept me around."

Most of Honky Tonk Man's fame came in a 15-month run as the WWF Intercontinental Champion during 1987-88. Farris lists many good workers as his opponents then, but he puts Bruno Sammartino, then past his prime, at the top of the list.

Being in the public eye for an extensive period has its drawbacks. There is so much going on that much is driven to the dark recesses of memory and cannot be automatically recalled. Farris reminisced about his championship run by saying, "Oh gosh, that was 300 days a year. I was listening to one of those rock 'n' roll guys the other day who was with the Grateful Dead and when he was doing testimony in court, he said, 'That was all a haze. You don't remember a whole lot about it.' There was not much time for humor because we all felt the same way—physically and emotionally drained day after day after day. That group of guys, we gave it all we had. We laid it all out there on the line."

Farris, like many wrestlers who have spanned generations in the ring, makes strong distinctions between those of a few decades ago and the current superstars. "The aestheticism of today's wrestlers is much better, but, as far as wrestling ability and knowing our craft, they're not as good. They are not as professionally trained to be skilled craftsmen in any way. I think most of the older guys from 20 or 30 years ago would probably agree. Sure, they're better athletes. They're in better condition; they're faster, stronger and they do a lot more flips and flops, but as far as honing their skills and being a skilled professional, they are not."

Most fans want to know who wrestlers consider the best workers in the trade. Farris said, "I was in with so many, it would be hard to say. For the things I did and crowd response, Ricky Steamboat was very, very good, bar none. He was right up there with the top guys as a very good worker. In those days, Jake Roberts was very good. Nowadays, Bret Hart is very good. I've wrestled him a lot of times. He deserves all the praise he gets."

Fans of old-time wrestling often criticize today's gimmicks and long for the "good old days." Farris, however, does not share the same affinity for bringing back those days, and he also points to a slight hypocritical attitude of the "purists." He explained, "There's nothing wrong with images, simply because it's show business. It is sports entertainment, theatrical athletics, a lower form of drama. The old-timers, they can say what they want, but there was Gorgeous George back then. There was Wild Red Berry, Killer Kowalski. Everyone had some kind of hook name or some gimmick that they personified. "It's a thing of marketability. Do we put blinders on or have tunnel vision and say let's only market guys in black trunks and black boots with big, round bellies, or do we try to give every segment of the population something out there to look at?

"We cross all boundaries. It always has. When we used to buy wrestling tights from K & H Wrestling Wear, their slogan was 'For Discriminating Individuals.' That was their hook line."

Farris again came to the forefront in the WWF in 1997. He was a manager of his supposed successor, Rockabilly, formerly Billy Gunn of the tag team the Smoking Gunns. Many thought this was a jump-start to the resurrection of the Honky Tonk Man, but Farris was cautious. At the time, he stated, "I would hope the Rockabilly character progresses instead of them trying to 'kill' my character. This is something the WWF is known to do. Bring a guy back who drew them good money or has a good, big name, and then kill it off. They are known to do that, and I'm monitoring that very, very close.

"I knew when I accepted McMahon's offer to come back and do business again, I was stepping into that area of killing the Honky Tonk Man, killing the character, or trying to put the character on to someone else."

Although Farris returned to the WWF as a manager and a mentor, he would not have minded grappling again. “I would wrestle as much as they would want me to, and obviously they don’t think there’s any dollar value in me trying to wrestle, for some unknown reason. You know, when you go there and you hear four months of television saying you’re the greatest intercontinental champ of all time, well, find out if he is. In our business, logic is an abstract way of thinking.”

One of the Honky Tonk Man’s signature gimmicks has been to smash his guitar over someone’s noggin, rendering the foe unconscious. However, there is a knack to this of which only Farris is the master. “They used the guitar more in a four-week

Mike Lano

Honky Tonk Man celebrates victory

period when I came back than it was used in four years when I was with the WWF earlier. It's a normal guitar you buy off the shelf. You can get them anywhere from 90 to 150 bucks, I guess. There's a certain way it's done. They've tried to duplicate it a few times, and they've injured some people. I thought they should have just called me and given me a consultant's fee. I would have shown them how to do it. There's a real mystique to that. They're constantly trying to get all that out of me so they can transfer it over to someone else."

Despite the on-again, off-again uncertainty about the Honky Tonk Man's future, Farris knows exactly what he will be doing for the rest of his life. "You kind of get, like the old term, 'once you get sawdust in your blood, you'll always do it.' I will always be involved somehow, whether it be only 10 or 20 times a year, with some kind of a part of wrestling. If it's nothing but making personal appearances and talking about wrestling, it will always be a part of my life. I don't envision going back into the classroom or things of that nature."

Farris is one of the most astute wrestlers in knowledge of the business, and he is realistic about the pushes in the trade and the inevitable "burying" of talent. He summarized his philosophy by stating, "You're here today, gone tomorrow. You just take each day as it comes."

Within a few weeks of the resurrection of the Honky Tonk Man, Farris' premonition came true. In the ring, his so-called heir, Billy Gunn, was persuaded by another wrestler to dump Farris as his manager. Gunn did just that: he dropped the Honky Tonk Man using his guitar to knock him out in the middle of the ring.

Despite the seeming demise of the Honky Tonk Man, he still shows up occasionally for WWF events. The 1998 *Royal Rumble* included the Honky Tonk Man as one of the 30 competitors in the yearly battle royal put on by the WWF.

Fortunately for Farris, the WWF only temporarily tarnished the image of the Honky Tonk Man as he is occasionally seen promoting that organization at autograph signings and other events.

Farris is well aware of the wrestlers of old and those of today who attempt to convey the history and the friendship coming from those who have graced the squared circle. He stated, "The camaraderie is such a big part of it. That's what grows on you. You get, if you want to call it that, an addiction to our sport for the guys who are in it. You miss the camaraderie when you're not around it.

"I go out and do these small independent shows and sometimes I'm the only star on the show or I might be the star along with maybe Greg Valentine, and we sit and reminisce. Some of the young guys doing full-time work now haven't come to realize the groundwork that was laid before each of us and each of them—the sacrifices made by the older wrestlers."

Professional wrestlers fit into a category all their own in many ways. For instance, if you get a bunch of retired wrestlers, even those who were once household names, in a meeting, such as the once-a-year Cauliflower Alley Club banquet, there is little, if no, pretense. If you took the same amount of famous people of other trades (writers, athletes of other sports, business people, etc.) and put them in one room, the jockeying for positions of importance would be stifling. In regard to this phenomenon, Farris mentioned, "The wrestling business has always been such a struggle as far as getting recognition from mainstream media or from the general population as a whole, so we learned to be grateful for what we had no matter what. I think you can see that when you talk to the other guys."

The camaraderie that wrestlers show in their meetings is evident, yet it is curious. Inside a building, the wrestlers will talk to each other about the old days and reminisce about their travels and matches. Outside the building, they appear to go their own ways until the following year when they meet again. Farris stated, "It's true. There really is not a big friendship outside the locker room or the once-a-year Cauliflower Alley Club meetings. Just after I left the WCW the guys came to town here in Phoenix. Nobody picked up the phone to call me, and I didn't go down to the arena to see them. Same way with the WWF.

"I never really understood that part of it. I came from a background in sports, a small town in Tennessee where everyone knew everyone. Everyone was friends with everyone. Everyone said hello to you all the time and you spoke frequently on the phone.

"Then again, the wrestling business is such an independent kind of sport. Still, I don't know why the guys only get together once a year and rehash old times. They'll exchange phone numbers right there, and even then, they still never go home and call each other. My wife says, 'You guys never even talk to each other when you're not around the business. If you're not in the dressing room, you don't even talk to each other.'"

Wrestlers fought for years with promoters for guaranteed contracts. Today many grapplers have these contracts, and they don't have to worry about losing money if they are injured and have to take time off. The positive side of guaranteed contracts also carries a negative aspect, according to Farris. "I find that the greed and the envy and all those things that go with pro sports and show business are more prevalent in the dressing rooms currently as opposed to the past. Our paychecks depended on the amount of attendance. With everyone on a guaranteed contract now, you get paid if there's one person or 10,000 people. The push and desire and dedication and hard work to get there and make sure there's plenty of people in

Mike Lano

Honky Tonk Man wrestling Vincent of NWO

the arena for the event have been diminished greatly. It's totally in the marketing part of it today.

"I remember people like Mario Galento and Sputnik Monroe, real legends down in the South, who would walk the streets with their gimmick on, their flashy outfits, and go out to the bars and go out to places and try to create disturbances and try to prove that they could beat up anyone, just so they could sell tickets. They would actually take it to that length. I thought, 'Gosh, these guys gotta be crazy. Why would you want to be recognized when you're out in the public?'

"Back then I really didn't understand it, but as I was in the WWF and doing my thing as the Honky Tonk Man, I made sure that every time I went out into the public, especially for an autograph session or some event like that, or went to a TV or radio station for an interview, I dressed in the flashy outfit and the stuff just like those old-timers did. I knew that if I did that, I would be more recognized than the wrestlers who might have gone with me wearing a T-shirt and a baseball cap. Indirectly, I guess I did pick something up from them."

Professional wrestling organizations have at times held an iron fist in the creative aspect of character development, yet at other times, they have listened to the input of the workers. Farris has wrestled mostly under people who have called all the shots, yet he is well aware of the changes currently in wrestling which, at times, allow the wrestlers to give their opinions. "When I was the Honky Tonk Man, there was really no creativity on our part at all. That's one thing I thought was lacking—probably where the WWF might have missed the boat back then. There were a couple of guys who had creative control over things . . . Piper and of course Hogan and Savage, but other than that, we were all kind of robotish—be there as good soldiers, shut up and do what you're told to do.

"As far as the creativity now, it's better because of the war going on between the WWF and WCW. They want input from the wrestlers. It's only during the last year or so that they've started asking for input from wrestlers. 'What do you want to do? What do you think about this?' It shocked me when I went back to the WWF in 1997 that they were asking guys what they thought about the ideas."

With the newly found creative freedom for the wrestlers, new problems arise, however. Lately, we have heard about wrestlers refusing to do a job for someone, or refusing to lose cleanly and so on. At times, chaos reigns in the bookers' offices. Farris, although he is all for the wrestlers having an input, thinks matters may have gone too far in the creative aspects of the wrestling trade. "You can't have the inmates running the whole thing. I don't think it's a great idea. You gotta have a general who's leading the whole thing, who makes the calls out on the battlefield. You gotta have the sergeants who carry them out and give them to the troops and you go do it."

One of the most talked-about subjects today in professional wrestling is the dramatic increase in the amount of injuries to wrestlers. According to Farris, "There are more injuries now than ever before. I don't think it's the owners' fault. After all, the wrestlers are on guaranteed contracts. Whether the promoters ask anything or not, the wrestlers are still going to be paid unless there's some performance clause in those contracts that I don't know about. I just think each wrestler is trying to outdo the other one. I never went out there and tried to outdo Ricky Steamboat or Jake "The Snake" Roberts in their match if I had a match with Jimmy Snuka. They didn't go out and try to outdo Hulk Hogan in his match. We all had a persona that we lived when we walked through the curtain that we executed that was enough for us to be able to go out and carry the match.

Lynne Gutshall, courtesy of Lanny Poffo

Jake "The Snake" Roberts

"I think it's a lack of their self-confidence in their persona in what they're doing. Take Stone Cold and Owen Hart. They're into their persona and know how to do it. You don't see them climbing up on the top rope and doing a double back-flip out in the first seats. Everyone wants to outdo each other. Maybe they do it to get their contracts renewed. If you're talented in what you do, and you know what you're doing and you know how to do it, you don't have to worry about anything else."

Farris is well known as the Honky Tonk Man from his WWF stints. However, he did bring the character to WCW in 1994 for a few months. "I was with WCW from August through December in 1994. I had a tremendously big push . . . a lot of TV time. I was in the transition group that was coming in with Hogan. I came in there with the impression that if I worked hard and did everything I was told to do and keep my mouth shut, that I'd get a contract. Obviously, I was wrong.

"They kept holding the carrot out in front of me and I chased it up until Christmas, at which time I made a stand and said, 'If you're not going to treat me like the rest of the players, then I don't want to be on the team.'

"In addition to the contract, another carrot was making me TV champion. That was a carrot that was dangled out there for four months. I chased it and finally made my stand. Bishoff took it as me holding them up for money."

In recent years, so many wrestlers have switched back and forth between the WWF and WCW that one may think there is a constant revolving door between the two groups' offices. Farris has worked for both groups and can give valuable insight into the similarities and differences of the organizations. "I group both of them (McMahon/WWF and Bishoff/WCW) in the same boat because they basically have the same job. I think McMahon is much more schooled, dedicated and meticulous in the things he does and the way he does it. McMahon will take a year, sometimes more than a year, to bring something to fruition. All you have to do is look back 12 months. Stone Cold Steve Austin was a nobody a year ago. He was just another guy on the card. Look at me. McMahon spent a year on me before I was turned loose to be the Honky Tonk Man and have main event matches. He's very patient compared to Bishoff, who's 'go get 'em right now.' Look at the latest WCW phenom, Goldberg. There was no slow buildup. It was right away. On the other hand, WCW runs a lot of television down there (Atlanta) and can't be as time-consuming as McMahon."

Some fans maintain that there is too much pressure being put on today's wrestlers to excel, but Farris believes the pressure is all self-induced. "I don't think they have to do more today. I think the wrestlers themselves think they have to do more. I think what has gone away and what's been forgotten in the dressing room or before you go through the curtain is, 'We know what the script is. We know what the finish is. The people out there don't know.' Why should we let the fans tell us what to do? It's our job to control them for 10 minutes, not them control us. You can't let the fans control the wrestlers.

"During the course of a Shakespearean play, the fans don't start hollering, 'Hogan, Hogan,' and the guy starts shaking and coming up. You don't say, 'Well, the hell with this, let's just drop Act II and finish this right now. If they want it, let's give it to them right now.' That's just not how this thing works.

"Back when I broke into the wrestling business, if a guy did not toe the line, they'd take you in the back room and close the door. There were a couple of cauliflower-eared guys in there. They and the promoter would lay the law down."

For some time now, the WWF has become more and more risque in their angles. Some people have criticized the contemporary angles, while others have embraced the new format. On this subject, Farris stated, "From a promoter's standpoint, if I was a promoter, I would say, 'How much further can we take this?' As far as my part of it, I don't live my life and my kids don't live their lives around that segment of society who gets off on urinating on somebody's motorcycle. To each his own. TV looks at ratings and promoters look at selling tickets, and if people are buying it, then of course, you do it. You can't knock success.

"For some reason, I don't know why parents or people in radio or TV or movies, they never come clean and say, 'Listen people, everything you see on television is fake and phony. There's nothing real here.' Only clips from CNN, and they only show you the clips they want to show you, are real . . . live shots of O.J. on the slow-speed chase, now that's real, that's happening. Otherwise, it's all prefabricated bullshit they feed us.

"We're not trying to tell anyone that this (wrestling) is real. But yet, we're not telling them it's not either. That's left up to you to decide. There are so many gullible people out there. If they believe in Bill Clinton, they obviously believe in pissing on motorcycles. If they buy it, go for it."

Farris also knows that persuasion runs two ways—wrestling promoters persuade the public and the wrestlers as well. "There are a few of us that were in the business who were not easily swayed by emotional pleas from promoters or different things a promoter might try. The majority of wrestlers are easily persuaded, however. It's the old pat on the back and 'what a great match,' and 'man, you're fantastic.' Well, fine, don't tell me that, put it in my paycheck. There's no one better at that than McMahon. The only good to him is your last box office. They can pat Stone Cold on the back right now and tell him how great he is, but a year from now, if he's not selling tickets, they'll boot his ass out.

"If you're easily persuaded, then you'll follow them down to the end where you do climb up on the top rope, do a double back-flip and break your goddamn neck. They'll roll you out in a wheelchair and say, 'Helluva match!'"

The chronicling of professional wrestling history is an enigma. The major organizations constantly change and rewrite their own histories in a self-serving manner. For instance, a couple of years ago, Mr. Perfect (Curt Hennig) was an announcer with the WWF. He, in cahoots with Hunter Hearst Helmsley, was part of a dastardly plot to relieve Marc Mero of the Intercontinental belt. The plot worked and Mr. Perfect was projected as a genius. Two weeks later, Hennig switched employers and showed up at a WCW show. All of a sudden, Mr. Perfect was shown as an idiot and an ingrate. In two weeks, history had been rewritten by the WWF. Farris finds this aspect of wrestling quite disturbing. He stated, "Years ago, before the WWF started squashing out all these little territories, you could go from place to place and history would follow you. You had a bio you sent a promoter, and he would put it in his program that you were the former champion here and the former champion there. It gave you the big buildup that you were coming in bigger and better and badder than the last guy who was in. Once McMahon started his takeover of the small places, it was like Sherman's march to the sea where he burned them all down. Along with doing that, went the history behind each person he took. It was never mentioned that Piper was a former champion anywhere, or that Hogan was AWA champion or I was a tag team champion or Southern Heavyweight champion. It was always only a mention of our names. It surprised me so much that they brought former NWA champions out and paraded them in front of a pay-per-view audience. In years gone by, if it wasn't WWF, it didn't exist.

"For instance, I'm still with the company. I'm on their payroll, yet when they send a guy out to hit another guy with a guitar, use my gimmick, they don't go, 'Shades of Honky

Tonk Man,' or 'Honky Tonk Man must have told him,' or 'Looks like a leftover Honky Tonk Man guitar.' I was never mentioned."

Wayne Farris has lived the past two decades in and around the wrestling world. Several years ago, he and his family moved to Phoenix, Arizona. He has picked up a new hobby that is not wrestling-related—golf. "Living here in Phoenix, I have taken up golf. My handicap is two broken legs—I'm still trying to break a hundred!"

Being an athlete, Farris is well aware that his golf game will not improve without instruction. He has this aspect of golf taken care of. "My boy has signed up for lessons. I'm gone so much I couldn't practice what they teach. He can come home and show me, and I can work on it. Golf is something he and I can do together. It's something we're both equal on, him being a 13-year-old and me being over 40. I go to the driving range or the course every day. I live on a PGA qualifying course and I recently joined."

Farris plays golf almost every day and shows up as Wayne Farris, not the Honky Tonk Man. What would happen if he tried to play a round of golf in his performing outfit? "It wouldn't fit the dress code."

*** ***

SCENE II

A GENIUS IN THE RING

"I was eight years old, and I was asking if I could be a midget wrestler."

— Lanny Poffo

There are many self-professed geniuses in the world, and there are those who actually have been certified as geniuses through the organization Mensa. Professional wrestling has its own authenticated genius in Lanny Poffo. Throughout his career, Poffo used the monikers Lanny Poffo, "Leaping" Lanny Poffo and The Avenger. His best-known character portrayal, however, was as "The Genius" in the WWF.

For a brief moment in his career, Poffo took to the ring donned in cap and gown and berated both his opponents and the audience in verse. His poetry was original and astute, so the name "The Genius" that was given to him by the promotion did in fact carry some validity.

The role of The Genius lasted only a few months, yet Lanny Poffo's career in the squared circle has spanned 25 years. Poffo hails from a wrestling family. His father Angelo was a main event performer and his brother Randy "Macho Man" Savage is still filling seats in auditoriums across the country.

Poffo did not have to go far from home for his training. His father is a world class trainer and began to work with Lanny at an early age. The young Poffo has been an admirer of professional wrestling as long as he can remember. "My earliest recollection of wrestling was my father against Pepper Gomez in Houston, Texas. I think it was 1960 or 1961. That would have made me five or six years old. I enjoyed it right away.

"When I was eight years old, I asked if I could be a midget wrestler. My father said, 'No. You're a boy, but you're not a midget. You're short enough, but nobody would take you serious as a midget.'"

As he became older, Poffo did not let his dream of becoming a professional wrestler falter. "I wrestled in high school and I was lifting weights all through then, too. I also have a gymnastics background. My father was training me all along through that time."

Despite his love of wrestling, Lanny, with brother Randy, had picked another choice of career. "Of course, the first priority for my brother and me was to be baseball players. Randy spent four years in the minor leagues. He had time with the Cardinals, then he went on to the White Sox and then the Cincinnati Reds. He never got higher than A ball. He hurt his throwing arm and they tried to get him to throw left-handed. He was a catcher at first and then he went to first base as a left-handed first baseman. I was a catcher and an outfielder in high school ball, but I went into wrestling right out of high school."

Not long after graduating from high school, Poffo performed in the ring for the first time. His inaugural professional match was held in Aurora, Illinois, on June 10, 1973. He lost to Freddy Rogers.

From the beginning of his career, Poffo achieved success in the ring. He said, "I got off to a very good start. Then, in 1985, I made it to the WWF.

"I always did well and made a pretty good living before the WWF. My father, my brother and I had our own business called International Championship Wrestling out of Lexington, Kentucky. We wrestled in about seven or eight markets. We were in business for five years with our promotion. We were independent opposition.

"We were opposition to Jerry Jarrett and then joined up with him. About a year later, Vince McMahon put Randy in the WWF and I went too. That was in 1985."

Initially, Poffo wrestled as Leaping Lanny Poffo in the WWF. He was a babyface with a gimmick of supplying Frisbees to the fans. Then Poffo's big push came. In 1989, Leaping Lanny Poffo the babyface was transformed into The Genius, heel extraordinaire. Instead of Frisbees, the crowd now received insults, in the form of poetry, from Poffo, who had donned the ring attire of a cap and gown.

The Genius quickly made his way to the top rung of the wrestling ladder. He wrestled and beat Hulk Hogan on NBC television. According to Poffo, "That match is now on a videotape called *Hulkamania Forever*, which chronicles Hogan's greatest matches. It was taped in Topeka, Kansas, on Halloween of 1989, and it was aired on Thanksgiving weekend of 1989.

"In the four months that I was on top in the WWF doing my thing with Hulk Hogan, I was in main events and was a partner in breaking two box office records. I'm not saying I did it alone, but I was part of it. One was at the Myriad in Oklahoma City, and the other was at the Los Angeles Sports Arena. Those were the only times I had been in a main event in those towns, and they were actual records —the most money ever drawn at the venues."

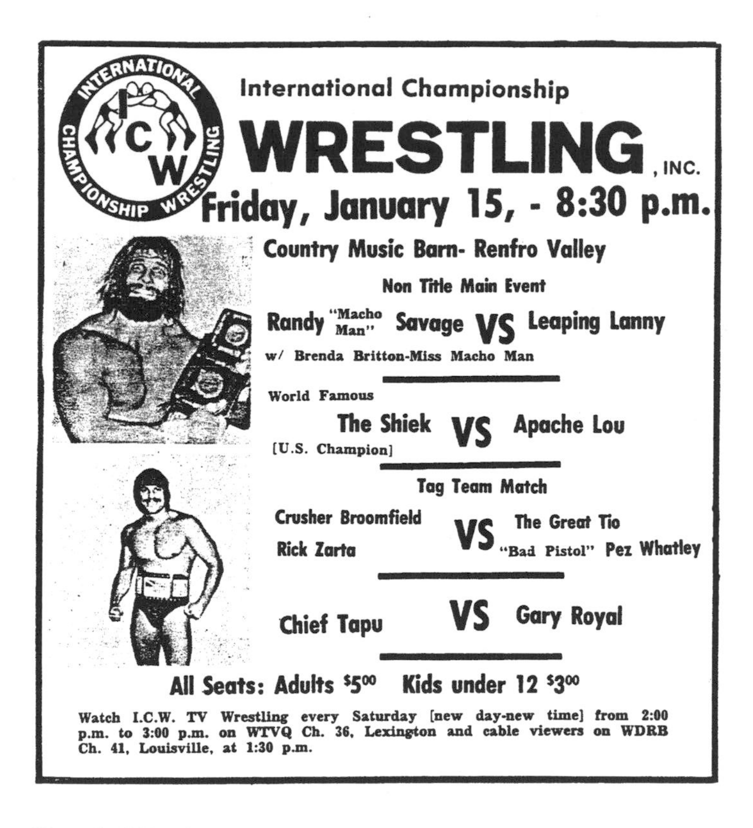

Randy "Macho Man" Savage vs. Leaping Lanny Poffo, Lexington, KY

From the time a young wrestler enters the ring for his first match, he becomes obsessed with a "push." The push makes a wrestler a star. Poffo, wrestling as The Genius, received as big a push as possible. However, the push can sometimes be accelerated and turn out to be a push right out the door. Poffo suffered this fate. He explained, "There are a lot of guys who get big pushes, and then you never hear from them again. Naturally, I was hoping that my push would last a little longer. I thought it would be the beginning of my career, not the end of it. Unfortunately, it was the end."

Actually, Poffo, now 43 years old, and in better shape than he was even at his peak of popularity, is still pursuing a wrestling career. "I haven't ruled out coming back as The Genius. I always keep my avenues open. Right now, I'm in an independent organization called the WPWF, and I'm their champion. They're based in the Gulf Coast area of Florida."

Most fans do not know that Poffo, at the time of this writing, has been under contract with WCW since 1996. The organization had various plans for him, yet they were

Mike Lano

Lanny Poffo with announcer Boyd Pierce

eventually scrapped. For now, his impending WCW career is on hold. According to Poffo, "I'm waiting for a phone call. For a while, they had me slated to be a Gorgeous George type. I even bleached my hair in anticipation of it, but it never occurred.

"Gorgeous George was great. Actually, I'm glad I'm not going to imitate him because I never could have followed him. He was first.

"Besides, my hair is dark and making it blond was causing it to break. I could have never kept up with the gimmick. It was a difficult gimmick and you have to keep going to the beauty parlor. When Gorgeous George took off his robe, he could wrestle. He wasn't all show and no go."

Wrestling ad, misidentifying Lanny and Randy Poffo as "The Poppo's"

At the beginning of their careers, Randy and Lanny Poffo wrestled as the Poffo Brothers. From 1975 to 1977, they wrestled in Charlotte, North Carolina, and in the Gulf Coast area of Florida. According to Poffo, "We did very well. We got the Gulf Coast championship and were very competitive in North Carolina."

Many times in various forms of sports or entertainment, brothers have participated and one has dominated more than the other. Take the Aaron brothers of baseball, for instance. They hold the record for the most amount of

Lynne Gutshall, courtesy of Lanny Poffo

Randy Poffo as
Randy "Macho Man" Savage

home runs hit by a brother combination. Hank, the all-time homer leader, hit 755 round-trippers, while his brother Tommy slammed 13 home runs in the major leagues. There was less disparity in the careers of Randy and Lanny Poffo, yet Randy went on to a lengthy star-studded career as the Macho Man.

The fact that his brother Randy may have overshadowed him in the ring does not bother Lanny Poffo in the least. "I'm not jealous of Randy. The fact that he's been more successful makes me happy for him. I'm happy for the success I have enjoyed. You can never be happy and jealous. You can only choose one. I don't have that green monster on my back.

"At least I got to drink from the silver chalice of success. It may not have been the gallons and gallons Randy has had, but I had a sip.

"Randy's always been a great brother to me, and he's a fantastic person. I'm happy for him. Don't forget, I was there when he failed in baseball, and it was just very inspirational that he went from a failure in baseball to a success in wrestling. Now all those who did succeed in baseball are watching him on TV. They're too old or retired. There's nobody his age playing major league baseball today."

When Vince McMahon suggested that Leaping Lanny Poffo become The Genius, the angle smacked of reality. Poffo enjoyed poetry and in 1988 had *Wrestling With Rhyme* published. The book was a collection of poetry which highlighted wrestlers and the angles of the day. Poffo described the progress which culminated in the publishing of his book: "My fifth grade teacher told me that an essay I wrote was really great. That kind of encouraged me to keep trying to write.

"I finally got interested in poetry. I liked to read and recite poetry. When I came to the WWF, I was a guest on a show called TNT, *Tuesday Night Titan*, hosted by Vince McMahon. I wrote a poem for that occasion. Vince told me, 'From now on, every

Leaping Lanny – the book

time you get in the ring, I want you to do a poem.' When I became The Genius, I just wrote nasty poems to evoke the ire of the people."

The book began to sell well, but the change from Leaping Lanny to The Genius cut into the popularity of the collection of rhymes. According to Poffo, "When I was Leaping Lanny, WaldenBooks had promised me a national contract. But when I became The Genius, they didn't want to do it any more because I had changed and was a villain. It was good for my career, but it was bad for book sales."

Lanny Poffo is well aware that in-ring performance is only a part of the success of a professional wrestler. He is astute in marketing and fan perception. According to Poffo, "As Leaping Lanny, I used to throw out Frisbees. I had an idea to put a poem on a Frisbee and send it out. The guy who was in charge of marketing in the WWF came up to me and asked, 'Do you mind if we market these?' I said, 'Go ahead.'

"After my matches, I would go to where they were selling souvenirs and be nice to the people. Frisbees were on sale for $3 each, but if they didn't have $3, or they didn't want to buy a Frisbee, I would just sign what they wanted. I would just be nice to the people.

"Pretty soon, I sold out of Frisbees every night. They sold almost $1 million worth of Frisbees at $3 a clip. I was really proud of it, but unfortunately, I never got anything else in the way of marketing. I never got a doll made of me or anything else. At least I was successful in that. One of my heroes is Sam Walton of WalMart, and he always said, 'Be nice to people.' If it wasn't for the fans, the sport wouldn't exist."

Poffo's career has spanned three generations of wrestlers. When he entered the trade, superstars from the sport's Golden Age were still appearing in the ring as well as those who represented the next era of professional wrestlers. Today Poffo is facing yet another group of wrestlers who have changed the look of the sport. What does Poffo think of the performers of today? "I see some wrestling that's phenomenal today. I see a lot of old-timers are knocking the stars. I see that as either stupidity or jealousy, but mostly stupidity."

Two common themes emerge when talking about wrestling today. First, the comparison of wrestling generations, which Poffo has addressed, followed by the similarities and contrasts of today's two big wrestling organizations, the WWF and WCW. Poffo has distinct thoughts about both promotions. "I wrestled for Vince McMahon for six years. He made my life more interesting. I got to go to Australia, New Zealand and all throughout Europe, all because of him. I hear terrible things about him because wrestlers who don't work for him any more want to piss in the soup so nobody else can have any.

"Look at him now. He's taking on Ted Turner. I think the WWF and WCW are both great organizations, but I think it's amazing how Vince is competing with such a blue-chip company. Vince said that nobody ever went broke by underestimating the taste of the public. If you look at the demographics, there is a wide spectrum of people who watch wrestling. You get the kids with the parents and that could be anybody. However, if they didn't have something on the ball, they couldn't afford the price of a ticket."

The WWF and WCW portray different images for the public. Their angles differ as well as the time it takes to bring them to fruition. Basically, the WWF will wait months until an angle attains maturity, while WCW is more immediate. One instance in particular shows how WCW will push an angle quickly—the crowning of Goldberg as its champion. Only a few months before Goldberg became champ, he was a mid-card performer whom the fans quickly admired. He was given a push and then made champion. According to Poffo, "I think the people wanted it and they got it. I think he's obviously what they want. They've probably got a banana peel in store for Goldberg in the future, but that's just going to make it all mean more."

With the advent of the Internet, Poffo has found a new passion that allows him another financial avenue. He researches the stock market daily and then makes his decisions about which stocks to buy or sell. His philosophy is to stick to the stocks that are steady. He would rather make a little over a long period than to risk all for the allure of a short-term high-percentage return.

With his diverse interests, what does Lanny Poffo consider himself—poet, business entrepreneur or entertainer? "I still consider myself to be a wrestler. I'm not going against the grain. The business will get along without me. They've proved that. If I can fit into the business, it will be my pleasure. I'll do the very best I can.

"I do have one thing going for me. A lot of the wrestlers are independent contractors, which means the promotions do not take taxes out when they pay you. At the end of the year, you have to pay the I.R.S. Many of the wrestlers can't pay their taxes at the end of the year because they're living like they're in Hollywood.

"I'm one guy who paid his taxes. If the phone rings for wrestling, I'll answer it, but if it doesn't, it's not catastrophic. I want more, but I don't need more.

"Lanny Poffo is very appreciative to the WWF and WCW and anybody else who crosses my palm with green. I'm not mad with anybody. I'm very happy for the career I've had, and I'm glad other people are enjoying it. I'm warning the wrestlers that most are not preparing for their futures, and they're going to wind up the way the majority of them wind up."

Growing up in a wrestling family is like perpetually being a kid in a candy shop. In his childhood, Poffo met many wrestlers from the Golden Age. One in particular sticks out as being the epitome of what a human being should be. "I met Killer Kowalski back in 1967. My father was teamed up with him in Hawaii. He was a vegetarian and a very devout health nut. Although I didn't become a vegetarian, and some of his philosophy I didn't prescribe to, I did appreciate the fact that he was digging for health and spirituality.

"A lot of the wrestlers are just drinking and smoking and living for the moment. They're not saving their money, and they act like there is going to be no tomorrow. Maybe there isn't, but it's just that Kowalski seemed superior to be with. He appeared to be above everything else. He's beautiful."

Sid Eudy (Psycho Sid, Sid Vicious, Sid Justice), one of the most muscular men ever to step into the ring, gives Lanny Poffo credit for getting him started in the wrestling business. This is a high accolade coming from a former two-time WWF heavyweight champion. Poffo is grateful for Sid's endorsement, yet he did not have to do much to get the big man started in

Mike Lano

Psycho Sid

grappling. "Sid was at Mid-South Coliseum and came up to me and asked, 'How do I get started with wrestling?' I said, 'Put on a tight T-shirt and hang around because you have the visuals. If they see your muscles, they're going to look at you and see money.' I told him, 'If I looked like you, I would hang around anywhere.' The guy was phenomenal."

Lanny Poffo has not allowed himself to be caught in the trap which snares many wrestlers—that of knowing nothing else but wrestling and then finding yourself starting life over again after retiring from the ring. "My goal is to be healthy, wealthy and wise—in that order. Without your health, all the money in the world won't help you. If you've got your health, you have your first million already. The second million is a little harder.

courtesy of Lanny Poffo

Lanny Poffo today – still in shape

Poffo, now divorced, was married for 12 years and has a 14-year-old daughter. "She's starting to become a wrestling fan, although it's nothing I've ever encouraged. It's not for everybody. She's starting to show some interest in it, but I don't think she'll be climbing into the ring. Nor will I encourage her to do so. It's just not the same career opportunity for a woman that it is for a man."

*** ***

Scene III

THE BABE RUTH OF WRESTLING

Kowalski had legs. He had wind.
He was a health fanatic.
He could wrestle when he's a
hundred. I swear.

— Cowboy Bill Halliday

To label someone the "Babe Ruth" of anything is a very subjective statement that is left open for many to criticize or question. That said, I have taken the liberty of calling Killer Kowalski the "Babe Ruth" of wrestling in this book. The reasons are many. Kowalski was parallel to Ruth in changing the concept of professional wrestling and during his day, his name held as much esteem as that of the late baseball player. Internationally, Kowalski was much more recognized than Ruth, especially in Japan, Australia and South Africa.

Kowalski was more than a professional wrestler. He was an artist. The ring was Kowalski's canvas (no pun intended), and his moves were his paintbrush and paints. It is evident when one watches a classic Kowalski match that he knew and controlled every square centimeter of the ring during the hectic activities being conducted like no one before or since.

ORIGINS OF THE KILLER

In 1927, a baseball player called Babe Ruth was transforming the game of baseball. In that year, he hit (what was considered impossible at the time) a total of 60 home runs. Before Ruth, baseball was a slow sport in which runs were scored by advancing base runners one base at a time. Ruth made it possible for one man to create runs with one swing of the bat.

During the same year that Ruth was rewriting baseball strategy, a person was born who would revolutionize another sport. Just across the river from Detroit, in Windsor, Ontario, Canada, Wladek (pronounced vla-dek) Kowalski, a son of Polish immigrants, came into the world. Wladek would become the legendary wrestler, "Killer" Kowalski.

Despite his tremendous athletic ability, the young Kowalski was not interested in sports. His hobby as a youth, continuing into his adult life, was photography. In fact, Kowalski has had his photographic works exhibited in Las Vegas, New York and Boston.

Physical fitness has always been at the forefront of Kowalski's agenda, even before he began to work the squared circle. This affinity eventually led him to a challenge which changed his life.

According to Kowalski, "There were about three of us guys working out at the YMCA, lifting weights in Windsor. One coach, an amateur wrestling coach who also wrestled professionally, came up to us one time and said, 'I could put a hold on you guys that would make you squeal.'"

The unimpressed Kowalski told the boaster that he and his friends did not believe him, and they ignored him for a time. The coach was persistent, so to stop him from issuing the ongoing dare, Kowalski eventually told him, "Okay. Put the hold on me." The result was painful. Kowalski said, "He put it on me and I DID squeal . . . ayhh, ayhh, ayhh, ayhh."

Kowalski and a friend were so impressed that they inquired about taking up professional wrestling. "There was a wrestling school in Detroit, Michigan, so we started training there."

After Kowalski completed his student stint, he began to wrestle on weekends, attempting to earn enough money to put himself through college. At the time, he worked in the electrical department of Ford Motor Company and aspired to be an electrical engineer, a career which would not have eluded him if he earned a degree.

Kowalski began to achieve success in the ring and received assignments which led him away from the Detroit area. He still wanted to become an engineer, so he asked for some time off. Ford did not share Kowalski's admiration of wrestling, so they refused his request. According to Kowalski, "They wouldn't give me the time off, so I quit. That was way, way, way, way back."

Kowalski spread his wings by wrestling in Ohio, Buffalo and Toronto. After a year, he returned to Detroit to choose the next step of his fledgling career. In those days, there were many wrestling organizations which covered various territories, but the one which was considered to be the closest to a "major league" was the National Wrestling Alliance (NWA). Kowalski was interested in joining the prestigious organization and took steps toward that end.

Joining the NWA created an opportunity for Kowalski to begin his journey to stardom. Soon after, he relentlessly rose in the ranks and became the nationally known wrestler whom we all remember.

Once Kowalski began to advance with the NWA, it was evident that he had to learn various fine points of wrestling that had so far eluded him. One of the aspects that he had to master was "shooting." A wrestler who is a good shooter is one who is respected by others. "Shooting" is another term for being tough. A good shooter has a hold, or variety of holds, that can intimidate other wrestlers.

When Kowalski began with the NWA, he was tutored by the legendary Lou Thesz. One day, Thesz pulled him aside and told him, "Walter, over the years you're going to be challenged. Some guys out there will try you out. They're big-headed, and they will see how tough you really are. You meet a wrestler who's a good shooter, and you don't mess with him because he can break your arm."

"Lou Thesz taught me how to shoot," Kowalski added. "He taught me how to take care of myself." Kowalski was an astute student of the master. Throughout his career, every wrestler he faced knew that Kowalski could have immobilized him at will if he chose.

When he was challenged, Kowalski always rose to the occasion. He reminisced, "One time I'm wrestling Antonio Inoki in Japan. (Inoki was and still is an idol to the Japanese, much as Michael Jordan or Ken Griffey, Jr. are to Americans.) This goes back to the '60s.

courtesy of Walter Kowalski

Kowalski, before the "Killer" tag was added

"I've been there for about eight weeks. After wrestling other people in Tokyo, I must go back to Osaka and wrestle Inoki in his hometown.

"Inoki picked me up and dropped me backwards on my head. Knocked me out . . . for about five seconds only. I come right out of it. He's got me pinned."

When the match appeared to be over—hometown hero beats foreign upstart—the mood swiftly transposed.

Kowalski continued, "Boy, he never made it. I hooked him. I hooked his leg, got him off me, and he could see the fire in my eyes and he was scared. I got up; we both got up. 'You son of a bitch,' I said. When he came at me, I hit him. I hit him as hard as I could, right in the head. I knocked him out completely."

Now Kowalski was in an unpredictable dilemma. His opponent was supposed to win, yet he was out cold in the middle of the ring.

"This was his hometown—he's gotta win!" said Kowalski, "so I reach down, picked him up off the floor, struggled, got him up, and when I lifted him up, I fell back with him on top of me. The referee goes one . . . two . . . three. I shoved him off me and started walking out of the ring. I turned around. There's the referee raising his arm, while Inoki's laying on his back, still unconscious."

The Japanese were not exactly filled with joy about Kowalski's manhandling their national hero, so they concocted a payback scheme for the next time he traveled to Japan. "When I went to Japan again, they put a sumo wrestler against me to get even for what I did to Inoki. Well, I didn't catch on. So I'm walking along the ropes and felt something hit me behind the ear. Knocked me out . . . for only about a tenth of a second. But I start staggering . . . I'm working now. I fall to the ground and I'm hunched over like I'm unconscious. My left foot was up. When he came close enough to me, I leg-dived him.

"There's a shooting way of leg-diving. I could leg-dive you with my thumb on your shinbone and knock you right down. Down he went! I'm getting up and moving around him.

"You know, sumo wrestlers have that big glob of hair behind all in a bundle. I grabbed that hair, put his head across my knee and hit him in the face. He went 'Rooooooaaar!' I hit him as hard as I could, and his nose crushed. Blood spurt all over the place. As I dropped him off, I stepped over him to get the referee. The referee got stuck underneath the rope and on the floor. So I went back and put my foot on the sumo wrestler's chest. The referee, from the floor, counted . . . one . . . two . . . three. I raised my own arm and went back to the dressing room."

Killer Kowalski began his wrestling career as Wladek Kowalski. In some areas, he was billed by the English version of Wladek, "Walter," Kowalski. One incident changed all that, however, and from then on, he would always be known as "Killer" Kowalski.

"Oh, that's an interesting story," Kowalski reminisced. "My first time wrestling in the Detroit area, I was wrestling under the name Wladek, that's Walter in Polish. So they always talked about Wladek Kowalski.

"Eventually, I wrestled a fellow named Yukon Eric in Montreal, Canada. During the match, I tied Yukon Eric's leg over the second rope and his toe underneath the bottom rope. Got him hooked like that.

"In the corner, I climb to the top of the turnbuckle, and the referee comes underneath me to unhook Yukon Eric's leg. At the same time, I jumped over the top of the referee onto

Yukon Eric to drop my shinbone across his chest. I was known for the knee-drop off the top rope.

"Well, he saw me coming and he turned away. I thought I missed him. My shinbone grazed his cheek and ripped the ear off the side of his head. The ear rolled across the ring."

The arbitrator then unhooked Yukon Eric and sternly admonished Kowalski by screaming, "I told you not to jump on him."

"Meantime, I backed up across the ring," continued Kowalski, "and the referee's arguing with me. I say 'What's that?' He picks it up. It's Yukon Eric's ear, still throbbing a little bit. We look over at Yukon Eric and blood's squirting out the side of his head like you wouldn't believe. Somebody threw a towel at him. He took the towel, put it over his head, and the towel was soaked within seconds."

Yukon Eric then walked down the steps and continued toward the dressing room. A perplexed referee looked at Kowalski and inquired, "What do I do?"

"Raise my arm. I'm the only one left," Kowalski quipped. As the arbitrator elevated Kowalski's arm, he stuttered, "Oh okay, okay, okay."

The infamous victory over Yukon Eric occurred on a Wednesday evening at the Montreal Forum. Kowalski was scheduled to go to the Forum on the following Friday to collect his paycheck from the promoter, Eddie Quinn.

Shortly after entering the office, Quinn asked Kowalski, "Been to the hospital?" "For what?" countered Kowalski. "Oh you dumb Polack. The least you could do is apologize," Quinn snapped. A puzzled Kowalski asked, "Apologize for what? These things happen." Quinn then told an office employee, "Take him over to the hospital."

Kowalski and the hireling walked to the hospital, which was only a block from the Forum. They climbed to the second floor, where Yukon Eric's room was. When they approached the room, Kowalski told the employee, "There's a bunch of people in there. I'm not going in. I'm leaving."

As Kowalski turned to walk away, the employee ran into Yukon Eric's room and loudly exclaimed, "Kowalski's out there!"

Kowalski wanted to save himself from embarrassment, so he approached the room and stood in the doorway. He said, "I never entered the room. I looked across the room, and there's Yukon Eric sitting on the edge of his bed with his feet on the floor, and his head was bandaged around and around and around.

"The first thing that came to mind was 'Humpty Dumpty sat on a wall.' So I start smiling. He smiled back. Then I start laughing. The more I thought of Humpty Dumpty, the more I laughed. He laughed and I threw my arms in the air and I swung 'em down. I walked out. That was it."

When Kowalski paid Yukon Eric the short visit, there was a newspaper reporter as well as a TV reporter on the scene. Kowalski did not think too much about the media presence until the next day. The headline of a Montreal paper read, "Wladek Kowalski visits Yukon Eric in the hospital and 'laughs' at him." There was no mention, however, that Yukon Eric laughed as well.

Kowalski's stint in Montreal included a match every Wednesday evening at the Forum. He was not expecting his next match to acquire the notoriety that it did.

According to Kowalski, "The following Wednesday, I'm wrestling. I don't remember who my opponent was, but they had it advertised all over. Big publicity about me tearing a guy's ear off. In fact, it made national news.

"Guys were writing columns. Mentioned the whole thing. One actually said I chewed a guy's ear off. I was a vegetarian. I've been a vegetarian for 45 years now. I don't chew ears. No meat or poultry. And I don't eat ears."

When he entered the ring, Kowalski understood the magnitude of the previous week's match against Yukon Eric. "As I walked in the ring for the match, people started throwing garbage at me. Something hit me. I looked down and it was a sow's ear. In indelible ink across it, it said, 'Yukon Eric.'

"People started hollering, 'You're a killer,' and pretty soon I was being called Killer Kowalski. That was it. From then on, I dropped every other name."

Because the wrestling game traditionally has exploited mishaps, both inside and outside the ring, the Yukon Eric incident was a natural to activate a years-long feud between Kowalski and Yukon Eric. They wrestled all over the United States and Canada in matches which were billed as "revenge matches." In the midst of misfortune, humorous moments sometimes occur. Kowalski told about one such incident when Eric and he main-evented a card in the Midwest several years after the infamous bout in Montreal. Kowalski and Yukon Eric stuck their heads out from behind the curtain and saw a quiet audience awaiting the evening's wrestling. Yukon Eric looked around and joked, "Shit, Kowalski, that's a lousy house. I might have to sacrifice another ear."

The Yukon Eric incident set the pace for Killer Kowalski's persona, but he represented much more to wrestling than just being a wrestler who caused another grappler to leave the ring with one ear less than when he entered. Only about once in a generation does an athlete emerge who changes the sport in which he or she participates. Killer Kowalski laid the foundation for the style of professional wrestling we enjoy today.

Kowalski's 6'7" frame made him a giant in the ring at the time. In addition to his being taller than most wrestlers, he was a finely conditioned, superb athlete, allowing him to wrestle full-out for a whole match. He was so intense that he forced his opponents to raise their performance levels.

A cartoon capitalizing on the "Yukon Eric" ear episode (from a Boston tag match promo, 1953)

The reason for Kowalski's success can be found in his conditioning. "I was a health nut. I wouldn't even take an aspirin. I just worked out and took care of myself. I didn't drink and never smoked in my life.

"One time, a few guys asked me to go to a bar. They said, 'C'mon. There's a lot of girls there.' I said okay. Then they asked me to drink a beer. Finally, I took the glass, drank a gulp, spit the whole thing out, and said, 'Who the hell can drink this piss?' Never tried beer again.

"Nobody traveled with me. I'm a nutball. No smoking allowed in my car. I didn't stop for beer."

The self-professed "nutball" elaborated on how his conditioning translated into revolutionizing professional wrestling. "I didn't eat meat. There is zero oxygen in meat. Because of that, I had tremendous energy.

"I was the guy who increased the speed of wrestling. Remember, many years ago, they would lay around for minutes with a hold. I didn't. I used to jump up and down, do the kangaroo hop. I increased the speed of wrestling. Guys would jump out of the ring and walk around. They were pooped.

"One big body builder with a tremendous physique threw up on me in the ring. I couldn't stop. I kept going."

The referee was a friend of Kowalski and asked, "What's up? He's turning blue."

Kowalski added, "I turned around . . . the guy's laying on the ground. I said, 'Holy shit!' I dropped him one-two-three. They had to get two guys to haul him back to the dressing room.

"That was back in 1973 or '74, and I was thinking about retiring pretty soon. So when I got back to the dressing room, the guy said, 'Gee. I didn't know who you were.' So I said, 'You sure know now.'"

Kowalski's reputation as a relentless competitor preceded him wherever he wrestled. "In Toledo, Ohio, one time I was putting on my wrestling shoes, and I had such a reputation everybody in the dressing room was just looking at me. I got up and said, 'What's happening?' Someone then said, 'Well, we heard you were coming here six weeks ago, and we all went to the gym to start working out.' I said, 'Why didn't you start working out before then?' One of them answered, 'Well, you get lazy a little bit. We wanted to at least look half decent against you in the ring when we get in there with you.'"

Bill Sprague, the journeyman who grappled from 1975-1985 under the name of Cowboy Bill Halliday, also promoted small independent cards in the Northeast. Although he never wrestled Kowalski during the Killer's mat career, he had occasion to become involved with him at various times. Sprague reinforces the aura of Kowalski's relentless pursuit of excellence in the ring, even after the Killer had retired from active wrestling.

According to Sprague, "Walter and I live in the same proximity, and he had a wrestling school in one of the rooms in the YMCA in Salem, Massachusetts. I would go up there a lot and work out with him, and we would put on shows. We got into some good fights, he being the referee, and I would take a swing at him. He would pick me up and throw me down. We had a few things going like that.

"When he throws his kicks and his knees, he puts a lot of aplomb behind them. The thing of it is, if you need a minute's rest, you do not get it.

"You don't see 60-minute matches like you used to. He could go 60 minutes. You'd try to get out and you just couldn't.

courtesy of Walter Kowalski

Kowalski hoists Haystack

He'd go out and throw you back in. The man had legs. He had wind. He was a health fanatic. He had the best wind in the business, bar none. He could wrestle when he's a hundred, I swear."

Kowalski was noted for his excellence in working with other wrestlers to protect them and himself, while producing an effect that would be fan-appealing. Despite his lack of interest in other sports, Kowalski occasionally worked with athletes in their own sports, attempting to show them advanced tricks of the trade. "When I first started wrestling, I read in the paper in Detroit that a former hockey player was complaining that hockey was fake. From that moment on, I knew it was a "work."

"I was a big star in Montreal. In fact, when they closed the Montreal Forum, they had a 15-minute segment on Killer Kowalski.

"Once, one of the hockey players asked me how to hit a guy with a stick without hurting him. I got a stick and came out of the office. I got one of the wrestlers. I took the stick and slapped the wrestler across the neck. The wrestler was working and took a big bump. The hockey player hollers, 'Hey! I can't do that.' The other guy jumps up and says, 'Didn't feel it. . . .'

"I showed him how to hit someone with a stick. He was with the Montreal Canadiens. I told him to wind up big so it looks big. They were very kind to me . . . all those players there."

Despite Kowalski's knowledge of protecting oneself in the ring, there is one move that is defenseless. When somebody asked the Killer how to protect himself against a 500-pound guy who jumps off the top rope, Kowalski simply said to the rookie, "Our Father . . . ."

There are those pundits who maintain that professional wrestlers do not get injured when they apply the skills of their trade. "Bullshit," Kowalski responded, "they get injured. Both my knees are gone. My hip is gone. I don't have full movement of my neck anymore. I've had my share of injuries. Despite the injuries, I never missed a main event. The night after an injury, I would be back in the ring."

In a sport that thrives on the combination of fantasy and fact, there are times when the line between the two becomes blurred. Kowalski was wrestling in Montreal when one such incident occurred. He said, "I took a bump. I landed on my head. My hip went out. Pinched the nerve. My legs went numb.

"I'm laying in the ring and I tell the referee that I can't move. I'm paralysed. They went and got a stretcher, put me on it, and took me back to the dressing room.

"It was two-out-of-three falls back then. There's a knock on the door and a guy says, 'I know what's the matter with him.' He comes running in and turns me over. Click! Puts my hip back in.

"I walk back to the ring, and all I hear is 'Fake! Fake!' I'm walking back to the ring, and I'm all right. When it's not fake, the fans thought it was."

A STELLAR CAREER

To me, it was important that my opponents were in tremendous physical shape. Kowalski was a guy I truly admired. Kowalski was in such great, great shape. I don't know how many people realized just what a phenomenally conditioned athlete this guy was.

To me, it was a great challenge to wrestle him, especially if you had to go an hour, because to go an hour, you knew it was going to be nonstop. It just was going to be hard work.

– Bruno Sammartino

Killer Kowalski's reign in the squared circle lasted almost three decades. He wrestled on several continents in every kind of arena imaginable. In addition to crisscrossing the United States many times, Kowalski plied his trade in Australia, Japan, South Africa, Indonesia, Singapore, Hong Kong, Malaysia, Zimbabwe [at the time, Rhodesia] and the whole of Canada from the westernmost province of British Columbia to the eastern stretches of New Brunswick.

It is virtually impossible to know what his exact record in the ring was, but Kowalski approximates his win-loss record at around 7,000 wins, 100 losses, 200 disqualifications.

Kowalski's demeanor in the ring was frantic, relentless and, at times, gruesome. He was the consummate "bad guy." In contrast to many of today's stars, he never changed to a babyface, only to revert to a heel. He was always the ultimate demon. His arsenal was extensive, but he will always be known for his knee drop off the top ropes and his devastating "claw hold," with which he could immobilize an opponent at will.

The claw hold was much more than just an agonizing hold that stretched an opponent's stomach muscles. It was a nerve hold that could paralyze. In a magazine called *Wrestling Annual #12* published in 1975, a feature article titled "Why Nerve Holds Must Be Banned" appeared, and Kowalski's claw hold was at the top of the list of devastating holds. According to the article:

> One of the reasons no official action has been taken against the nerve hold is its close relationship to the claw hold. While the claw also grabs at certain muscles, it is very difficult for anyone without a medical degree to clearly tell the two apart. There are those, like Killer Kowalski, who are proficient at both holds, and can cripple with either.

> "I'm great in all things," Kowalski declares, "so it's no surprise I can apply the nerve hold better than anyone else. Anyone who has brains can apply the claw as easily as the nerve hold. Anyone who doesn't do both is a fool."
>
> Does it bother Killer Kowalski that the victim of the claw hold may be crippled for life?
>
> "No," Kowalski answered coldly.

That in-character interview was conducted almost at the end of Kowalski's long career, yet he was so successful with the claw hold that it held a foremost position in the minds of wrestling fans and journalists alike.

In the final year of Kowalski's wrestling career, a magazine, *The Best of the Wrestler—Fall 1976*, ran an article written by a psychologist, Dr. Manfred E. Wilson, in which he described the mental attributes of "The 10 Most Dangerous Men in Wrestling." Of course, Killer Kowalski was a major player in Dr. Wilson's assessment. According to Dr. Wilson's article:

> Killer Kowalski is a psychiatrist's dream—the foremost example of a split personality. Never have I met a man in whom the split personality runs along such textbook lines.
>
> Outside the ring, Kowalski is a mild-mannered, soft-spoken individual with the gentleness of your neighborhood minister. He does not drink, or smoke and is the kind of man mothers might point to and say, "I hope my son grows up to be just like him." He is pleasant, refined and good company.

WRESTLING
MONDAY, JUNE 22, 1970, 8 P.M.
MAIN EVENT
WILD BULL
CURRY
VS
KILLER
KOWALSKI
SEMI-FINAL
TAG TEAM MATCH
LORD CHAS.
MONTAGUE
AND
BOB
ORTON
VS
MIL
MASCARAS
AND
RONNIE
ETCHINSON
SPECIAL EVENT
EDUARDO
PEREZ
VS
MARK
STARR
PLUS OTHER GREAT MATCHES
TICKETS ON SALE
NORTH SIDE
COLISEUM
CALL EARLY FOR RESERVATIONS
MA 4-7269

Kowalski billings

(left: Fort Worth, Texas, 1970, below: St. Louis, Missouri, 1975)

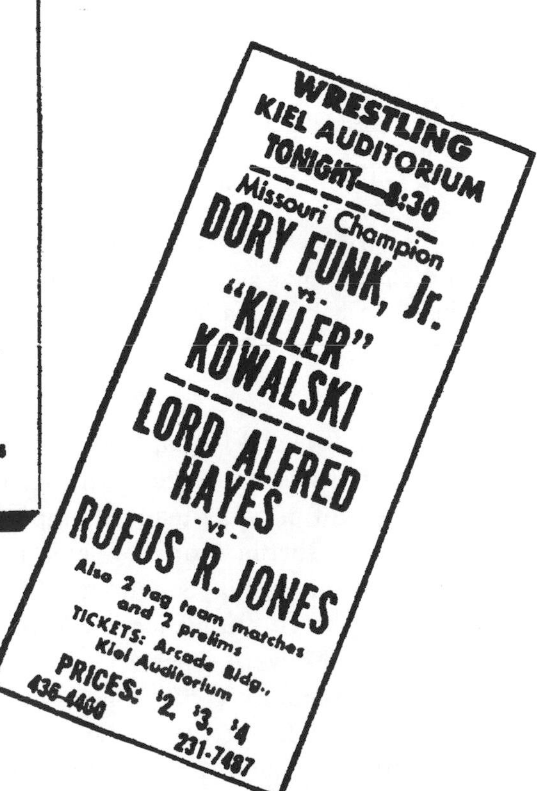

WRESTLING
KIEL AUDITORIUM
TONIGHT—8:30
Missouri Champion
DORY FUNK, Jr.
-VS-
"KILLER"
KOWALSKI
LORD ALFRED
HAYES
-VS-
RUFUS R. JONES
Also 2 tag team matches
and 2 prelims
TICKETS: Arcade Bldg.,
Kiel Auditorium
PRICES: $2, $3, $4
436-4400
231-7487

But once he puts on a pair of trunks, Kowalski turns into a ruthless, sadistic individual who delights in torturing his opponents. He'll stop at nothing, as the famous incident when he actually tore off an opponent's ear indicates.

As I said earlier, Kowalski was almost a perfect textbook case. The reason for his split personality dates back to his very first match when he was thrown in against an experienced and particularly brutal veteran. He absorbed a horrible beating.

And although he was wrestling clean at the time, he vowed that never again would someone do to him what had been done in that first match. In effect, every time Killer wrestles, he sees himself wrestling that very same opponent who hurt him so badly. He has no conception of whom his opponent for a particular evening might be. To him, they are all one man—that wrestler who nearly murdered him in his first match and almost ended his career before it began.

Kowalski is dangerous. Make no mistake about that. But he's dangerous only when wrestling. Most fans, however, believe that's enough.

Most of Kowalski's career consisted of him in singles matches, but twice he teamed up with other wrestlers and became one-half of a tag-team championship unit. According to Kowalski, "Gorilla Monsoon and I were WWF tag-team champions for one solid year in the 1960s. Later on, Big John Studd and I were champions when we wrestled as The Executioners. We were masked men. I was 'Executioner #1' and he was 'Executioner #2.' We held the WWF tag-team title for a whole year. In fact, they took the title away from us by bending the rules. No championship could change hands on a disqualification, but we were so ruthless, they took the title away from us. They disqualified us."

Despite his success as part of a tag-team unit, Kowalski favored wrestling in singles matches. "I preferred one-on-one. Most of my prime was one-on-one."

For much of Kowalski's career, there were various organizations which were split up into territories, so the rights to being called "champion" were much more diverse than they are today. Kowalski held many variations of championship belts over his career. He stated, "Every place I went, they made me the champ.

"Buddy Rogers was NWA champion. I'm wrestling Buddy Rogers in Montreal. In the match, I drop-kick him. He fell out of the ring onto the floor and broke his ankle. So he crawled back into the ring and says, 'My ankle's broken.' I said, 'Oh shit!' I start jumping in the air and I start jumping on his other leg. Fighting, screaming, he finally gave up. So they give me the NWA title in Canada. From there on, I take all his bookings. I dropped all the small towns I used to wrestle in and took over the big towns.

"I'm wrestling Lou Thesz in Houston, Texas. They didn't recognize me as champion. I was at the time the world champion for the outfit I was wrestling for in Montreal. So when I beat Buddy Rogers, they would not recognize me as NWA champion.

"I wrestled Lou Thesz in Houston. We went 90 minutes. He couldn't beat me. I couldn't beat him. A draw. I was in good shape.

"Finally, Buddy Rogers comes back . . . his ankle got better. He wrestled me back in Montreal. He beat me and got his title back. Then he wrestled Lou Thesz in Toronto and gave

Lou Thesz the title. I've never been recognized as official NWA world's champion."

Killer Kowalski and Bruno Sammartino were intense rivals in the ring. Their in-character relationship can be equated to that of Hitler and Churchill or Martin Luther King, Jr. and J. Edgar Hoover. Despite the overwhelming animosity in the ring, Kowalski has fond recollections of Sammartino. "Here's the kind of guy Bruno Sammartino was. I wrestled him, he was the champion. I put him over (lost to him) everywhere. I put him over all over.

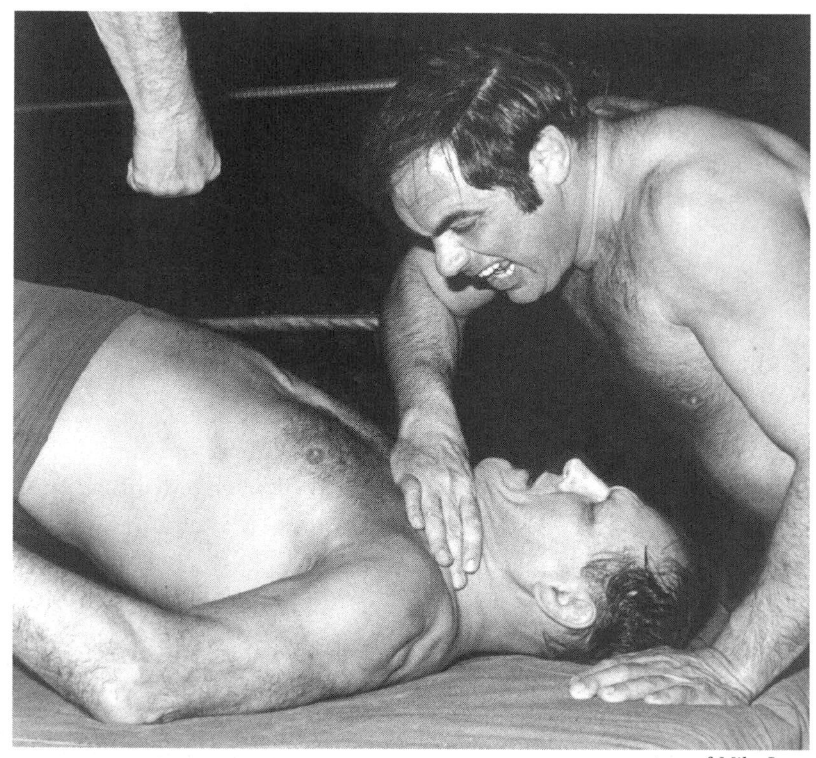

courtesy of Mike Lano

A bad day at work for "The Killer"
(Kowalski vs. Tolos, 1972)

"I was the world's champion in Canada, however. Bruno had such a big name that they brought him up there. Right in the middle of the ring, I said we'll have a double count out. He said, 'Bullshit! Bullshit.' Right in the middle of the ring, I pinned him in the middle of the ring. He wouldn't take anything else. That's Bruno Sammartino.

"I was also the world's champion in Australia. They brought him down for a two-month tour. We worked angles on TV and everything. We worked the matches down there. He put me over. He was a real, real nice guy. Today, it's a bit different."

The difference today that Kowalski mentioned is the egos of some wrestlers. He stated that they always want to win, but he maintains that the victories will come if a wrestler is competent and works hard. Kowalski thinks that the importance some wrestlers affix to winning all their matches is superfluous.

He reminisced about the attitudes today compared to those prevalent in his prime. "It goes in cycles. In my day, I had to sleep in my car. I wrestled for $35, $40 or $50.

"The cycle is downward right now. House fights. No loyalty. Money talks. In my day, a basketball team owner wanted to start his own promotion. I got a phone call and was offered $2,000 a week. I was only making five or six hundred. He wanted me to come over to him. I refused. I was working for Vince McMahon, Sr. at the time and I stayed with him. In fact, I started wrestling with the father of McMahon, Sr. He treated me nice and kind. When he passed away, McMahon, Sr. used me for a long time. If a guy was kind to me, I loved him back."

Kowalski was a giant in the ring and rarely wrestled men who possessed a larger stature than he; however, a couple of his opponents were in the giant category—Haystack Calhoun and Andre the Giant. Kowalski was successful against both men despite some of his contemporaries not being able to contain the two titanic grapplers. He attributed his mastery against big men to his technique. “Many good wrestlers do not know how to wrestle against a big man. Against Haystack Calhoun, I had to increase my speed. He couldn’t keep up.

“Andre the Giant was a different story. When he first came from France, he went to Montreal. I was champion there. We wrestled quite a bit and I was beating him. He was a big,

WWWF, courtesy of Mike Lano

Andre the Giant showing his strength

powerful, strong guy and if I got too close to him, he'd think he had a basketball, and he would bounce me around. The only way I could handle him was to increase my speed and try to outsmart him.

"Later on, Vince McMahon, Sr. squared away Andre's working papers and had him come to the United States where he became a superstar. Our feud spilled across the U.S./Canada border, and we wrestled in the United States. At a match in Pittsburgh, Andre whispered in my ear, 'Slam me.' I thought, 'Bullshit! I can't even lift his arm.' He said, 'Slaaaaaam me!' I knew he meant it, and if I didn't try to slam him, it would have been the end of me.

"I crotched him. Up he went. The people went, 'Ohhhh.' They were flabbergasted. I walked around the ring and flexed my muscles like I was Superman.

"Wrestling, unlike other sports which keep accurate records, has a tendency to write and rewrite its own history. In 1987, Hulk Hogan slammed Andre the Giant, and his action was heralded as the first time that Andre had ever been slammed. I slammed him more than a decade earlier. I was years before everybody and everything in professional wrestling."

Today if an athlete approaches the end of his or her playing days, all sorts of celebrations and good-bye tours are planned. In Kowalski's day, there was no such fanfare. According to the Killer, "The last match I had was in Providence, Rhode Island, in 1977. They put me against some schlep and I beat him and that was that. I retired."

Kowalski himself eloquently encapsulated his career by saying, "There was a time not so long ago, in an America starved for larger-than-life heroes, when I was as close as anyone could become to being the ultimate public villain. For almost 30 years, I was one of the most hated celebrities in

America. They called me Killer Kowalski, and mine was not the gentlest of professions.

"When I entered sporting arenas in the United States, Canada, Japan and Australia, women and children screamed their darkest thoughts at me. Male and female fans attacked me with knives. There were lawsuits and death threats.

"At the height of my career in the late 1950s and early '60s, I received a thousand letters a week with the vilest of suggestions. Small riots would accompany my appearances. On several occasions, armed cops formed human walls to protect me. But I loved every minute of it.

"I loved stalking the professional wrestling rings across America and the world. I absolutely revelled in twisting, smashing and pounding my opponents in brutal mayhem that made me one of the most loathed and feared men alive.

"For a strange, turbulent, golden era—more than a quarter of a century—Killer Kowalski singularly dominated professional wrestling as no man did before him, and as no man has since. I was the man America loved to hate.

"I was, in fact, America's premier antihero. And I worked hard at being bad because it taught me the way to peace."

THE MARK TWAIN OF PROFESSIONAL WRESTLING

Killer Kowalski was one of the most skilled wrestlers ever to step inside a ring. He possesses another skill, however, that puts him head and shoulders above most athletes—he can tell comprehensive, outrageous stories. Mark Twain was arguably the finest storyteller the world has ever encountered, yet Kowalski can relate incidents in an almost as astute manner as the man from Hannibal, Missouri. Kowalski may have won and lost world titles, but he will always retain the designation of being "The Mark Twain of Professional Wrestling." Let's take a look at recollections of Killer Kowalski's career, as he tells some of his famous stories about action inside and outside the squared circle. Some are familiar to longtime wrestling fans, while others appear here for public consumption for the first time.

Today the two main professional wrestling television programs, WWF's *Monday Night Raw* and WCW's *Monday Nitro*, use ploys at the end of the shows that keep the viewer on edge until the next week's offerings. This technique is not new, and at one time it was more spontaneous because the wrestlers could implement their own twists to the plots.

In Boston, Massachusetts, television station WBZ was a pioneer in presenting professional wrestling to the public in the 1950s. Killer Kowalski was a primary player in WBZ's early days of spreading the "gospel."

According to Kowalski, "We used to do live television on WBZ back in 1958 . . . in the studio. I used the claw hold and the knee-drop too.

"We had a guy named Pepper Gomez—a man with a cast iron stomach. He challenged everybody. He used to say, 'You could hit me with a baseball bat in the stomach.' So working on TV, I come up with a bat and hit him in the stomach. It didn't phase him at all. He starts charging me and says, 'You could jump on me or use your claw hold. It wouldn't work.'

"So I asked him, 'Can I jump on your stomach?' He was cocky and said, 'Sure you can jump on my stomach.'

"I looked over and saw we had three minutes to go before we went off the air. I had him lay down near the turnbuckle. I climbed the turnbuckle and looked over to the guy, and he gave me a signal that there's two minutes to go.

"I climbed down on the mat again, pulled over a little bit. I looked over at the guy, climbed back up, and I again looked over and he said, 'Ten seconds to go.'

"Everybody thought I was going to jump on his stomach, but I leaped off the top turnbuckle and knee-dropped him across the throat. We went into the black (off the air).

"People went crazy. They called the police and reported a murder. The police came down and asked what happened. 'Somebody get killed?' No, we had a wrestling show. The police left.

"They made a match out of Pepper Gomez and me. A big challenge match—everything goes. We sold out Boston Garden three days ahead of time. Big sign—NO TICKETS LEFT.

"We had a gimmick with another wrestler. Frank Scarpa was his name. He would just sit there and watch me wrestling. They mentioned that he was a wrestler and this, that and the other thing. So he's sitting down. Finally, I put the claw hold on my opponent. He's screaming with pain.

"Frank Scarpa jumps into the ring. I jump up . . . look at him. He hits me—knocks me out. We go into the black, off the air. I'm unconscious. We make a match at Boston Garden—Frank Scarpa vs. Killer Kowalski. Again, sold out three days ahead of time."

When Killer Kowalski wrestled in the 1950s, the crowds were more outspoken than those of today. In fact, it was not uncommon to hear about incidents in which the wrestlers' lives or well-being were put into jeopardy. Montreal was one city in which the fans occasionally attempted to take matters into their own hands.

According to Kowalski, "There was a guy who worked in the Montreal office. We called him 'Wonder.' The guy was 6'3" tall, ordinarily. I say 'ordinarily' because he had artificial legs below the knees. He had a bit part in a Western movie once, where the villains tied his legs to a railroad track, and it was made to look like the train had run over his legs.

"Anyway, Wonder was a powerful man and packed one helluva wallop. We called him Wonder because we would often see him walking around the wrestling office without his artificial legs, and his arms reached the ground.

"After a match of mine in Montreal, a riot ensued. Both my opponent and I had trouble making it to the dressing room, and Wonder came out without his artificial legs and got behind the fans who were causing the ruckus and blocking our exit.

"Boom! He began throwing uppercuts to their balls, and people were dropping like flies. I and my opponent looked down. There was Wonder smiling because he knocked the shit out of everybody. He didn't even have to bend over because he was already there—just nailed them in the nuts and down they went."

Most athletes can tell you about the most grueling contest in which they appeared during their careers. Kowalski is no exception. He participated in the squared circle more than 7,000 times, yet one bout stands above all others in its tenacity.

"My most grueling match was against Bruno Sammartino in Pittsburgh, Pennsylvania. He was just starting out. It was his hometown. He was a championship weightlifter and all that jazz, so I figured I'm going to teach these people here a lesson. I'm going to show them what real professional wrestling is all about. I'm going to pick on this geek here, this Italian geek, and let him see what Killer Kowalski is all about.

"We wrestled and we wrestled, and we went up and down, go, go, go. He stayed with me all the way. One whole hour. The bell rang. The match was finished.

"I went back to the dressing room. I was sitting there gasping, and one of the other guys came up and asked, 'How is it?'"

An exhausted Kowalski told the other wrestler, "Another three minutes and I would have quit . . . let him take the match." The wrestler laughed.

Kowalski continued, "He went across the hall to the other dressing room. Later, he came back and said Bruno was laying there, gasping, and had told him, 'To tell you the truth, another two minutes, I would have quit and given him the fucking match.'

"He was laughing and I asked him, 'Is that his dressing room across the hall?'" The wrestler answered, 'Yeah.'

"I went out of there and kicked the door open," said Kowalski. "I was doing pushups and said, 'You fucking Dago, just can't give me a workout.' So he kicked the door and said, 'Go to hell, you damn Polack.' That's called one-upmanship."

During his career, Kowalski made many trips overseas. In some of the foreign countries, he was held in as high esteem as their own national heroes.

In the 1960s, Japan was virtually a required stop for American professional wrestlers. The Japanese were infatuated with the American stars, even though they had a fine group of homegrown talent.

According to Kowalski, "In 1963, we all went to Japan. It was my first trip there. Haystack Calhoun had just started wrestling only a short time ago. Gorilla Monsoon was on the trip as well as Fred Atkins. There were guys from Mexico, Hungarians and Australians. We all met in Los Angeles Airport.

"I didn't know most of these guys, so I was standing around, and Haystack Calhoun came up to me. I was his hero. I used to wrestle in Dallas, Texas, and this fat little kid used to be out there. This little kid sitting at ringside, it was Haystack Calhoun. He grew older and became interested in wrestling himself.

"At that time, the 707 jets stopped at Honolulu to refuel. Those planes didn't have the long range they have today. We all got off the plane for a while and then got back on, one hour before flight time.

"I had been in Honolulu before, so heck, I know what it's all about. I love it there.

"My seat was right in the separation behind the first class section, in the economy class. We were all in the economy class. Actually, with the separation, you have all the leg room there. Each of the eight wrestlers had an aisle seat, and the two seats behind him were empty. The rest of the plane was packed.

"Haystack came up to me and said, 'Boy, I could live there (Hawaii) forever. All those concession stands. Boy, I had a quart of pineapple juice, a quart of guava juice, a quart of papaya juice. Man, I could live there forever.'"

Kowalski went on to say, "Calhoun weighed 600 pounds—he was 6'5" up in the air and 6'5" sideways. He hadn't seen his balls since he was born. To keep all that weight on, he only took a crap about once a month. As the plane took off, I was reading a magazine. About a couple of hours into the flight, the stewardess ran by me in a panic. I looked down the aisle, and she went straight to the cockpit. Pretty soon, she came running back in a panic again.

"A few minutes later, she's walking by and she's laughing with her hands over her mouth. So I turned around and I saw two wrestlers—one on each side of the aisle. Each was holding a blanket covering the entrance to the galley.

"I asked one of the wrestlers what was going on. 'Haystack has to take a shit!' he responded. I said, 'How the hell is he going to do that?' Pretty soon I hear this guy say, 'Holy shit! What a stink!' He dropped the blanket and ran right out.

"Right away, I went back. Here's what I saw—Haystack Calhoun, nude, standing in a mailbag. He couldn't squat too well. It stunk like a son of a bitch.

"All the people in the back of the plane said, 'Oh my God, what a stink!' They left and took all the empty seats near us. A bunch of people went to the first class seats."

The Haystack Calhoun saga was just beginning. When the group arrived in Japan, the wrestlers soon discovered that toilets in Japanese hotels differ considerably from their American counterparts. According to Kowalski, "All the toilets in Japanese hotels and inns at that time were flush to the floor. Haystack couldn't squat, so he would put his back up against the wall to take a crap. It would hit the floor and stink up the whole place. People complained. Finally, we asked for hotels with Western-style toilets. We finally got one, and Haystack sat down on it . . . and crushed it! The guys were picking pieces of porcelain out of his ass."

After a few days in various cities, the group made its way to Okinowa. On the agenda for the wrestlers was the chance to view a cobra-mongoose fight. Kowalski explained, "I was a bit of a photographer. I had my 8mm and my Hasselbad with me. I was taking pictures, and one of the wrestlers asked, 'What's a mongoose?'

"I said, 'You dummy. It's a small chicken.' I didn't know what a mongoose was, but I told him it was a small chicken.

"When we walked into the hotel, we saw in the middle of the granite floor a thing about three feet high and square . . . all glass . . . open top. That's where the cobra and mongoose were going to fight. All the guys got chairs and got up close. Haystack Calhoun pulled up this big, big chair, like a lounge chair. He was squeezed into it, stuck in it.

"Pretty soon, here comes the guy with a wicker basket. He dumps it open and out falls this mongoose. It looked like an oversized rat. The guy who asked me what a mongoose was looked over at me and said, 'A little chicken? You dummy!'

"Finally, the guy puts his hand in another wicker basket and grabs the snake. As he lowers the snake past Haystack, Haystack screams. He was deathly afraid of snakes. He screamed and pushed his chair all the way back to the carpeting. He got stuck in the carpeting. He started panicking and we all laughed about it."

The mongoose and the snake went at it for a few minutes, with the inevitable result of the mongoose winning. When the snake went limp, the wrestlers were told that it died from its own venom.

When the snake-handler showed the dead snake to the wrestlers, Haystack Calhoun panicked and pushed his chair backwards, tipping it over. According to Kowalski, "It took four guys, one guy on each leg and one guy on each arm, to straighten him up. He was stuck in the chair."

After the exhibition, Gorilla Monsoon and Kowalski left to play sightseers in town. "We came to this one part of an open mall. It stunk like hell—like dried fish in the open air. There was a coral snake all coiled up. Gorilla Monsoon looks at it. I look at it. We look at one another. He says, 'You thinking what I'm thinking?' I said, 'Yep. Wrap the snake up.'

"We put the paper around the snake and bought a little suitcase for three dollars. We put the snake in there and went back to the hotel.

"There was nobody at the hotel. The wrestlers all stayed downtown. We asked the maid to open the door to Haystack's room. She asked if we had a key. No key. She said, 'No key, no open door.' Monsoon kicked the door, and the whole building shook. She screamed and she opened the door. We walked in, and she was watching us.

"We took the bedspread and pulled it back; took the sheets and blanket and put them back; took the snake out and put it in the middle of the bed. We were nice guys; we made the bed. We had to hold its head down. It kept popping up. The maid screamed and ran away.

"We finally made the bed so it looked pretty doggone good—thumped up the bedspread and the pillows a little bit. We went out to get something to eat.

"It was almost 8:30, and we knew they closed the doors to the hotel at 8:30, so we rushed back. When we got back, we noticed the interpreter's room—his door was cracked down the middle. We looked around and nobody was around. Usually, on each floor, they have a lounge area where all the guys sit and talk about wrestling—wrestling in Hungary, wrestling in Australia, wrestling in Mexico. Now there's nobody around.

"I look at Monsoon and he looks at me. I say 'Oh, oh!' One of the doors opens, and one of the wrestlers comes out.

He asks, 'Where you guys been?' I say, 'Just shopping around. Got a bite to eat. Why? What's going on?' He says, 'Haystack Calhoun is going home. Haystack quit.'

"Holy shit! By this time Haystack Calhoun had opened his door, and he's screaming and hollering. We don't want to go back home. We have no bookings at all back in the United States. This was only the third of five weeks.

"I said, 'What's happening?' Monsoon's only been in the business for a year and a half, and I've been in the business for 13 years, longer than anybody, so I'm the veteran, according to them.

"Haystack told me, 'One of these no-good sons of bitches put a snake in my room. I hadn't been laid in months. I find myself a beautiful girl, and I brought her back. She's got her clothes off, and as I went to take the spread back, this snake head pops up. The girl screamed, grabbed her coat and ran out. The snake stunk like a son of a bitch. I was so mad, I grabbed the snake. I rushed in and crashed it into the door. I threw the snake out and said I'm going home.'"

"The guys called up the office, called the promoters and asked if they would take the tour without Haystack. They said 'NO! Six-foot-five up and down. Six hundred pounds.' He was a real freak to the Japanese. They wanted to see this guy. They could care less about any other wrestler. So that was it. They were going to cancel the tour.

"I said, 'Oh shit!' I told Haystack I would take the blame. I did it. Gorilla Monsoon backed up. He wouldn't say a word.

"'Let the other guys stay here. You go ahead. They don't have any bookings. I'll take the blame,' I told Haystack.

"Haystack put his arm around me, and tears came to his eyes. He said, 'You're just trying to be a martyr for one of these no-good sons of bitches. I'll tell you what, you stay here. Don't go home, and I'll stay here. You guys better get on your knees and thank Kowalski.'

"Haystack goes back in his room. Fred Atkins, he looks around and says, 'It was you, you fucking Polack and this four-eyed baboon.' He pointed to Monsoon. 'You were the two guys who did it.' I said, 'shhh . . . shhh . . . shhh.'"

Later on the tour, Kowalski and one of the other wrestlers met two Japanese girls in a club and brought them back to the hotel. According to Kowalski, "I had 34 cents, the cost of cab fare, invested in her. When we entered the room, some of the wrestlers and Haystack Calhoun were there. Haystack was sitting in a chair against the wall. His shirt was open, and he had little shorts on. This woman, when she saw the hair on Haystack's chest, she started rubbing her cheek against his chest. We were thrilled with what we saw. Most Japanese men have no hair on their chests. Calhoun said, 'This girl is mine.' I told him, 'You can't have her.' 'I'll buy her off you,' he replied. Haystack wasn't used to Japanese money, and after joking and telling him that he couldn't afford her because I already had spent a lot of money on her, I took 100 yen from him. He said, 'That's only 28 cents.' I said, 'Good enough,' and walked out. I figured that I was only out six cents now.

"After I left, the girl finally got bored and left. When we all got back to the States, we heard stories about it. Rumors spread that Kowalski found girls in Japan for 28 cents. Calhoun got even with me. He used to tell everybody, 'Kowalski's a pimp too. He's selling girls for 28 cents.' Guys were coming and telling me about it."

Haystack Calhoun died before his time in 1989. When Kowalski tells stories about the gentle giant, his voice changes subtly. There was a strong bond between the former "fat kid," as Kowalski described him when he first saw him, and the master. Kowalski said, "He was a dear friend."

Mike Lano

**Killer's ring compadres –
Haystack Calhoun and Gorilla Monsoon**

Ivan Putski experienced a long and fruitful professional wrestling career. In fact, in 1995, he was elected to the WWF Hall of Fame. In the beginning of his career, however, he experienced matches that were not as glamorous as those in which he participated after he became a star. Kowalski takes us back to one such match in which Putski became "em-bear-assed."

"I was wrestling in Texas," Kowalski reminisced, "and I'm going to Amarillo. I go into the building. I'm quite early, look at the poster . . . a big poster that says Killer Kowalski vs. I don't remember who, John Valentine maybe. Underneath . . . special attraction, 600-pound bear vs. . . . it named two guys (two wimps) and Ivan Putski.

"So I walk in and the promoter comes in, looks around, looks at me and gives me a big jar of honey. I put the honey in my bag. I pull out a book and start reading.

"Pretty soon, the guys start coming in, drifting in. The promoter comes in again. I said, 'Excuse me. I would like a very special favor.' He asked, 'What is it?'

"You got me as the last match. The bear sheds hair and there will be a stink in there. Can you put me on before the bear and the bear on last?' He said, 'No problem. We'll have intermission right after your match.'

"By that time, they got the bear out of the van and by the time they got everything set up, it will be fine. I said, 'Great!'

"At that time, Ivan was just starting. He was a real green guy. I walked over to him and told him in Polish, 'Ivan, I'm a very experienced wrestler. What you do is listen to me. You're very well built . . . a nice body. Let the other two wimps go in the ring first. When you come in, all the people will start looking at you. I bet even the bear will notice you.' He said, 'Yeah, yeah.'

"After my match, I had a quick shower. By that time, the bear's in the ring. Ivan's in the doorway and I told him, 'I'll tap you when it's time to go out.'

"Everybody's waiting. The bear goes in the ring hungry. If he eats, he goes to sleep, so he's hungry as hell.

"I get the top off the honey jar. I scoop my hand inside, take a big gob, rub it on his ass and say, 'Go get him Ivan.'

"Well, the bear was hunched down on all fours. There's a collar around his neck with a big hook, and the guy's got the chain. They're holding the bear. He's all drooped down, wants to go to sleep. Ivan starts walking out there, and the bear smells that honey. He comes up off the ground, jumps up, has his paws in the air and he roars, looking at Ivan.

"The wrestlers were shaking. The bear was growling, and these guys are having a hard time holding the bear back. Ivan walks around the ring, walks up the steps, gets one foot over the middle rope, and the bear lunges and the collar straightens out.

"Ivan tried to pull out and he never made it. The bear grabbed his leg and pulled him in. As he pulled him in, he turned him over and hit him with his tongue—hit him with the tongue in the ass.

"The other two guys start panicking, thinking the bear was tasting him before he ate him. The other two guys ran out of the building.

"I'm laughing. Finally, the referee put another collar around the bear's neck. They were trying to pull the bear off, and he's licking his ass. He's hungry as hell.

"Finally, Putski got away . . . almost. The bear pulled him back, turned him over and hit him in the ass with his tongue. Finally, they got the hook back on, and the referee, with more help, pulled the bear off Ivan Putski.

"People have seen it all now. There's nothing else left. Ivan Putski comes back to the dressing room and said, 'He likes me. He likes me.' I said, 'No, Ivan. He LOVES you.'

"Years later, when Putski started working for the WWF, I told the story. He said, 'Gee, it's true, it's true. But I didn't know about the honey.'"

Kowalski thinks some of the current wrestling stars worry too much about their won-loss records. He maintains that their egos, at times, get in the way of the big picture.

In his day, Kowalski had a different attitude about winning and losing. "I just want to show how big-headed I wasn't. Today, some of the guys have to win every match. You can't even talk to them.

"I was going to wrestle Bruno Sammartino in Madison Square Garden in two weeks, but before that, I was scheduled to wrestle Arnold Skaaland in White Plains, New York, his hometown. The place is packed. We're wrestling, going along, and I'm making him look good. I make a comeback.

"People were screaming and hollering, so I said, 'Arnold, backslide me.' He puts me down. Just before the count of 'two,' I glued my shoulders to the ground. He tried to push me over, but he couldn't make it. The referee goes, 'one . . . two . . .' and momentarily stopped the count waiting for me to kick out before he finally said 'three.' He went to Arnold and exclaimed, 'You beat him, you beat him!'

"When the referee went to raise Skaaland's arm, he said, 'Bullshit! I could never beat him. Don't believe it.'

"I have my head on the ground, feigning pain and I'm laughing like hell. Skaaland thought he was going to get fired. I crawled out of the ring, selling big time. It was a big auditorium there, and the dressing rooms were above the stage part.

"I was waiting for him in the dressing room when he came in and stated, 'I'm going to get fired. What did you do that for?'

I said, 'It's your hometown, for Christ's sake. Let me put you over.'

"He said, 'Jesus Christ, you're a helluva guy, but I'll get fired.' I told him, 'Those guys (promoters) are upstairs playing cards. They didn't even see the match.'

"I knew the guys in the office, so I went upstairs and said, 'How was the match?' A response came: 'Perfect, perfect. C'mon, deal! deal!'

"To this day, when I mention the story, I say, 'Boy, that Arnold was a real shooter. The son of a bitch wouldn't put me over in his hometown. He beat the hell out of me.'" Skaaland recalls a slightly different scenario, however. When talking about the match, he says, "Bullshit! It was the other way around. He put me over because it was my hometown."

KOWALSKI AS MENTOR

Killer Kowalski may be retired from wrestling, but his schedule is almost as hectic as it was when he performed in the squared circle. Unlike many retired athletes, he spends countless hours giving something back to the sport which was, and still is, his lifelong passion.

Currently, he owns and operates a wrestling school in Massachusetts and occasionally travels to WWF venues in the capacity of advisor for matches that appear on television. In addition, the health expert works with the wrestlers in training, conditioning and injury rehabilitation.

Unlike many old-time wrestlers, Killer Kowalski does not reminisce about the "good old days" and tell everyone that athletes were better in his day. When asked about the modern wrestlers, he stated, "Well, there are a lot of flyers. Quite interesting. They fly all over the place. You're giving people what they want. They are very skilled, very athletic."

Kowalski has been running a school for aspiring wrestlers since 1979. Several current superstars have graduated from his academy, including Hunter Hearst Helmsley, Matt Bloom and Perry Saturn. In addition to teaching these superlative athletes the trade, Kowalski was the tutor for the Amazon-like "wrestling bodyguard," Chyna.

Kowalski also runs independent promotions in the northeast. "For the promotions, I use available WWF superstars and then the rest are my own people. I've had my school since 1979. I tried to quit one time, but I couldn't. The guys cried, 'We need someone to teach us.'

"I was the first wrestling school out there. It's in Malden, Massachusetts. Unfortunately, today there are so-called schools popping up all over the place. There are guys who graduate from a school, don't know their ass from a hole in the ground and set up their own school."

Kowalski is well aware of this notoriety and is thankful for all the fans who remember him. "Fans are very enthusiastic. Today I was in a restaurant getting a bite to eat and a very old woman comes up to me and says, 'You're Killer Kowalski!' I'm still remembered.

"I went to an event, and a bunch of young kids came up to me for autographs. I asked, 'How did you know about me?' 'My father told me about you.' For crying out loud, my name is still there. I'm still remembered. I've been passed on. Somebody told me, 'You're the Babe Ruth of wrestling,' and I said, 'Thank you very much.'"

The legendary Hulk Hogan is still a huge name in professional wrestling. There are those who maintain that he has hurt the image of wrestling as much as he has helped it, but Kowalski has nothing but good words for the "Hulkster." He recalled, "Hulk Hogan called me one time. He says, 'Walter, I got a guy down here in Florida who wants to start wrestling. We'll send him up to you.' I said, 'Fine. Send him up.' 'What are you going to charge me?' Hogan asked. I said, 'Nothing. I wouldn't charge you a dime.'

"You know, he never forgot that. Finally, he called me back and said, 'To tell you the truth, Walter, this guy changed his mind.' So I said, 'No problem.'

"Hogan made a movie. He had a patch over his eye and someone asked, 'Who did it?' Hogan answered, 'Killer Kowalski.' He was putting me over. He put me over in two of his movies because I was kind to him. I have nothing but good things to say about Hulk Hogan."

In November 1996, Killer Kowalski was awarded with what is considered to be the ultimate accolade for an athlete—he was inducted into the Hall of Fame for his sport. On the evening prior to the WWF presentation of its annual *Survivor Series*, Hunter Hearst Helmsley, the reigning WWF Intercontinental Champion at that time and a former Kowalski student, escorted the Killer to the podium to accept his induction.

Killer Kowalski has entertained millions of fans over the years. He is still in the public eye, although not as much as he was during his active career. To many, Kowalski has given inspiration through speeches and talks. The man has contributed much more to humanity than he has taken. Perhaps his greatest legacy is the pinnacle for what a human being could desire—the world is a much better place for his having been a part of it.

Walter Kowalski is a man with extraordinary insight into the psyche of human beings. Lately, he has taken pen in hand and written heartfelt poetry, of which the following is a classic example.

I AM A PROFESSIONAL WRESTLER

I am a professional wrestler,
A World Champion wrestler!
I am tough, I play rough.
Money is my bread;
I want to get ahead.
I could give you a clothesline,
Which would make me feel just fine.
I do it all—just for love.

I am a professional wrestler,
A World Champion wrestler!
You fans are great;
You love and hate.
Take sides—boo or cheer;
But it's ME you always fear.
I make the people wild;
I get them all up-riled.
Some people call me crazy,
But I sure as hell ain't lazy.
I do it all—just for love.

I am a professional wrestler,
A World Champion wrestler!
I would grab and twist your arm,
But I'd mean no harm.
I'll give you a leg-dive;
Your head to the mat I'll drive.
My next one is a suplex;
Our bodies will be duplex.
Another hold is the Boston Crab;
With your feet, your head I'll grab.
I do it all—just for love.

I am a professional wrestler,
A World Champion wrestler!
I would grab you with a claw hold,
And the pain will make you fold.
I could put you in a head lock,
Then it's time for you to drop.
Another is a sleeper;
When you'll meet the Grim Reaper.
I could drop-kick you in the face,
Which would get you out of pace.
I do it all—just for love.

I am a professional wrestler,
A World Champion wrestler!
I will throw you with a slam;
You go down—"BAM, BAM, BAM!"
All these actions I do play;
I mold your body like it's clay.
If your body is all flab,
I will flatten it into a slab.
All the girls call me "Honey,"
Cause they know I'm worth the money.
I do it all—just for love.

I WAS a professional wrestler,
A World Champion wrestler!
Many friends I met along the way,
Which made me happy, I should say.
All the world has seen me go;
From country to country I would flow.
I did it all just for glory,
But, now, I say, "I am sorry."
They all thought that I was bad,
Which made me very sad.
I DID it all—just for love.

I was a professional wrestler,
A World Champion wrestler!

When I was billed as the main event,
You found your money was well-spent.
All the arenas were always packed;
This was a well-known fact.
My autograph to everyone I would give;
This was worth it—just to live.
You always recognized who I was
Because my future had a cause.
I did it all—just for love.

I was a professional wrestler,
A World Champion wrestler!
Time now marches on.
Where have all the memories gone?
Everything I did is in the past.
But, here "I am"—at last.
The legend is still living.
My love, "I am" always giving.
My star will always be—in the sky!
Killer Kowalski "am I."
I DID IT ALL—JUST FOR LOVE.

Killer's Photographic Legacy

During the latter part of his ring career, Kowalski took his trusty Hasselblad camera along with the associated lighting and backdrop equipment to his wrestling engagements. Scene III concludes with some results of his endeavors to capture the spirit of the wrestling stars of his day. Although Kowalski has enjoyed at least one exhibition of his work, these photographs have rarely been seen by the general public.

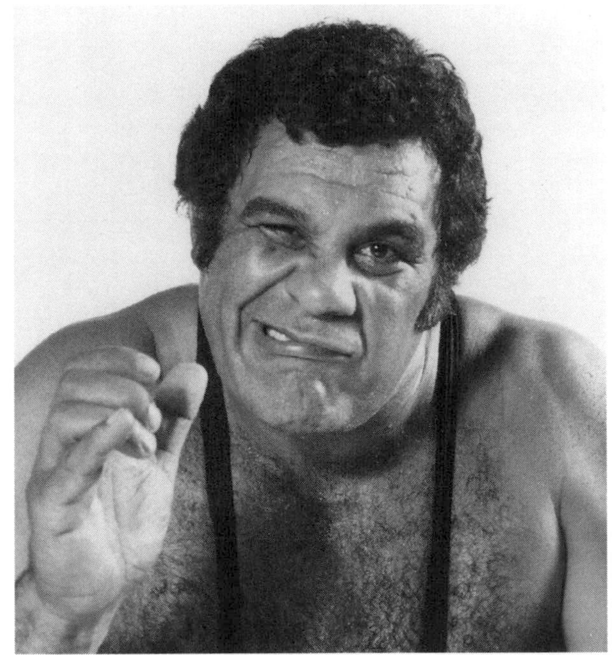

Walter Kowalski

Angelo Mosca

Walter Kowalski

Nikolai Volkoff

Walter Kowalski

Bruno Sammartino

Walter Kowalski

Chief Jay Strongbow

Walter Kowalski

Lou Albano

Walter Kowalski

Mr. Fuji

Walter Kowalski

Tony Garea

Walter Kowalski

Superstar Billy Graham

Walter Kowalski

George "The Animal" Steele

Chief Peter Maivia

Walter Kowalski

Mr. Fuji and Prof. Toru Tanaka

***   ***

Scene IV

MR. BACKLUND FOR PRESIDENT

"I can eat more marijuana than anybody else in the world, if that's what it takes to be president."

— Bob Backlund

Professional wrestling is a mixture of reality and fantasy—worked angles and shoots. Most professional wrestlers have never wrestled at an amateur level, yet they relish being called the "Champ" of a professional wrestling organization.

One famous professional wrestler, Bob Backlund, actually did come from the amateur ranks and excelled in professional wrestling—both as a supreme babyface and a crazed heel. When talking to Backlund, the line between reality and a work becomes very, very thin. Some of his quotes are "in-character," while others can stand on their own at any time. This tribute to him relies on that fine line to depict his career and his future. After all, I should be able to have as much fun in writing certain parts of this book as the in-ring performers do in bringing you the best in sports entertainment.

Of all modern professional wrestlers, Bob Backlund has been one of the most diverse and enigmatic contestants to grace the squared circle. Over a span of more than two decades, he has been the All-American Boy; retired for eight years; come back and won the WWF championship for a second time; and become one of the most colorful heels ever to perform in front of an audience of grappling fans.

Backlund hails from the small town of Princeton, Minnesota, where he excelled in sports, primarily wrestling and football. After high school, he attended Waldorf Junior College in Forest City, Iowa, and he finished his college education at North Dakota State University in Fargo, North Dakota, graduating in 1972. He received All-America honors at Waldorf for his performance on the football field and the wrestling mat. When he transferred to North Dakota State, Backlund diverted all his sports attention to wrestling and again was awarded NCAA All-America distinction, making him a four-time All-America choice and giving him the right to call himself the nation's premier amateur wrestler.

Following graduation, Backlund gave thought to turning professional in the ring. In 1974, he began to wrestle professionally in Louisiana for independent promoters. Eventually, Backlund became acquainted with promoter Leroy McGirk, who saw much potential in the rookie. McGirk, then affiliated with the NWA, took him under his wing and arranged matches farther afield for the future champ. According to Backlund, "Every three months I moved around the country."

After logging hundreds of thousands of miles, Backlund received a big break in 1977. His work and travel had paid off to the extent that he signed with the WWF. Initially, he made many television appearances in an effort to gain recognition. According to Evan Ginzburg, a wrestling journalist from New York, "Backlund was the All-American boy at the time. Basically, they fed him people like Mr. Fuji, and he worked his way up the ladder. In the old programs, they used to call it, 'stepping stone to the throne.' He beat some of the mid-level guys, and in the eyes of the fans had earned a title shot because he went through one guy after another, after another . . . on TV and at the arenas."

On February 20, 1978, Bob Backlund secured his big chance. He was scheduled to meet Superstar Billy Graham for the WWF title. The pundits thought the match would be a mere formality with Graham easily defeating the upstart. To make matters worse for Backlund, the contest was to be held in Madison Square Garden in New York. Backlund was from a small town and had never been involved with such notoriety. He said, "There were more people in the building than there were in my home town."

The experts were wrong. Backlund, in possibly one of the biggest upsets in sports history, defeated Graham. According to Backlund, his image helped because most of the top-name wrestlers of the day were much bigger than he, and he was not taken as seriously as some of the giants. In keeping with his amateur roots, he said, "I was sort of a shy, not-so-muscular technical wrestler."

In 1978, Ginzburg, was a teenager who had attended almost all the wrestling cards held at Madison Square Garden since 1974. He observed the Backlund win, but was not impressed with the performance of the new champ. According to Ginzburg, "Backlund won the title on February 20, 1978. It's amazing that I can remember a date just like that, but that's because of how memorable it was. Superstar Billy Graham at the time was this incredibly colorful, larger-than-life character, and it was almost unheard of that a villain was equally loved and equally hated. He had an unbelievable following and was an incredible box office draw. For me, Backlund's win was a disappointment because I was a big Billy Graham fan at that time. Backlund was almost colorless, compared to Graham, who was sort of like a more savage Gorgeous George type. He had the charisma but also the power to go with it."

Putting aside all the differences in styles, Backlund's win was no fluke. For virtually the next six years, he did not relinquish his championship belt. He defended the title against all comers.

In December 1983, Backlund's streak came to a halt. During a grueling match with the Iron Sheik, Backlund's manager, Arnold Skaaland, threw in the towel while the Sheik had Backlund in a compromising position.

To this day, Backlund is bitter about the events which caused him to lose the title. Despite being the recipient of the "Camel Clutch," a difficult hold to break, he maintained that his style of technical wrestling would have enabled him to eventually reverse the hold. He adamantly insists that Skaaland's submission on behalf of him was premature. According to Backlund, "It cost me 10 years of my career."

For the next few years, Backlund dabbled in various fields. He coached wrestling at Central Connecticut State University in New Britain, Connecticut, and later coached high school wrestling. In addition, he started and ran a construction business in Connecticut.

His absence from the ring led Backlund to appreciate wrestling even more than he did during his active career. He elaborated by saying, "Amateur wrestling did a lot to mold me into the person I am today. It's a one-on-one sport. It's just like life."

Mike Lano

Backlund vs. Koloff

In 1992, Backlund's life again changed radically. He received a phone call from the wrestling coach at North Dakota State University asking his advice about which professional wrestling organization would be the best to promote an event at the opening of a new athletic facility at the institute.

Without hesitation, Backlund recommended the WWF. During the negotiations, a WWF official talked to Backlund about the event and then surprised him by asking if he would like to make a comeback in professional wrestling. A perplexed Backlund told the official, "I never wanted to quit."

Shortly after, Backlund again donned his trunks and ever-present towel and came out of retirement. On a WWF *Superstars* broadcast in 1993, announcer Vince McMahon told a surprised TV audience, "And here comes Bob Backlund. He's attempting a comeback." The fans cheered him vociferously as Backlund easily won his first match in the ring in almost a decade.

Backlund was still a fan favorite, keeping his previous followers while gaining the adoration of a new generation of fans. He would offer his hand to his opponents prior to and after their matches. In other words, he was still the All-American boy, only a few years older.

All of this may sound familiar—retired athlete comes back and tries to regain his former status—but there is a twist to Bob Backlund's story. A match on July 3, 1994, at Ocean Beach, Maryland, caused him to drastically alter his views on wrestling and life.

Bret Hart was the WWF champion at the time and was scheduled to meet Backlund, giving him a chance to regain the title. The match was unusual because two fan icons rarely square off when the championship belt is on the line. Most often, a fan favorite is pitted against a less-than-popular, yet highly skilled, opponent.

Vince McMahon stated, "This is Bob Backlund's final chance for a title shot." Hart and Backlund shook hands in the middle of the ring, waited for the bell to sound and began a methodical, scientific wrestling match. Backlund toiled, countering almost every move Hart threw at him and finally saw his chance. He reversed a Bret Hart hold and pinned him. The referee, however, was slow in getting on the canvas, and when he did, he prolonged the beginning of the count. When he finally began to count, he administered the count sluggishly, allowing Hart the chance to dismiss himself from the hold just prior to the count of "three."

Backlund was basking in glory. He thought he had won and held his arms triumphantly aloft, only to see the referee holding two digits up, designating that the match was still on. Shortly after, Hart pinned Backlund and, before a second had elapsed, the arbitrator counted Backlund out. He had entirely reversed his cadence from a lethargic count against Hart to a faster-than-the-speed-of-light count against the challenger.

After the match, a dejected Backlund shook Hart's hand. Then Hart asked for another handshake. The TV fans only saw the scenario which followed; they never heard Bret Hart berating the former champ.

Backlund, forever a gentleman in the ring, then atypically lost his composure. He threw a mysterious hold on Hart that incapacitated him. "Bret was flippant towards me . . . laughing while I was trying to shake his hand. I tried to be a nice guy, but it did not work. I had to make a statement and make people realize I was not going to be a nice guy anymore."

Later, opponents would come to fear the odd-looking hold which was coined the "cross-face chicken-wing." Backlund explained the concept behind what has come to be acknowledged as one of the most deadly holds in the history of professional wrestling. "I used the cross-face chicken-wing in the past, but not as a staple of my repertoire. The chicken-wing was always an illegal hold in amateur wrestling, but I dabbled with it in the pros. In 1982, I put the chicken-wing on an opponent, and I crossed his face. It was painful."

For the next few months, the wrestling world saw a different Bob Backlund. In keeping with his revised philosophy of not being a "nice guy," he defeated opponent after opponent with the cross-face chicken-wing. For the first time in Backlund's career, the fans began to cheer for his adversaries, but he dismissed the change of heart of the fans.

At last, on November 23, 1994, at the WWF *Survivor Series*, Bob Backlund earned the chance to redeem the past 11 years of his life in his quest to regain the championship belt that he felt had been unfairly taken from him. The match was against his archenemy, Bret Hart, however, there was an idiosyncratic stipulation—the match was to be lost by the wrestler who threw in the towel first. This amendment referred to the method in which Backlund had lost the title in 1983 when his manager, Arnold Skaaland, threw in the towel. To augment the symbolic atmosphere, the towel Backlund brought to the ring in his championship endeavor was the actual towel used in the 1983 match to designate his submission.

Because the corner men would hold the towels of Backlund and Hart and would have to make the decision of when to throw in the towel, they became as important as the combatants in deciding the victor. Each wrestler had to choose someone in whom he could put his total trust.

In Backlund's corner was Owen Hart, brother of the champ, Bret Hart. Owen had disassociated himself from his brother a few months before and vowed never to throw in the towel on behalf of Backlund. Bret Hart designated his brother-in-law Davey Boy Smith (aka the British Bulldog) to be the keeper of his towel. Smith was just as adamant as Owen Hart in stating that the towel in his possession would never be thrown in.

During the match, Owen Hart and the Bulldog were attempting to intimidate each other with outside-the-ring chicanery. Smith fell, smashing his head against the steel steps leading to the ring. He was knocked unconscious.

Back in the ring, both wrestlers were attempting to soften each other up for their final submission holds. Bret Hart had Backlund in the "sharpshooter" for a few minutes and it appeared that Backlund was close to submission, but only a throwing in of the towel, even if the combatant submitted, could stop the match. Owen Hart kept his word and never thought of parting with Backlund's towel. Eventually, calling on his ring savvy of more than two decades, Backlund dismissed himself from the painful hold.

After a few more minutes of exhausting grappling, Backlund secured his prime hold on Hart. With the cross-face chicken-wing solidly in place, Backlund began to administer increasing doses of pain on the champ. Because there was no one to throw in the towel on Bret's behalf, the fans were becoming concerned after he was in the throes of the dreaded hold for more than five minutes. Apprehension ran rampant that Hart may become permanently injured.

After Bret Hart had been incapacitated for more than five minutes, his brother, Owen, appeared to have a change of heart. He approached his mother, Helen, and pleaded with her to throw in the towel, the only act that would terminate the torture Bret was experiencing. Owen kept telling his mother, "He's my brother. I didn't think this was going to happen."

Eventually, Helen grabbed the towel and threw it in the ring, ensuring a Backlund repeat championship—a moment he had anticipated for over a decade.

After the victory, a previously concerned Owen Hart was mirthful as he told everyone that he had plotted for his mother to throw in the towel, under the guise of being distressed that his brother Bret would be permanently injured. Critics have stated that Backlund may not have won if there were no fraudulent actions taking place outside the squared circle. Backlund dismissed these Monday-morning quarterbacks, however. "At that point, I could have pinned him, or if the match continued and I kept the cross-face chicken-wing on him, he would have passed out. Once I got the chicken-wing on him, he was in my hands."

Ironically, Backlund (then 46 years old) regained the world title only days after a 46-year-old George Foreman shocked the world by winning back the World Heavyweight boxing title he had lost two decades before.

Bob Backlund's efficiency cost him dearly. He had injured Bret Hart to the point that Hart had to take two months off from his trade and his contractual bouts, which included several rematches with Backlund, had to be rescheduled. A match was quickly called for November 26, 1994, at Madison Square Garden, pitting Backlund against Diesel (Kevin Nash, the original Diesel), an almost seven-foot-tall wrestler who was quickly making progress in the WWF.

Diesel quickly defeated Backlund in a record-breaking eight seconds, putting a swift halt to his right to be called "Champ." Backlund is a scientific wrestler with no peer in the mental execution of the sport, yet he let his guard down at the beginning of the contest. He lamented, "I was embarrassed. I went to shake his hand, he kicked me in the stomach and then he jackknifed me. I should have known better."

Evan Ginzburg is one of the few people who was in attendance at Madison Square Garden in 1978 when Backlund first became champ and also on November 26, 1994, when Backlund lost the strap. According to Ginzburg, who was not impressed with Backlund's initial championship victory, "My feelings had changed entirely. This guy (Backlund) is an incredible villain. The heat in the Garden on November 26

(1994), was unbelievable. The fans despised him, and I thought it was criminal to take the belt from him, especially in an eight-second match to a big lumbering guy who is probably the most overpaid mediocrity in the history of wrestling. Diesel was no wrestler. I mean he has charisma and is certainly large, and in the WWF, that's the way it's been—bigger is better.

"I just thought they (WWF) made a tremendous mistake not milking Backlund's heat for as long as they could because the reaction was unbelievable. I had never seen anything like that. To take it from him after a very, very short title reign and give it to a guy who doesn't know 10 holds, just seems an incredible waste of an opportunity."

For the next few months, Backlund went through opponents like a hot knife through butter, all the time fine-tuning the cross-face chicken-wing hold. The list of those whom he vanquished is long and notable—Lex Luger, Doink the Clown, Razor Ramon (Scott Hall), Bob Holly and others. According to Backlund, "Things were going pretty good."

With the success of his new hold, Backlund at times did not discriminate between opponents in the ring and innocent bystanders outside. Among those who felt the wrath of the cross-face chicken-wing were his former manager, Arnold Skaaland, and a WWF journalist covering matches at ringside. When Backlund was interviewed by WWF broadcaster/wrestler Jerry "The King" Lawler, he told Lawler that once his magical hold was in place no one could escape. Lawler, usually a Backlund ally, agreed with Backlund but added, "Everyone but me." Backlund, in a rage, screamed, "Everyone!" and then proceeded to put the cross-face chicken-wing on Lawler. When confronted by ring announcer/WWF owner Vince McMahon about his lack of discretion, Backlund told him, "Before I retire, I will put the cross-face chicken-wing on you."

Backlund's actions and habits were becoming more erratic as each day passed. In addition to stating that no WWF wrestler could relinquish the cross-face chicken-wing once it was applied, he stipulated that every future opponent must state, "I give up, Mr. Backlund," before he would release the grip. He made it clear that no one was to address him as "Bob." From now on, everybody had to call him "Mr. Backlund."

In early 1995, Backlund, who still maintained that he was robbed of the WWF belt, and on occasion in fits of dementia thought he was still champ, gained a title shot for another strap, the Intercontinental Championship. His methods of attaining the title shot were unorthodox, yet they worked.

Jeff Jarrett (Double-J), one of the WWF's top villains at the time, was the reigning Intercontinental Champion. After a non-title match in which Jarrett easily defeated journeyman Barry Horowitz, the loser demanded a rematch. Jarrett not only offered Horowitz a rematch, but he told him, "To show you the kind of guy Double-J is, I'll put the title on the line." Jarrett then pulled out a contract, signed it and put it on the ring apron for Horowitz to sign. With pen in hand, Horowitz was about to pick up the document when Backlund seemingly came out of nowhere and put the cross-face chicken-wing on the would-be challenger. All the time, Jarrett was cheering on Backlund. His jocularity was short-lived, however. As soon as Backlund dispensed with Horowitz, the former WWF champ grabbed the contract and affixed his signature to it, making him the legal challenger for the Intercontinental title.

The following week, millions of fans viewed what some have called one of the most memorable matches in WWF annals. On nationally televised *Monday Night Raw*, two heels fought for the Intercontinental title. The match was arduous, yet uncharacteristically clean by bad-guy standards.

Both fought as laboriously as ancient warriors, yet they fought by the book. For a few minutes, each wrestler was successful in applying astute holds and moves on the other. Eventually, Jarrett made a mistake and Backlund raised his hands, the preceding motion to his cross-face chicken-wing, and was about to expose Double-J to the dreaded hold.

Razor Ramon, who was to face the winner of the match in two weeks, thought it best to interfere in the match and cause a disqualification. He jumped in the ring and grabbed Backlund from behind as he was only centimeters away from doing Jarrett in. Backlund won on a disqualification, but the belt could only have changed hands with a pin or submission, so Double-J was still champ. Camaraderie among heels now prevailed as Backlund and Jarrett gave Razor Ramon a taste of their opinion of him. Backlund secured the cross-face chicken-wing on Ramon while Double-J repeatedly kicked him in the stomach.

Backlund agreed that the contest with Double-J was a classic. He stated, "He didn't poke me in the eyes, and I didn't do it to him either."

The tension was building for a rematch with Bret Hart. During *Wrestlemania* (1995), the WWF's premier annual event, they were scheduled to square off again. The stipulation of this match would be that the winner would be declared when his opponent stated over a microphone, "I quit!"

When the wrestlers were introduced, the fans let it be known that they were on the side of Bret Hart, hoping he could avenge his November 1994 loss to Backlund. After the introductions, Hart grabbed a questionable immediate advantage. According to Backlund, "I always said Bret Hart was one of the biggest cheaters in the WWF. He jumped me before the bell."

After the initial setback, Backlund came to form and methodically wore Hart down. He gradually softened Hart up for his pièce de résistance. Finally, Backlund, who resembled a jungle cat stalking his prey, saw his chance and implemented the cross-face chicken-wing. For a few moments, it appeared that history would repeat itself as Hart was immobile and showed no signs of recovering from Backlund's hold. When victory appeared imminent for Backlund, Hart quickly reversed the hold and won the match. A disoriented Bob Backlund left the ring stating, "I see the light."

The fans were as confused as Hart. A seeming Backlund victory was swiftly reversed. In his exit to the locker room, Backlund appeared to have something on his mind other than the wrestling match.

Nobody knew what Backlund meant by his, "I see the light" statement, but speculation ran rampant. Shortly after *Wrestlemania,* Backlund told the wrestling world that he had an announcement to make in May, but he gave no clues about the subject of his proclamation. Many observers assumed that he was going to announce his retirement.

On May 15, 1995, on *Monday Night Raw*, Backlund heralded something to the world, but it was not his retirement. After several attempts at trying to state his case, Backlund walked away from the microphone and pondered his forthcoming disclosure. Eventually, ring announcer Vince McMahon stated, "I know this is an emotional moment for you. Will you please tell us what you have to say, Mr. Backlund."

His voice was quivering as he told the live audience and millions of television viewers, "I'm . . . I'm . . . contem . . . contemplating . . . running for the office of president of the United States." The audience was stunned to silence and momentarily a marching band emerged, playing "Hail to the Chief." Months later, Backlund said, "Everybody was in a frenzy. People thought I was going to turn into a good guy, but I have no intention of that."

Backlund here provides for the first time exclusive information concerning his match with Bret Hart—information that explains his loss as well as his "I see the light" statement. Prior to divulging these facts, no one had been told of the reasons for his baffling loss to Bret Hart and the ensuing statement. According to Backlund, "During the match, while I had Bret Hart in the cross-face chicken-wing, I decided I wanted to declare for the presidency." With thoughts of a presidential run in his mind, Backlund found it difficult to sustain the intensity of his dreaded hold. "I kind of loosened up and he reversed the hold. I wanted to get out of the ring and get on with business."

Shortly after his presidential announcement, Backlund began to campaign in earnest. He is steadfast in his principles and does not believe in compromise for the sake of gaining supporters. He said, "I am not worried about making enemies. I have them already. I will not placate them to get a vote."

Certain aspects of Backlund's change in philosophy came to the forefront. He stated that before he announced his prospective candidacy, he was virtually an autograph-giving machine. "I probably signed more autographs than anyone ever in professional sports. I would wait until the last person had left, sometimes after dawn of the following day. Now, people who want to procure my autograph must recite the presidents of the United States from Washington to Clinton, or they must tell me the names of all the planets in the solar system and the diameter of the Earth." Since his new regulations have come into play, Backlund has signed fewer than a dozen autographs.

Why the dramatic change in Bob Backlund? He mentioned that most Americans are not living up to their full potential in the realm of brainpower, and he is attempting to enlighten them. Since 1991, he has been acquiring knowledge, and his entire attitude toward life has been modified. According to the presidential aspirant, "I was a Plebeian until four years ago. I was as much an idiot as anyone else. But now, my life has changed. I feel I can do anything in the world."

Backlund summed up his philosophy in an abbreviated form: "Knowledge is freedom."

According to him, "You should be a champion within yourself." Backlund stated that it is better to finish sixth in an athletic event, knowing you have done your best, rather than finish first with outside help, such as steroids.

Backlund wished to portray his candidacy much in the same manner in which he conducts his out-of-the-ring (both wrestling and presidential) life. He stated, "I'm very disciplined. I've never paid a penny of interest in my life. If I become president, I would run the office like that."

Believe it or not, Bob Backlund actually gained the endorsement of a political publication in September 1995. *The Alternative*, a San Diego, California magazine, endorsed Backlund in its editorial. The publication is a small bimonthly radical magazine that reports mostly on non-mainstream or underreported events. Its September 1995 editorial[1] titled "Mr. Backlund for President" read:

> Since the publishing of our first newspaper in May 1993 and the change to magazine format in May 1995, *The Alternative* has never endorsed a candidate running for political office. Our reasons have varied from skepticism of the electoral process to the lack of integrity of those who

1. © 1995, *The Alternative*. Reproduced by permission.

were running for office. We are now breaking tradition and are proudly endorsing a prospective candidate for the office of President of the United States. Our endorsement represents possibly the earliest endorsement by any publication in the United States of a person considering running for the presidency in 1996.

Our person for the office is Mr. Bob Backlund. Despite his notoriety, it is just possible that some readers have not heard of Mr. Backlund and his intentions, so we will give you a little background.

Mr. Backlund is currently employed as a professional wrestler with the World Wrestling Federation (WWF). Before he turned professional, Mr. Backlund was a National Collegiate Athletic Association (NCAA) champion. From the years 1978-1984, he reigned as WWF champion.

After his unparalleled stint as champ, Mr. Backlund retired, only to come out of retirement a couple of years ago to try to regain his championship belt, which he successfully accomplished in November, 1994. Unfortunately, his newly won championship lasted only three days.

A few months ago, the world expected to see Mr. Backlund retire in front of a nationwide TV audience, but he shocked those in attendance by announcing his intention to run for president.

Our reasons for endorsing Mr. Backlund are varied. First, he is not a professional politician (he has never run for public office), therefore, corruption is not a daily part of his life.

How does he stand on the issues? Currently, he is still fine-tuning his platform, but he has stated that he will be strong in the areas of education and culture. In the future, he will be announcing more of his stands.

A Backlund presidency could save billions of dollars in defense spending. There is a possibility that he will challenge the leader of any country that the United States appears to be on the verge of war with to a wrestling match —winner take all. When he beats the tar out of the opponent, most countries would think twice before messing with U.S. interests.

To conclude, Mr. Backlund has spent most of his adult life entertaining millions of people. In spite of his inescapable 'cross-face chicken-wing' hold, he shows no signs of overt violence. What's more, he is not in the hands of any special interest group. Mr. Backlund's record is clean, so we would wholeheartedly endorse him if he were to run for the office of president of the United States.

Why would a politically progressive magazine endorse Backlund for president? When the staff of *The Alternative* was interviewed, it became apparent that they were all professional wrestling fans, despite the stigma attached to adults who follow the exploits of those who grapple for a living.

In collaboration with the WWF, *The Alternative* had scheduled a press conference for April 1, 1996, in San Diego, in which Mr. Backlund would speak about his candidacy. As part of the card, a former California state legislator was booked to debate Mr. Backlund on the issues. Unfortunately, the WWF had diminished its role in Backlund's presidential bid early in 1996, and the organization backed out of the event. At the time, the defections of Scott Hall and Kevin Nash to World Championship Wrestling (WCW) forced the company to reevaluate its strategies and Backlund's push was temporarily

Todd Strom

A wrestling fan holds the Sept. 1995 issue of *The Alternative,* which endorsed Bob Backlund for President

over. Ironically, the state legislator whom Backlund was scheduled to debate currently is serving a prison term for having unlawful sex with a 14-year-old girl.

The alteration of Backlund's persona led him to develop new avenues for his character. For years, he was considered "Mr. Clean," gaining the adoration of the fans. Since 1994, however, he has been on a rampage, threatening to put the cross-face chicken-wing on everybody. In late 1995, he raised the tempo to new heights. During a two-week stretch, he ambushed and cross-face chicken-winged Bret Hart as he was being interviewed; put the deadly hold on announcer Jim Ross because he addressed him as "Bob," not "Mr. Backlund;" and almost severed the left arm of a sound engineer who had cut Backlund's microphone as he was rambling about "wanting to be God again."

Following these incidents, Gorilla Monsoon, president of the WWF, announced that free psychiatric help had been offered to Backlund through the Human Resources section of the WWF. Backlund refused the benevolent proposal.

Actually, Backlund's character is loaded with enigma. In his message, he states that we need "order, discipline and authority," yet his actions absolutely contrast his ideas of an ideal society. Backlund flaunts every authority he confronts, whether it be referees or WWF administrators. In essence, his actions would make an anarchist envious. His enigmatic deeds are not unique in professional wrestling. Other wrestlers are paradoxical, yet Backlund exceeds all his comrades in portrayals of contrasts.

With the change in Backlund, the WWF discovered a new outlet for the former champ as well as allowing more fan involvement. About 20 minutes prior to the beginning of a WWF card, Backlund would emerge from the locker room. He would not be in a confrontational mood—he slowly perused the crowd—yet within seconds, thousands of fans would rush to the area and engulf Backlund with insults. He was only too willing to return the ridicule, and within a minute or so, he would begin to make the rounds of the arena, pointing his finger at fans while he consistently argued. In effect, a situation which appeared to be confrontational was actually mystical as the fans felt cleansed after they had admonished Backlund. By his actions, Backlund had warmed up the crowd as no one else could have, ensuring the first match of the night to be almost as exciting as the main event.

In the midst of his campaigning, Backlund was also called upon to occasionally take to the squared circle. For instance, former WWF wrestler Man Mountain Rock used to play hard-rock guitar prior to his matches. Backlund, who has stated that he would outlaw rock 'n' roll music if he became president, took offense at the antics of Rock, so he smashed his guitar, leading to a series of grudge matches in which the former champ taught the musician a few wrestling lessons.

In addition, Backlund fought Bret Hart, bringing back painful memories to the on-again, off-again champ from Canada. The match was a non-title bout, much to the chagrin of Backlund. After more than 10 minutes of slam-bang action, Hart attempted to put his signature hold, the sharpshooter, on Backlund, who was trying to make it difficult for Hart to affix the submission move. The British Bulldog (now an enemy of Bret Hart) ran toward the ring and when Hart saw him, he relinquished his hold and confronted the Bulldog. Immediately, Backlund threw the cross-face chicken-wing on Hart and held it in place for minutes. It took a dozen officials to pry Backlund loose from Hart. Even ring announcer Vince McMahon screamed to those in the ring, “Get that idiot off Bret Hart!”

As the elections drew near in 1996, Backlund broadened his political agenda. For months, he talked mostly about education and discipline, yet on August 12, 1996, he began to address social issues. On that date, on *Monday Night Raw*, he emerged and harshly stated to Vince McMahon that America was in trouble, and he had a message for his countrymen. When McMahon asked about the message, Backlund announced, “You can prevent AIDS by wearing a condominium.”

Backlund eased off his presidential campaign and became a manager. He teamed with his old foe the Iron Sheik, who was the trainer of the new Backlund protege, to assist a reworked Fatu, now called the Sultan, in gaining the WWF championship belt. The Sultan was given a mild push as he beat all mid-level opponents. However, in time, he was delegated to putting over future WWF stars on their way up in the organization, and Backlund disappeared from the managerial scene.

courtesy of Bob Backlund

Backlund, during his presidential campaign

Backlund did not fare well in the 1996 elections, but he is still hinting at running for president. On December 6, 1996, on the WWF show *Live Wire*, he rambled about politics and inferred that his hat was still in the presidential ring as he stated somewhat less than poetically:

> I can eat more marijuana than anybody else in the world, if that's what it takes to be president!

Nobody can predict Bob Backlund's future actions. However, a sign in the rafters of an arena where a December 1996 *Monday Night Raw* was held may give us some insight. In the uppermost part of the venue, a fan proudly held aloft a placard that read . . . *BACKLUND FOR PRESIDENT IN 2000!*

Wrestlers Running the USA?

Despite Mr. Backlund's novel attempt at gaining office, he was not the first person with a professional wrestling background to declare a political candidacy. In 1990, Jesse "The Body" Ventura was elected mayor of Brooklyn Park, Minnesota (pop. 60,000). Many considered his election to be a fluke and one-off occurrence.

In 1998, however, Ventura experienced a transformation to Jesse "The Mind" Ventura and shocked the country by winning a three-way election to become the governor of Minnesota. He defeated two politically savvy opponents and showed that the time was ripe for the election of a "normal person" to the top statewide office. The pundits had a field day with Ventura's election. Some laughed at the results and said it was meaningless in the larger political picture, while others proclaimed a new political scene in the United States.

Not to be outdone by an old foe, in November 1998 Hollywood Hulk Hogan announced that he would run for U.S.

president in the year 2000. At first, it appeared to be an angle, but many mainstream newspapers published articles in which they seriously analyzed a Hogan candidacy. Ventura's win jolted the establishment to the point of rampant speculation about future electoral endeavors by professional wrestlers.

Only time will tell Hogan's plans. In contrast to Backlund's presidential aspirations, Hogan, with the backing of his boss, billionaire Ted Turner, may conceivably be a serious candidate.

Currently, those who run for political office supply the voters with endless facts and figures on their backgrounds and experience. Future candidates may have to show professional wrestling experience on their resumés to be considered legitimate by the voters.

*** ***

Scene V

The Best Superstar That Never Was

"Louie Spicolli was a real gung-ho kid. He was loyal to me 'til the day he died. He was a very loyal, faithful student and friend."

— Bill Anderson

In early 1998, I was talking to a sheet editor about Louie Spicolli and his performance in WCW. At that time, he had just signed with the group and had made only a few ring appearances. From his few matches, I could tell that he was going to eventually receive a push, although I did not know the angle. The editor disagreed with me and said he thought that Spicolli was only an average wrestler. I then assured the journalist that Spicolli's charisma transcended that of wrestling ability alone. He told me that he would watch him more closely.

On February 16, 1998, the aforementioned editor called me and said, “Louie Spicolli is dead.” There was not much to say after that.

Let’s go back to 1995. Spicolli (real name Louis Mucciolo) was introduced to the fans of the WWF as Rad Radford, grunge rocker from Seattle. He bounced and jerked his way to the ring, all the time performing spastic-like gyrations. In the ring, he was deceivingly quick as well as powerful. His mastery of holds was above that of most modern wrestlers. At first, his matches were meaningful, whether he won or lost.

Unfortunately, the WWF did not see Radford as a major player and assigned him mid-level matches. His biggest push came when the character of Radford wanted to be accepted into the Bodydonnas, a tag-team with Sunny, who eventually became a big star in the WWF, as manager. His portrayal of a bad-guy wannabe in the WWF preceded what could have been larger things to come in WCW a few years later.

By the end of 1995, Radford was at the end of his WWF contract and was being buried in what Vince McMahon calls, “time-honored tradition.” He was appearing at house shows against Ahmed Johnson. Johnson made Radford look like a total fool. He laughed at him and prompted the crowd to humiliate Radford. When their matches were over, Radford was lying unconscious in the middle of the ring. Knowing that Johnson did not exactly possess a great amount of finesse in the ring, we can look back and question whether Radford was working or really KO’d.

The enthusiasm which Radford displayed while being buried during the last months of his WWF contract was admirable. He went along with the angle and put all he had into it. At that point in his career, all he had to do was show up, get beat up and leave, but he actually immersed himself into the part as if he were auditioning for a major role in the organization.

Let's fast-forward to early 1998. After a stint in ECW, the former Rad Radford reemerged in the WCW as Louie Spicolli. At first, he was merely a nondescript jobber, but something happened to change all that. On a *Monday Nitro* broadcast, he entered the ring while Scott Hall was talking and professed to Hall his desire to be his gofer, valet, shoeshine boy or whatever else Hall had in mind for him. He even volunteered to take on Hall's opponents. The script was similar to the one played when he attempted to join the Bodydonnas in the WWF, only this time it appeared that the character was going somewhere.

When his image began to emerge, striking similarities could be observed between Spicolli and Michael J. Pollard. If you remember, the famed actor played a part in the movie *Bonnie and Clyde* and later in *Little Fauss and Big Halsey*, in which he met "bad guys" and immediately became attached to them. Ironically, certain facial features of Spicolli resembled those of Pollard. (Another famous actor who came to an untimely end was similar in style and physical characteristics to Spicolli—Chris Farley. It had been reported that Spicolli actually patterned his WCW character after that of Farley.)

Eventually, Spicolli had entrenched himself in a role in which he was a stooge for the NWO, the ultimate bad guys. A decision was made that would have catapulted Spicolli to top-level status in WCW. One Monday evening, he took the microphone and broadcast play-by-play in a comedy heel role. His performance was nothing short of fabulous.

WCW was so impressed by Spicolli's presentation, that it changed the angle and decided to make Spicolli a full-time announcer and elevate his in-ring status as well. Quickly, plans were made for him to appear on the promotion's next pay-per-view event, taking on Larry Zybysko. It appeared that Spicolli had finally made the big time. Then he died.

When the news hit that Spicolli was dead, the wrestling world was numbed. From the first reports, it was indicated that he had taken an enormous amount of a muscle-relaxing drug called "Soma" on the evening before his death. In addition, he had been drinking quite heavily. It was believed that the drug, combined with alcohol, produced adverse side effects such as nausea, vomiting and diarrhea.

A couple of years before, Spicolli had received a warning when he collapsed outside a friend's house. At that time, it was inferred that the combination of Soma and alcohol had contributed to his losing consciousness.

Spicolli had been taking Soma for some time because of the pain he suffered in the ring. Friends and associates had warned him about the effects of the drug, and he finally quit taking it. Unfortunately, he began ingesting the drug shortly before his death when he learned that his mother had cancer.

Shortly after his death, something happened that nobody could have predicted. Within a couple of days, the Internet was abuzz with accolades and stories about Spicolli. He had turned into a cult figure along the lines of James Dean, Jimi Hendrix and Buddy Holly. The analogies are all there—a performer who dies young and who still had the best of his talents yet to give to his fans.

Among the onslaught of messages on the Internet, one, in particular, stood out: "Louie's dream has come true; he is finally over with all the Internet fans." Like most others who die young, Spicolli's talents were more appreciated after his death.

Spicolli's death devastated his longtime friend and mentor, Bill Anderson, who was in India when Spicolli died. Anderson was Spicolli's instructor, but their relationship transcended that of student and teacher.

Anderson vividly recalls the first time he saw Spicolli. He was on his way down the aisle at the Los Angeles Sports Arena going to the seat where he was to perform his ring announcing duties for a WWF show in early 1988 when a 16-year-old young man jumped out of the stands to approach him. According to Anderson, "Louie had gotten my name and number from Wildman Jack Armstrong and was at the event. He saw me coming down the aisle and, after he caught up to me, he asked me if I could help him get into wrestling. It was his dream."

courtesy of Bill Anderson

Sabu (left) with Louie Spicolli & crew at Bill Anderson's School for Hard Knocks

Many young wrestlers strive to make it in the trade. The business, however, has a way of turning the most naive young person into a cynical critic, making him old beyond his years. Spicolli had an innocence about him until the day he died. Anderson said, "He was the biggest wrestling fan I ever met. I used to laugh at him sometimes because of his 'being a mark.'

Mike Lano

Spicolli circles the squared circle

However, it was his innocence that I was jealous of because he didn't know some of the garbage out there in the business, but he was to learn all that later. He really enjoyed the business and had great respect for it."

Shortly after introducing himself to Anderson, Spicolli enrolled in his wrestling school. His advancement was atypical to that of most young wrestlers. Within a few months, Anderson thought Spicolli was ready for a WWF television taping, yet the youngster had not even had one match under his belt. According to Anderson, "I had such faith in Louie that I took him to Duluth, Minnesota, for a WWF TV taping. His first match was against Outlaw Ron Bass.

"I remember so well because I was so proud of him and his performance. Chief Jay Strongbow was in charge of hiring the undercard people for the event. He told me, 'Billy, I don't want any green guys.' I told him, 'Chief, I'll take care of you. You know me. I'd never give you a green guy.'

"He used Louie and told me after the match, 'Hey, Billy. This kid is good. How long did you say he's been working?' I told him, 'A couple of years, Chief.' It wasn't until about five years later that I told Strongbow that Spicolli had his first match that night.

"I risked my reputation on that. He had been training for only about four months. Normally, it takes a minimum of six months, and that's working out two or three times a week, for a guy to be ready. For some, it's up to a year, and some, never."

At the time he first trained Spicolli, Anderson was still a regular performer in the squared circle. He and Tim Patterson formed a duo called "The Mercenaries," and they wrestled throughout Mexico utilizing a gimmick in which they wore camouflaged army fatigues and masks.

Two-man tag-teams are the norm in the United States, yet Mexico is big on three-man teams, so Anderson had to add a new member to The Mercenaries. Without hesitation, he picked Spicolli. Anderson stated, "Louie was working in independent promotions in Arizona, and I thought it was perfect for him to do some work in Mexico, under a mask, so if he messed up real bad, he would be covered. I knew he had a lot of potential and that he was going to go places. I didn't want him to be ruined by this gimmick or anything, but the gimmick was very successful. We were the three-man champions of Mexico for two-and-a-half years. Louie held up his end real good."

Professional wrestling is a nasty business at times. There are numerous stories about wrestlers backstabbing each other, but Spicolli was impeccable in his dealings with wrestling's social mores. Anderson added, "When Tim Patterson, Louie and I were on the road all over the Southwest, Mexico and Japan, I trusted them with my reputation in the dressing room. I never expected any backstabbing from them, and I never received it. That's unlike a lot of guys today who train a couple of guys to become a tag-team and, behind each other's back, everybody's griping and arguing with each other.

"Louie spent many years with me, and I tried to instill in him the values of getting along with people and always being a friend, always doing good, never a guy who wants to shoot with somebody. Some trainers teach guys how to really be an asshole to people. I don't believe in that, never have and never will. I will retire from the business before I push that attitude with the boys. Louie was basically a fan and a friend of everybody."

Spicolli gained international success with Bill Anderson, wrestling in Mexico and Japan. By the early part of the 1990s, he was ready to attain a higher level in the United States, but he had a major hurdle to overcome—he was so good as a jobber, that it would be difficult to become a part of the mainstream in the WWF. Anderson explained, "I took him to many WWF tapings in the early '90s. They saw him so often and he made such an impression that the WWF would ask for him—'Billy, give me eight guys. Make sure Spicolli is one of them.'

"In the early '90s, the WWF realized that they had a kid who was really looking good. The bad part about this business is that he had been a job guy, so they thought they couldn't bring him in. He was overexposed as a loser. I hate that philosophy because it's a shame that a guy busts his butt and gets labeled a loser for it."

For Spicolli to have a chance in the WWF, he had to take time off to ensure the fans would not recognize him as the astute jobber that he had become. According to Anderson, "The WWF told him that the only way they could bring him in was to have him take some time off. I really hated taking a bunch of guys to tapings without Louie. My instinct was that he was turning paydays down, but I realized he had to do that to get a break. Part of me hated it and part of me accepted it. He took some time off, but he was still doing the Mercenaries thing, which remained hot until 1995.

"Finally, he and the WWF got in touch. They let him sit out long enough and said they had to develop a gimmick for him. At first, Louie wanted to be kind of like a Richie Rich character—the typical California stereotype of a rich kid. Then suddenly they didn't know what they were going to do with the character and eventually, Rad Radford became Louie's gimmick."

Unforeseen conditions contributed to the character of Rad Radford not becoming the main-eventer that Anderson and others thought he should be. Anderson added, "He got a push, but never a big push. Circumstances really messed him up there. The big thing that messed him up was the demise of

Mike Lano

An ECW event –
Louie Spicolli finishes The Death Valley Driver

Smokey Mountain Wrestling. Half the boys there were friends of promoter Jim Cornette. When SMW quit running, Cornette joined the WWF and brought in all his friends.

"What happened was that a lot of other people had to take a back seat. Three who got pushed down to a near nothing position were Louie, Hakushi and Barry Horowitz. That's when they brought in the Bodydonnas, Isaac Yankem and the Harris Twins. Because of their size and the political favors they got in the office, somebody had to take a back seat."

After his less-than-glorious demise in the WWF, Spicolli went to Extreme Championship Wrestling (ECW), an organization which is more violent and graphic than the WWF or WCW. He did receive a push, but nothing exceptional. At this time, his use of drugs was becoming evident. Anderson said, "By this point, Louie was already becoming messed up. He had already experienced what the new drug in the business was—Soma.

"He said he had pain. A lot of his complaints toward the end were about Ahmed Johnson, the injuries he got from him, his hip and his back. Every night that he took the Pearl River Plunge from Johnson, Louie said he hurt his back. He worked with him 40 nights in a row.

"He told me he got off Soma. Even as good a friend as I was, I did not know. We talked three or four times a week on the phone. He always said he was okay. He called me from every country he ever went to and told me to tell all my students that he was doing well. But at that point, he was beginning to change. He was being influenced by guys like Razor Ramon and Diesel and Owen Hart.

"He was hanging around on the road with them. If they were late for a show, he would make sure he came in late with them. He got caught up in that peer pressure. I told him many times, 'You're not Owen Hart. You can't just come in late. They're not going to fire Owen. They're going to come down on you.' I told him that was the nature of the business.

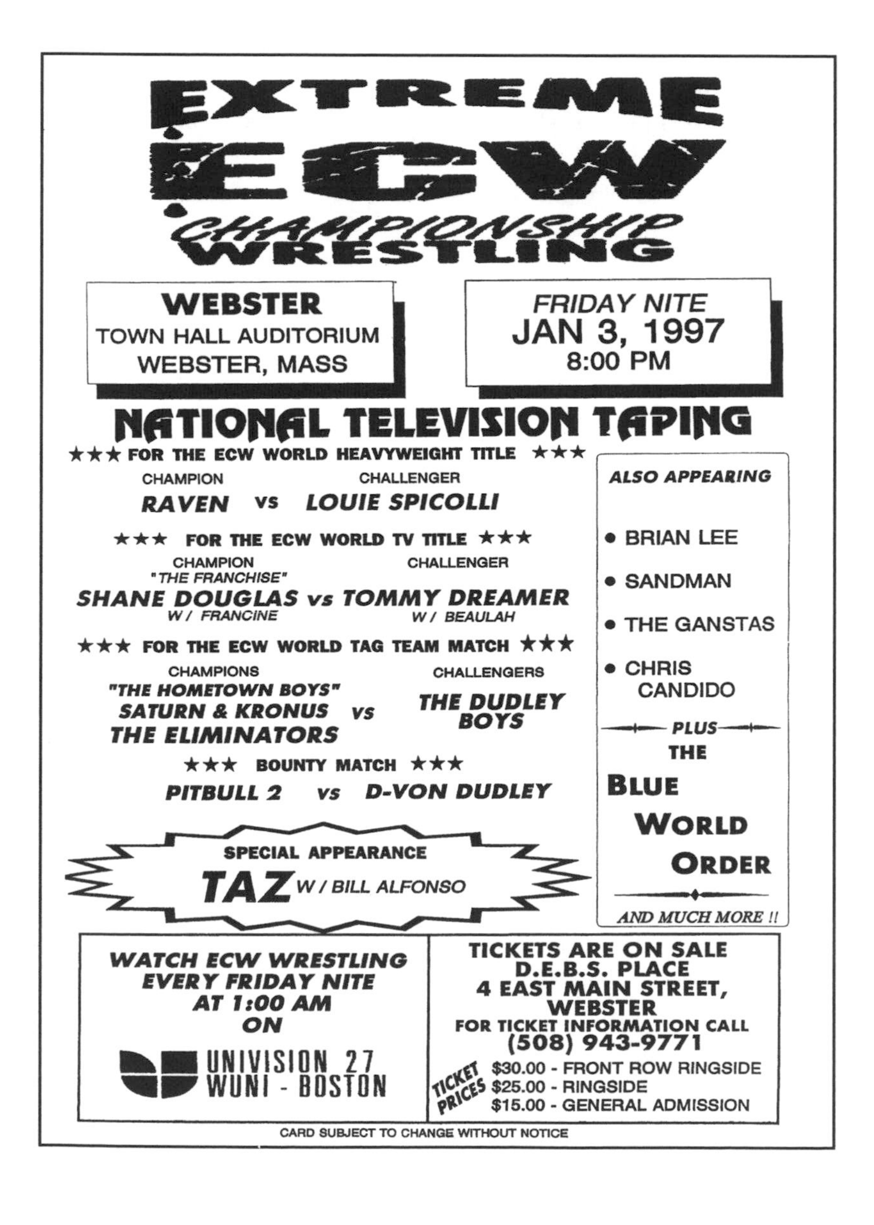

"He was a good kid, except he got caught up with these guys. That's where the garbage in his body started. He would drink alcohol with it."

Spicolli's death hit independent promoter, manager and wrestler Dale Pierce, then of Arizona, very hard. He was emotional, almost to the point of incoherence, when he stated, "On the afternoon of February 16, I got home and had a garbled message from the Navajo Kid which sounded like, 'Dale, I got a pencil in the forehead.' I'd known that he just had a bout in California, but I thought, 'What the hell kind of message is that? Was he working with The Sheik?' Then, after a second listen-to, I got, 'Louie Spicolli passed away.' I would have preferred, 'I got a pencil in the forehead.'

"Right away, I started calling around, but it was news to most people. I called Billy Anderson's school, as he had trained Spicolli, but there was no answer. Anderson was evidently on some kind of religious crusade. Finally, I did get a hotline that had 'the scoop' for what it is worth. The result was not pretty to hear."

Pierce was filled with sadness, but also anger at the hypocrisy which quickly emerged concerning Spicolli's career. He said, "Two things aggravated me the most. First, I have no ambition ever to go to the WWF, WCW or ECW and doubt very much that I would last long there with my attitudes, even if they wanted to take me. I am happy with the so-called 'small time.'

"Most people do not share this view. It angers me that Spicolli would spend nearly a decade trying to get into the doorway to the big time. There are 10,000 wrestlers who would have committed ritual sacrifice to have gotten his opportunity. However, he did get into the WWF and, for all practical purposes, let personal problems blow his chance for him.

"So it was back to the small time, a brief stint in ECW and then, finally, a second chance at the big time with WCW, which again got blown with no chance for a retake. This is what angers me. It was a dumb way to die, a waste of talent and a waste of life. It's something people should look back on and learn from. It's a tragedy one man brought on himself which, I hope, others can learn a lesson or two from.

"The second thing that really pisses me off is the majority of sheet writers, smart-mark hardcore pukes, Internet geeks and so on. On and on, over the past few years, I've sat back and listened to these self-professed experts ramble on and on, running Spicolli down, and now that he's dead, they try to erase what they've said. Now, all of a sudden, he's a fallen star, a great loss to the wrestling world.

"It's particularly angering to hear it from the same geeks who were bashing him and his workrate just a week or so before his death. Well, that's life. It happened with the Von Erichs, with Gilbert, with Art Barr, with Jerry Graham, with Adrian Adonis and so many others. My only thoughts are that these two-faced bastards should have died choking on their own barf instead. We'd be better off without them.

"I remember a couple of things about Spicolli. I remember when he first started out. He was called 'Pillsbury Doughboy' behind his back because he still had baby fat on him, but I always thought he had a lot of potential. I remember a while back, Billy Anderson saying in a letter, 'Louie is going to the WWF. Now the kid can finally make some money.' I was glad to see it happen."

After the anger and sadness subsided, Pierce talked of more humorous times concerning Spicolli. Over the years, the two had met and been involved with angles in the squared circle. According to Pierce, "Two stories come to mind concerning him. One was when I was managing my guys,

Special Forces, who were in the main event with Spicolli and Anderson at this American Legion Hall in Phoenix. To pop the crowd, they got hold of me and dotted me all over with a bingo marker. It took three showers to get the damn purple ink off me.

"Another time, again in Phoenix, Anderson and crew were coming from California to work at Toolies Nightclub.

"It was a good opportunity, but promoter Bill Johnson was blowing it. It was obvious this was going to be the last Toolies show, and we were pretty much fed up with the promoter, so we decided to say to hell with it.

"Anderson, Spicolli, The Ranger, The Black Mambo, Thrillseeker, myself and some others all went across the street to get blitzed before the show. It was not until about eight years later (I was 'suspended' from managing, so I was being a biased commentator at the time) that I saw what all went down. God, did I talk up a storm. I also tripped over the ropes on the way into the ring, and I'm sure the fledgling hardcore geeks thought it was intentional.

"Then I referred to Louie Spicolli as 'Louie Spaghetti' and got drop-kicked. Later, while in back of the announcer's table, Spicolli came up and in his interview said to me, 'Your cigar stinks,' to which I responded, 'So does your wrestling.' I remember thinking, even in my groggy state, 'Touché, greenhorn. Don't mess with the old guys.' He managed to keep a straight face and go on with the interview.

"Even though everyone was lit and Bill Johnson was ready to have a heart attack out of fear of what was going on, we did a pretty good show. Louie did the main event fine. The only bad spot came when The Ranger had his bout. On the video, you can see him in a leglock, and he'd motion the waitress to try to grab a drink off her tray. At least the rest of us weren't that bad.

"That was one of my favorite Louie Spicolli stories. It's too bad the future won't hold any opportunities for any additions to it."

courtesy of Bill Anderson

Louie Spicolli
1971–1998

Louie Spicolli's career was not as glamorous or as lengthy as that of many legendary stars, but his career was notable because of the determination he showed in wanting to be a professional wrestler as well as the irony of his premature death. The question "What if" is the foremost query one could ask about Louie Spicolli.

Louie Spicolli did not draw the line between fantasy and reality, between childhood and adulthood. To him, the world was about wrestling. In every match in which he appeared, he performed with energy, skill and enthusiasm. He wanted to give a performance that would have matched his expectations of wrestlers when he was a 12-year-old fan. He was a rare individual in that he did not suffer from the genetic deficiency which hits most of us—aging. He approached the world through the eyes of someone who had never been infected with the sometimes ugly disease of adulthood.

Angelo Marino

*** ***

CURTAIN CALL

Sorry folks, the performance has ended.

As you vacate the building, we offer our explanation of why the likes of Lex Luger, Diamond Dallas Page and Kevin Nash are not given prominence in this theatrical setting. These and others mentioned in this Curtain Call are more than welcome to appear on our stage at any time.

In the meantime, we wish you good luck in your further quest for wrestling-related regalement.

YOU CAN'T ALWAYS GET WHAT YOU WANT

Whatever happened to Bob Backlund? My publisher asked me that question after reading the first draft of this work (roughly a year after Backlund's gimmick had run its course). I told him, "They have no place for him. He's out." He was surprised by the crass manner in which a wrestler is dumped once a promotion thinks the grappler can no longer make it money. I then told him that the promotions do not explain someone's demise, even a person like Backlund who has wrestled for the WWF since the 1970s. They just . . . disappear!

With that response, my publisher asked me to include something about the impersonal parts of the wrestling business. There are many, so I will highlight just a few. Actually, the aloof attitude that is prevalent at the top end of the wrestling promotions did affect this book and its scope.

In 1995, Bob Collins, a front-office person with the WWF, visited me in California. I had just had a book published and told him I was thinking about writing a book on professional wrestling. Collins is from the old school of "protect the business," and he told me he thought that few, if any, wrestlers would talk to me. He said, "It's like a magician revealing his secrets." With the information in hand, I started my quest in earnest in 1996. After almost 500 pages, you can see that Collins was a little off in his assessment.

Once I began to interview people for this book, I thought that I must go right to the top and talk to Vince McMahon of the WWF and Eric Bishoff of WCW. Piece of cake, I pondered.

Over two years later and many phone calls and sent fax messages, I am about as close to having an interview with the big cheeses of WCW and the WWF as Adolph Hitler is to having a posthumous award given to him by the B'nai B'rith. I began with the WWF. I called Bob Collins to see if he could get me an interview with McMahon. He told me to call the man in charge of scheduling the interviews, Jay Andronaco. I called him several times and talked to his answering machine. No return calls. One day, I lucked out and he answered the phone. "Send me a fax with the book's outline," he told me. That day, I sent him the desired information. He never called, faxed or wrote back to me. My publisher sent him a fax, mentioning deadlines for the book. Again, no answer.

My experience with WCW was as fruitless. After talking to someone in public relations, I was told to fax them a request and outline. I did. A month later, I called. The woman told me they couldn't find the fax and to submit another. Another fax and still no reply.

I had given up hope of talking to anyone in these organizations when Hulk Hogan told Killer Kowalski that he would call me for an interview. "To hell with Bishoff and McMahon," I thought. A Hogan interview would well make up for the losses I had encountered. Hogan never called. As a last desperate measure, I called J. J. Dillon of WCW. His voice was on the answering machine, stating how important all calls were and that he would return them. He did not call, so I again called and left a detailed message. No response. My publisher called and received the same silence.

If any other trade ran its affairs in the same manner as the WWF and WCW in not responding to inquiries, it would not be in business long. For some reason, the wrestling business today still attempts to "protect the business" by not admitting they exist to journalists. Their responses are mostly the same: the press is out to get us, so we won't cooperate.

Those days are gone. Many legitimate writers and journalists who write about professional wrestling are not out to declare that wrestling is "fake." The only problem is that the promotions still live in the 1950s in this respect and do not realize that becoming involved with real journalists or writers would enhance their positions, not detract from them.

Professional wrestling is glamorous to the fan, but most never see the seamy side of the sport. As I am writing this, a young professional wrestler, who is a friend of mine, is sitting in an empty Atlanta apartment. There is only a chair in the flat. He is an accomplished wrestler on the independent circuit and, after looking at a videotape of a few of his matches, he was told by WCW that he would get a tryout, or at least a look-at, if he came to Atlanta. He moved and acquired an apartment, only to be told by the same people who suggested they would look at him that he would not even be able to train at their gym. Somehow, their memories of the promise went blank.

Not everything about professional wrestling is bad or seedy, but not all is glamorous either. For young wrestlers to make it to the big time, they must endure much suffering—physical and mental. Why do they stay around so long in attempting to fulfill their dreams? It's in their blood.

Some small independent promotions today are beginning to change the attitude of the business. They treat the wrestlers like human beings, not cattle, because they know without the wrestlers, there would be no promotions. It may take some time, but eventually that attitude may make its way upwards and become entrenched in the WWF and WCW.

In closing, we are not always able to do the things in life that we may want. I would have liked to have included information about women's wrestling and midget wrestling. Moreover, I am not remiss in knowing that Lou Thesz, Gorgeous George, Bruno Sammartino, Moolah, Ed "Strangler" Lewis, Verne Gagne, Antonio Rocca, Buddy Rogers, Andre the Giant, Randy "Macho Man" Savage, Ray Stevens, Nick Bockwinkle and many, many others have played very important parts in the development of professional wrestling. If I had included them, the book would have taken another five years to finish, and it would have been the size of a set of encyclopedias. If there is a sequel, it will include those people, and others, whom I have only briefly mentioned.

Fortunately, there is an optimistic endnote here. A Rolling Stones song announces:

"You can't always get what you want . . ."

I have delved into that issue. Now let's invoke the conclusion of the verse to accurately assess this book:

" . . . but if you try sometime,
you might just get what you need."

BACKSTAGE (APPENDIX)

This appendix has been included to give the reader information about various subjects in the professional wrestling business. There is a myriad of information that will be useful to the wrestling fan.

Because professional wrestling does not keep accurate records, statistics of the sport have been compiled by historians and fans. At times, specifics differ from one historian to the next. Much of the time, however, there is a consensus. The information in this appendix has been accepted as being accurate. The title histories have been updated to reflect the latest information available at the time of printing.

WWF WORLD HEAVYWEIGHT TITLE

05-17-63 **Bruno Sammartino**
d. Buddy Rogers, New York, NY

01-18-71 **Ivan Koloff**
d. Bruno Sammartino, New York, NY

02-08-71 **Pedro Morales**
d. Ivan Koloff, New York, NY

12-01-73 **Stan Stasiak**
d. Pedro Morales, Philadelphia, PA

12-10-73 **Bruno Sammartino**
d. Stan Stasiak, New York, NY

04-30-77 **Superstar Billy Graham**
d. Bruno Sammartino, Baltimore, MD

02-20-78 **Bob Backlund**
d. Superstar Billy Graham, New York, NY

12-26-83 **The Iron Sheik**
d. Bob Backlund, New York, NY

01-23-84 **Hulk Hogan**
d.The Iron Sheik, New York, NY

02-05-88 **Andre the Giant**
d. Hulk Hogan, Indianapolis, IN

03-27-88 **Randy Savage**
d. Ted DiBiase, Atlantic City, NJ

04-02-89 **Hulk Hogan**
d. Randy Savage, Atlantic City, NJ

04-01-90 **Ultimate Warrior**
d. Hulk Hogan, Toronto, Canada

01-19-91 **Sgt. Slaughter**
d. The Ultimate Warrior, Miami, FL

03-24-91 **Hulk Hogan**
d. Sgt. Slaughter, Los Angeles, CA

11-27-91 **The Undertaker**
d. Hulk Hogan, Detroit, MI

12-03-91 **Hulk Hogan**
d. The Undertaker, San Antonio, TX

01-19-92 **Ric Flair**
won a 30-man Royal Rumble, Albany, NY

04-05-92 **Randy Savage**
d. Ric Flair, Indianapolis, IN

09-01-92	**Ric Flair** d. Randy Savage, Hershey, PA
10-12-92	**Bret Hart** d. Ric Flair, Saskatoon, Canada
04-04-93	**Yokozuna** d. Bret Hart, Las Vegas, NV
04-04-93	**Hulk Hogan** d. Yokozuna, Las Vegas, NV
06-13-93	**Yokozuna** d. Hulk Hogan, Dayton, OH
03-20-94	**Bret Hart** d. Yokozuna, New York, NY
11-23-94	**Bob Backlund** d. Bret Hart, San Antonio, TX
11-26-94	**Diesel** d. Bob Backlund, New York, NY
11-19-95	**Bret Hart** d. Diesel, Landover, MD
03-31-96	**Shawn Michaels** d. Bret Hart, Anaheim, CA
11-17-96	**Psycho Sid** d. Shawn Michaels, New York, NY
01-19-97	**Shawn Michaels** d. Psycho Sid, San Antonio, TX
02-16-97	**Bret Hart** d. The Undertaker, Chattanooga, TN
02-17-97	**Psycho Sid** d. Bret Hart, Nashville, TN
03-23-97	**The Undertaker** d. Psycho Sid, Chicago, IL
08-03-97	**Bret Hart** d. The Undertaker, East Rutherford, NJ
11-09-97	**Shawn Michaels** d. Bret Hart, Montreal, Canada
03-29-98	**Steve Austin** d. Shawn Michaels, Boston, MA
06-28-98	**Kane** d. Steve Austin, Pittsburgh, PA
06-29-98	**Steve Austin** d. Kane, Cleveland, OH

11-15-98 **The Rock**
d. Mankind, St. Louis, MO

12-29-98 **Mankind**
d. The Rock, Worcester, MA

01-24-99 **The Rock**
d. Mankind, Anaheim, CA

01-26-99 **Mankind**
d. The Rock, Tucson, AZ

02-15-99 **The Rock**
d. Mankind, Birmingham, AL

03-28-99 **Steve Austin**
d. The Rock, Philadelphia, PA

05-23-99 **The Undertaker**
d. Steve Austin, Kansas City, MO

WWF INTERCONTINENTAL TITLE

04-21-80 **Ken Patera**
d. Pat Patterson, New York, NY

12-08-80 **Pedro Morales**
d. Ken Patera, New York, NY

06-20-81 **Magnificent Muraco**
d. Pedro Morales, Philadelphia, PA

11-23-81 **Pedro Morales**
d. Magnificent Muraco, New York, NY

01-22-83 **Magnificent Muraco**
d. Pedro Morales, New York, NY

02-11-84 **Tito Santana**
d. Magnificent Muraco, Boston, MA

09-24-84 **Greg Valentine**
d. Tito Santana, London, Ontario, Canada

07-06-85 **Tito Santana**
d. Greg Valentine, Baltimore, MD

02-08-86 **Randy Savage**
d. Tito Santana, Boston, MA

03-29-87 **Rick Steamboat**
d. Randy Savage, Pontiac, MI

06-02-87 **Honky Tonk Man**
d. Rick Steamboat, Buffalo, NY

08-29-88 **Ultimate Warrior**
d. Honky Tonk Man, New York, NY
04-02-89 **Rick Rude**
d. Ultimate Warrior, Atlantic City, NJ
08-28-89 **Ultimate Warrior**
d. Rick Rude, East Rutherford, NJ
04-23-90 **Curt Hennig**
d. Tito Santana, Austin, TX
08-27-90 **Kerry Von Eirch**
d. Curt Hennig, Philadelphia, PA
11-19-90 **Curt Hennig**
d. Kerry Von Erich, Rochester, NY
08-26-91 **Bret Hart**
d. Curt Hennig, New York, NY
01-17-92 **The Mountie**
d. Bret Hart, Springfield, MA
01-19-92 **Roddy Piper**
d. The Mountie, Albany, NY
04-05-92 **Bret Hart**
d. Roddy Piper, Indianapolis, IN
08-29-92 **Davey Boy Smith**
d. Bret Hart, London, England
10-27-92 **Shawn Michaels**
d. Davey Boy Smith, Terre Haute, IN
05-17-93 **Marty Jannetty**
d. Shawn Michaels, New York, NY
06-06-93 **Shawn Michaels**
d. Marty Jannetty, Albany, NY
09-27-93 **Razor Ramon**
d. Rick Martel, New Haven, CT
04-13-94 **Diesel**
d. Razor Ramon, Rochester, NY
08-29-94 **Razor Ramon**
d. Diesel, Chicago, IL
01-22-95 **Jeff Jarrett**
d. Razor Ramon, Tampa, FL
04-26-95 **Jeff Jarrett**
d. Bob Holly, Moline, IN
05-19-95 **Razor Ramon**
d. Jeff Jarrett, Montreal, Canada

05-22-95 **Jeff Jarrett**
d. Razor Ramon, Trois-Rivieres, Canada
07-23-95 **Shawn Michaels**
d. Jeff Jarrett, Nashville, TN
10-22-95 **Razor Ramon**
d. Dean Douglas, Winnipeg, Canada
01-21-96 **Goldust**
d. Razor Ramon, Fresno, CA
04-01-96 **Goldust**
d. Savio Vega, San Bernadino, CA
06-23-96 **Ahmed Johnson**
d. Goldust, Milwaukee, WI
09-23-96 **Marc Mero**
d. Farooq, Hershey, PA
10-21-96 **Hunter Hearst Helmsley**
d. Marc Mero, Fort Wayne, IN
02-13-97 **Rocky Maivia**
d. Hunter Hearst Helmsley, Lowell, MA
04-28-97 **Owen Hart**
d. Rocky Maivia, Omaha, NE
08-03-97 **Steve Austin**
d. Owen Hart, East Rutherford, NJ
10-05-97 **Owen Hart**
d. Farooq, St. Louis, MO
11-09-97 **Steve Austin**
d. Owen Hart, Montreal, Canada
12-08-97 **Rocky Maivia**
d. Steve Austin, Portland, ME
08-30-98 **Hunter Hearst Helmsley**
d. Rocky Maivia, New York, NY
10-12-98 **Ken Shamrock**
d. X-Pac, Uniondale, NY
02-14-99 **Val Venis**
d. Ken Shamrock, Memphis, TN
03-15-99 **Road Dogg**
d. Val Venis, San Jose, CA
03-29-99 **Goldust**
d. Road Dogg, East Rutherford, NJ
04-12-99 **The Godfather**
d. Goldust, Detroit, MI

05-25-99 **Jeff Jarrett**
d. The Godfather, Moline, IL

WWF TAG TEAM TITLES

06-xx-71 **Luke Graham & Tarzan Tyler,** New Orleans, LA
12-06-71 **Karl Gotch & Rene Goulet,** New York, NY
02-01-72 **Baron Scicluna & King Curtis Iaukea,** Philadelphia, PA
05-22-72 **Chief Jay Strongbow & Sonny King,** New York, NY
06-27-72 **Mr. Fuji & Toru Tanaka,** at Philadelphia, PA
05-30-73 **Haystack Calhoun & Tony Garea,** Hamburg, PA
09-11-73 **Mr. Fuji & Toru Tanaka,** Phildelphia, PA
11-14-73 **Dean Ho & Tony Garea,** Hamburg, PA
05-08-74 **Jimmy & Johnny Valiant,** Hamburg, PA
05-13-75 **Dominic Denucci & Victor Rivera,** Philadelphia, PA
08-26-75 **Blackjack Lanza & Blackjack Mulligan,** Philadephia, PA
11-18-75 **Louis Cerdan & Tony Parisi**, Philadelphia, PA
05-11-76 **Executioners (Studd & Kowalski),** Philadelphia, PA
12-07-76 **Chief Jay Strongbow & Billy White Wolf,** Philadelphia, PA
09-27-77 **Mr. Fuji & Toru Tanaka**, Philadelphia, PA
04-14-78 **Dino Bravo & Dominic Denucci,** Philadelphia, PA
06-26-78 **Yukon Lumberjacks (Eric & Pierre),** New York, NY
11-21-78 **Larry Zbyszko & Tony Garea,** Allentown, PA
03-06-79 **Jerry & Johnny Valiant,** Allentown, PA
10-22-79 **Ivan Putski & Tito Santana,** at New York, NY
04-02-80 **Samoans (Afa & Sika),** Philadelphia, PA
08-09-80 **Bob Backlund & Pedro Morales,** at New York, NY
09-09-80 **Samoans (Afa & Sika),** Allentown, PA
11-08-80 **Rick Martel & Tony Garea,** Philadelphia, PA
03-17-81 **Moondogs (Rex & King),** Allentown, PA
07-21-81 **Rick Martel & Tony Garea,** Allentown, PA
10-13-81 **Mr. Fuji/Mr. Saito,** Allentown, PA
06-28-82 **Chief Jay & Jules Strongbow,** New York, NY
07-13-82 **Mr. Fuji & Mr. Saito,** Allentown, PA
10-26-82 **Chief Jay & Jules Strongbow,** Allentown, PA
03-08-83 **Samoans (Afa & Sika),** Allentown, PA
11-15-83 **Rocky Johnson & Tony Atlas,** Allentown, PA

04-17-84	**North-South Connection,** Hamburg, PA
01-21-85	**US Express,** Hartford, CT
03-31-85	**Iron Sheik & Nikolai Volkoff,** New York, NY
06-17-85	**US Express,** Poughkeepsie, NY
08-24-85	**Dream Team,** Philadelphia, PA
04-07-86	**British Bulldogs,** Chicago, IL
01-26-87	**Hart Foundation,** Tampa, FL
10-27-87	**Strike Force,** Syracuse, NY
03-27-88	**Demolition,** Atlantic City, NJ
07-18-89	**Brainbusters,** Worcester, MA
10-02-89	**Demolition,** Wheeling, WV
12-13-89	**Colossal Connection,** Huntsville, AL
04-01-90	**Demolition,** Toronto, Canada
08-27-90	**Hart Foundation,** Philadelphia, PA
03-24-91	**Nasty Boys,** Los Angeles, CA
08-26-91	**Legion of Doom,** New York, NY
02-07-92	**Money Inc.,** Denver, CO
07-20-92	**Natural Disasters,** Worcester, MA
10-13-92	**Money Inc.,** Regina, Canada
06-14-92	**The Steiner Brothers,** Columbus, OH
06-16-93	**Money Inc.,** Rockford, IL
06-19-93	**The Steiner Brothers,** St. Louis, MO
09-13-93	**The Quebecers,** New York, NY
01-10-94	**1-2-3 Kid & Marty Janetty,** Richmond, VA
01-17-94	**The Quebecers,** New York, NY
03-29-94	**Men on a Mission,** London, England
03-31-94	**The Quebecers,** Sheffield, England
04-26-94	**Headshrinkers,** Burlington, VT
08-28-94	**Diesel & Shawn Michaels,** Indianapolis, IN
01-22-95	**1-2-3 Kid & Bob Holly,** Tampa, FL
01-23-95	**Smoking Gunns,** Palmetto, FL
04-02-95	**Owen Hart & Yokozuna,** Hartford, CT
09-25-95	**Smoking Gunns,** Grand Rapids, MI
03-31-96	**Bodydonnas,** Anaheim, CA
05-19-96	**The Godwinns,** New York, NY
05-26-96	**Smoking Gunns,** Florence, SC
09-22-96	**British Bulldog & Owen Hart,** Phildelphia, PA
05-26-97	**Steve Austin & Shawn Michaels,** Philadelphia, PA
07-14-97	**Steve Austin & Dude Love,** San Antonio, TX
09-07-97	**The Headbangers,** Louisville, KY

10-05-97 **The Godwinns,** St. Louis, MO
10-13-97 **The Legion of Doom,** Topeka, KS
11-24-97 **The New Age Outlaws,** Fayetteville, NC
03-29-98 **Chainsaw Charlie & Cactus Jack,** Boston, MA
03-30-98 **The New Age Outlaws,** Albany, NY
07-13-98 **Kane & Mankind,** East Rutherford, NJ
07-26-98 **The Undertaker & Steve Austin,** Fresno, CA
08-10-98 **Kane & Mankind,** Omaha, NE
08-30-98 **The New Age Outlaws,** New York, NY
12-14-98 **Big Bossman & Ken Shamrock,** Tacoma, WA
01-25-99 **Jeff Jarrett & Owen Hart,** Phoenix, AZ
03-30-99 **X-Pac & Kane,** Uniondale, NY
05-25-99 **The Acolytes,** Moline, IL

WCW WORLD HEAVYWEIGHT TITLE

01-11-91 **Ric Flair**
d. Sting, East Rutherford, NJ
07-14-91 **Lex Luger**
d. Barry Windham, Baltimore, MD
02-29-92 **Sting**
d. Lex Luger, Milwaukee, WI
07-12-92 **Vader**
d. Sting, Albany, GA
08-02-92 **Ron Simmons**
d. Vader, Baltimore, MD
12-30-92 **Vader**
d. Ron Simmons, Baltimore, MD
03-11-93 **Sting**
d. Vader, London, England
03-17-93 **Vader**
d. Sting, Dublin, Ireland
12-27-93 **Ric Flair**
d. Vader, Charlotte, NC
07-17-94 **Hulk Hogan**
d. Ric Flair, Orlando, FL
10-29-95 **The Giant**
d. Hulk Hogan, Detroit, MI
11-26-95 **Randy Savage**
won a 60-man Battle Royal, Norfolk, VA

12-27-95 **Ric Flair**
d. Randy Savage, Nashville, TN
01-22-96 **Randy Savage**
d. Ric Flair, Las Vegas, NV
02-11-96 **Ric Flair**
d. Randy Savage, St. Petersburg, FL
04-22-96 **The Giant**
d. Ric Flair, Albany, GA
08-10-96 **Hulk Hogan**
d. The Giant, Sturgis, SD
08-04-97 **Lex Luger**
d. Hulk Hogan, Auburn Hills, MI
08-09-97 **Hulk Hogan**
d. Lex Luger, Sturgis, SD
12-28-97 **Sting**
d. Hulk Hogan, Washington, D.C.
02-22-98 **Sting**
d. Hulk Hogan, San Francisco, CA
04-19-98 **Randy Savage**
d. Sting, Denver, CO
04-20-98 **Hulk Hogan**
d. Randy Savage, Colorado Springs, CO
07-06-98 **Goldberg**
d. Hulk Hogan, Atlanta, GA
12-27-98 **Kevin Nash**
d. Goldberg, Washington, DC
01-04-99 **Hulk Hogan**
d. Kevin Nash, Atlanta, GA
03-14-99 **Ric Flair**
d. Hulk Hogan, Louisville, KY
04-11-99 **Diamond Dallas Page**
d. Ric Flair, Tacoma, WA
04-26-99 **Sting**
d. Diamond Dallas Page, Fargo, ND
Diamond Dallas Page
d. Kevin Nash, Fargo, ND
05-09-99 **Kevin Nash**
d. Diamond Dallas Page, St. Louis, MO

WCW US HEAVYWEIGHT TITLE

01-01-91	**Lex Luger** (awarded title)
08-25-91	**Sting**
	d. Steve Austin, Atlanta, GA
11-19-91	**Rick Rude**
	d. Sting, Savannah, GA
01-11-93	**Dustin Rhodes**
	d. Rick Steamboat, Atlanta, GA
08-30-93	**Dustin Rhodes**
	d. Rick Rude, Atlanta, GA
12-27-93	**Steve Austin**
	d. Dustin Rhodes, Charlotte, NC
08-24-94	**Rick Steamboat**
	d. Steve Austin, Cedar Rapids, IA
09-18-94	**Steve Austin**
	by forfeit over Steamboat, Roanoke, VA
09-18-94	**Hacksaw Jim Duggan**
	d. Steve Austin, Roanoke, VA
12-27-94	**Vader**
	d. Jim Duggan, Nashville, TN
06-18-95	**Sting**
	d. Meng, Dayton, OH
11-13-95	**Kensuke Sasaki**
	d. Sting, Tokyo, Japan
12-27-95	**One Man Gang**
	d. Kensuke Sasaki, Nashville, TN
01-28-96	**Konnan**
	d. One Man Gang, Canton, OH
07-07-96	**Ric Flair**
	d. Konnan, Daytona Beach, FL
12-29-96	**Eddie Guerrero**
	d. Diamond Dallas Page, Nashville, TN
03-16-97	**Dean Malenko**
	d. Eddie Guerero, Charleston, SC
06-09-97	**Jeff Jarrett**
	d. Dean Malenko, Boston, MA
08-21-97	**Steve McMichael**
	d. Jeff Jarrett, Nashville, TN
09-15-97	**Curt Hennig**
	d. Steve McMichael, Charlotte, NC

12-28-97 **Diamond Dallas Page**
d. Curt Hennig, Washington, D.C.
04-19-98 **Raven**
d. Diamond Dallas Page, Denver, CO
04-20-98 **Goldberg**
d. Raven, Colorado Springs, CO
07-20-98 **Bret Hart**
d. Diamond Dallas Page, Salt Lake City, UT
08-10-98 **Lex Luger**
d. Bret Hart, Rapid City, SD
08-13-98 **Bret Hart**
d. Lex Luger, Fargo, ND
10-26-98 **Diamond Dallas Page**
d. Bret Hart, Phoenix, AZ
11-30-98 **Bret Hart**
d. Diamond Dallas Page, Chattanooga, TN
02-08-99 **Roddy Piper**
d. Bret Hart, Buffalo, NY
02-21-99 **Scott Hall**
d. Roddy Piper, Oakland, CA
04-11-99 **Scott Steiner**
d. Booker T., Tacoma, WA

WCW TAG TEAM TITLES

01-01-91 **Butch Reed & Ron Simmons** (awarded titles)
02-18-91 **The Steiner Brothers,** Montgomery, AL
02-24-91 **The Fabulous Freebirds,** Phoenix, AZ
09-05-91 **The Enforcers,** Augusta, GA
11-19-91 **Rick Steamboat & Dustin Runnels,** Savannah, GA
01-16-92 **Arn Anderson & Bobby Eaton,** Jacksonville, FL
05-03-92 **The Steiner Brothers,** Chicago, IL
07-05-92 **Steve Williams & Terry Gordy,** Atlanta, GA
09-21-92 **Dustin Rhodes & Darry Windham,** Atlanta, GA
11-18-92 **Rick Steamboat & Shane Douglas,** Macon, GA
03-03-93 **The Hollywood Blonds,** Macon, GA
08-18-93 **Arn Anderson & Paul Roma,** Daytona, FL
09-19-93 **The Nasty Boys,** Houston, TX
10-04-93 **Marcus Bagwell & Too Cold Scorpio,** Columbus, GA
10-24-93 **The Nasty Boys,** New Orleans, LA

05-22-94 **Cactus Jack & Kevin Sullivan,** Philadelphia, PA
07-17-94 **Pretty Wonderful,** Orlando, FL
09-25-94 **Stars & Stripes,** Atlanta, GA
10-23-94 **Pretty Wonderful,** Detroit, MI
11-16-94 **Stars & Stripes,** Jacksonville, FL
12-08-94 **Harlem Heat,** Atlanta, GA
05-03-95 **Harlem Heat,** Orlando, FL
05-21-95 **The Nasty Boys,** St. Petersburg, FL
06-21-95 **Dirty Dick Slater & Bunkhouse Buck,** Atlanta, GA
09-17-95 **Harlem Heat,** Asheville, NC
09-18-95 **The American Males,** Johnson City, TN
10-11-95 **Harlem Heat,** Atlanta, GA
01-22-96 **Sting & Lex Luger,** Las Vegas, NV
06-24-96 **Harlem Heat,** Charlotte, NC
07-24-96 **The Steiner Brothers,** Cincinnati, OH
07-27-96 **Harlem Heat,** Dayton, OH
09-23-96 **Public Enemy,** Birmingham, AL
10-01-96 **Harlem Heat,** Canton, OH
10-27-96 **The Outsiders,** Las Vegas, NV
01-25-97 **The Steiner Brothers,** Memphis, TN
01-27-97 **The Outsiders,** awarded titles on *Monday Nitro*
02-23-97 **Lex Luger & The Giant,** San Francisco, CA
02-24-97 **The Outsiders,** awarded titles on *Monday Nitro*
10-13-97 **The Steiner Brothers,** Tampa Bay, FL
01-12-98 **The Outsiders,** Jacksonville, FL
02-09-98 **The Steiner Brothers,** El Paso, TX
02-22-98 **The Outsiders,** San Francisco, CA
05-17-98 **The Giant/Sting,** Worcester, MA
06-14-98 **Sting & Kevin Nash,** Baltimore, MD
07-20-98 **The Giant & Scott Hall,** Salt Lake City, UT
10-25-98 **Rick Steiner & Kenny Kaos,** Las Vegas, NV
02-21-99 **Curt Hennig & Barry Windham,** Oakland, CA
03-14-99 **Chris Benoit & Dean Malenko,** Louisville, KY
03-29-99 **Billy Kidman & Rey Mysterio, Jr.,** Toronto, ON
05-09-99 **Raven & Perry Saturn,** St. Louis, MO
05-31-99 **Diamond Dallas Page & Bam Bam Bigelow,** Houston, TX

PRO WRESTLERS' REAL NAMES

The following compilation consists of the ring identities of professional wrestlers followed by their real names.

123 Boy .... **Justin Hansford**
1-2-3 Kid, Lightning Kid, Syxx, X-Pac .... **Sean Waltman**
2 Cold Scorpio, Flash Funk .... **Charles Skaggs**
911 .... **Al Poling**
Afa .... **Alfa Anoia**
Adam Bomb, Nightstalker, Wrath .... **Bryan Clark**
Adrian Adonis .... **Keith Franke**
Anibal .... **Ignacio Carlos Carillo**
Animal (Road Warriors) .... **Joe Laurinautis**
Arn Anderson, The Enforcer, Super Olympian .... **Marty Lunde**
Tony Atlas, Saba Simba .... **Anthony White**
Brian Anderson .... **Brian Rogowski**
Ole Anderson .... **Al Rogowski**
The Living Doll Michael Anthony, Michael Lee .... **Michael Hubbard**
Vittorio Apollo .... **Vincente Denigris**
Brad Armstrong, Arachnaman, Candyman, Bad Street, Fantasia .... **Robert James, Jr.**
Steve Armstrong .... **Steven James**
Road Dogg, The Roadie, Brian Armstrong, Jesse James .... **Brian James**
Scott Armstrong .... **Scott James**
Bob Armstrong .... **Bob James**
Bert Assirati .... **Bernardo Esserati**
Fred Atkins .... **Fred Atkinson**
Buddy Austin .... **Francis Gabor**
Stone Cold Steve Austin, Stunning Steve Austin .. **Steve Williams**
Demolition Ax, Axis the Destroyer, Bolo, Masked Superstar .... **Bill Eadie**
Ali Baba .... **Arteen Ekizan**
Black Knight, The Hood .... **Jeff Gaylord**
Mr. Backlund .... **Robert Backlund**
The Barbarian, Sionne .... **Sionne Vailahi**
Marcus Alexander Bagwell, Buff Bagwell .... **Mark Bagwell**

Beetlegeuse, The Juicer, The Love Machine .... **Art Barr**
Bobby Becker .... **John Emmerling**
Paul Bearer, Percy Pringle .... **William Moody**
The Berzerker, Nord the Barbarian .... **John Nord**
Beau Beverly .... **Wayne Bloom**
Blake Beverly, Mean Mike Enos ....**Mike Enos**
Bam Bam Bigelow, Crusher Yurkhov .... **Scott Bigelow**
Big Titan .... **Michael Bogner**
Jan Blears, Lord James Blears .... **James Blears**
Eli Blu, Jared Grimm, Ronald Bruise, Skull .... **Ron Harris**
Jacob Blu, Jason Grimm, Donald Bruise, 8 Ball .... **Don Harris**
Booker T ....**Booker Huffman**
Ludvig Borga ....**Tony Halme**
Horace Boulder .... **Mike Bollea**
Justin Hawk Bradshaw, Bradshaw .... **John Hawk**
Dino Bravo .... **Adolpho Bresciano**
The Brain, Bobby Valiant,
Bobby Heenan .... **Raymond Louis Heenan**
Bobo Brazil .... **Houston Harris**
Bruiser Brody .... **Frank Goodish**
Bad News Allen, Bad News Brown .... **Allen Coage**
Big Boss Man, Big Bubba, Guardian Angel .... **Ray Traylor**
Bunkhouse Buck .... **Jimmy Golden**
King Kong Bundy .... **Chris Pallies**
Mildred Burke .... **Mildred Bliss**
Cactus Jack, Mankind, Dude Love .... **Michael Foley**
Haystack Calhoun .... **William Calhoun**
Negro Casas .... **Jose Casas**
Chainz, Brian Lee, Prime Time Brian Lee .... **Brian Harris**
Cobra, Sting II .... **Jeff Farmer**
Crush, Brian Adams .... **Bryan Adams**
Dark Patriot .... **Doug Gilbert**
Paul E. Dangerously .... **Paul Heyman, Jr.**
Jimmy Del Rey, Jimmy Grafitti .... **James Backlund**
Paul Diamond, Max Moon, Kato .... **Tom Boric**
Iron Mike DiBiase .... **Mike DiBiase**
The Million Dollar Man, Ted DiBiase .... **Theodore DiBiase**
Dick the Bruiser .... **Richard Afflis**
Diesel, Big Daddy Cool, Oz, Vinnie Vegas .... **Kevin Nash**
Dirty White Boy, T.J. Hopper .... **Tony Anthony**

Disco Inferno .... **Glen Gilburnetti**
Shane Douglas, Dean Douglas, The Franchise .... **Troy Martin**
The Duke of Dorchester, The Golden Terror .... **Pete Doherty**
Doink the Clown, Big Josh, Maniac Matt Borne ..... **Matt Osborne**
Brooklyn Brawler .... **Steve Lombardi**
Ray Apollo, Doink .... **Ray Liccachelli**
Tommy Dreamer .... **Tom Laughlin**
Duke "The Dumpster" Droese, Rocco Gibraltar .... **Mike Droese**
J.C. Ice, Jamie Dundee .... **Jamie Crookshanks**
Bill Dundee, Squire William .... **William Crookshanks**
Steven Dunn .... **Steve Doll**
The Dynamite Kid .... **Tom Billington**
Earthquake, Avalanche, Shark, Big John Tenta .... **John Tenta**
Robbie Ellis, The Sports Illustrated Legend .... **Robert Elowitch**
El Santo .... **Adolfo Guzman Huerta**
Fatu, Tonga Kid, The Sultan .... **Solofatu Anoia**
Farooq, Ron Simmons .... **Ron Simmons**
Fire Cat .... **Brady Boone**
The Nature Boy Ric Flair .... **Richard Fliehr**
Flyin' Brian, Yellow Dog, The Loose Cannon .... **Brian Pillman**
Mr. Fuji .... **Harry Fujiwara**
Bobby Fulton .... **James Hines**
Jackie Fulton, The Eagle .... **George Hines**
Jimmy Jack Funk, Jesse Barr .... **Ferrin Barr**
Terry Funk .... **Terrence Funk**
Dory Funk, Jr. .... **Dorrence Funk, Jr.**
Rugged Ronnie Garvin .... **Roger Barnes**
The Giant .... **Paul Wight**
Giant Baba .... **Shohei Baba**
Robert Gibson .... **Rueben Kane**
Giant Gonzalez, El Gigante .... **Jorge Gonzalez**
Hot Stuff Eddie Gilbert .... **Thomas Edward Gilbert, Jr.**
Henry O. Godwinn .... **Mark Canterbury**
Phineus I. Godwinn .... **Dennis Knight**
Golden Phoenix, AC Golden .... **Mark Freer**
Goldust, Dustin Rhodes, The Natural .... **Dustin Runnels**
Superstar Billy Graham .... **Eldrige Wayne Coleman**
Eddie Graham .... **Eddie Gossett**
Grappler .... **Len Denton**
Johnny Grunge .... **Michael Durham**

Chavo Guerrero .... **Salvador Guerrero**
Eddie Guerrero, Black Tiger .... **Eddy Guerrero**
Hector Guerrero, LazorTron .... **Hector Guerrero**
Gory Guerrero .... **Salvador Guerrero Cuesada**
Mando Guerrero... **Armando Guerrero**
Stan Hansen .... **John Stanley Hansen**
Hawk .... **Michael Hegstrand**
Michael PS Hayes, Doc Hendrix .... **Michael Seitz**
Hunter Hearst Helmsley, HHH,
Jean-Paul Levesque .... **Paul Levesque**
Mr. Perfect .... **Curt Hennig**
Hercules, Hercules Hernandez, Assassin 2........... **Ray Hernandez**
Hulk Hogan, Hollywood Hogan,
Terry Boulder, Sterling Golden .... **Terry Bollea**
Bob "Spark Plugg" Holly,
Thermon Sparky Plugg .... **Robert Howard**
The Honky Tonk Man .... **Wayne Farris**
Wild Bill Irwin, The Goon .... **Bill Irwin**
I.R.S., Mr. Wallstreet, Capt. Mike .... **Michael Rotundo**
Tokyo Tom, Antonio Inoki .... **Kanji Inoki**
The Iron Sheik, Col. Mustapha .... **Kozrow Vaziri**
Chris Jericho .... **Christopher Irvine**
The Ugandan Giant Kamala, Kamala .... **Jim Harris**
Kane, Dr. Isaac Yankem, Unibomb .... **Glen Jacobs**
Kendo the Samurai I, White Lightning .... **Tim Horner**
Billy Kidman, Kidman .... **Pete Gruner**
Brian Knobbs .... **Brian Yandrisovitz**
Konnan, K-Dogg .... **Carlos Ashenoff**
Killer Kowalski, Wladek Kowalski .... **Walter Kowalski**
Lady Angel .... **Geneva Huckabee**
Nature Boy Buddy Landel .... **William Ansor**
Ed "Strangler" Lewis .... **Robert Frederick**
Jushin "Thunder" Liger .... **Keiichi Yamada**
Rio Rogers, Brother Love .... **Bruce Pritchard**
Lex Luger, The Narcisist .... **Larry Pfohl**
Mabel, King Mabel .... **Nelson Frazier**
Magnum TA .... **Terry Allen**
Dean Malenko .... **Dean Simon**
The Model Rick Martel .... **Richard Vignault**
Mantaur, Jack Neu .... **Mike Hallick**

Meng, Haku .... **Uliuli Fifita**
Shawn Michaels .... **Michael S. Hickenbottom**
Rey Mysterio, Jr. .... **Oscar Gonzales**
Mo, Sir Mo .... **Bobby Horne**
Gorilla Monsoon, Gino Marella .... **Robert Marella**
Aldo Montoya, P. J. Walker .... **Peter Polaco**
The Fabulous Moolah .... **Lillian Ellison**
Moondog Rex .... **Randy Collins**
Hugh Morris, Crash the Terminator .... **William DeMott**
Mortis, Chris Canyon .... **David Ashford Smith**
Mr. Moto .... **Masaru Charles Iwamoto**
Mr. Wrestling I, The Assassin .... **Jody Hamilton**
The One Man Gang, Akeem .... **George Gray**
Diamond Dallas Page .... **Page Falkenberg**
Col. Robert Parker, Robert Fuller .... **Robert Welch**
Papa Shango, Kama, The Godfather .... **Charles Wright**
The Patriot, The Trooper .... **Del Wilkes**
Man Mountain Rock, Maxx Payne .... **Darryl Peterson**
Pierre, Jean-Pierre Lafite .... **Karl Ouelette**
Rowdy Roddy Piper .... **Rod George Toombs**
The Genius, Leaping Lanny Poffo .... **Lanny Poffo**
Raven, Johnny Polo, Scotty The Body .... **Scott Levy**
Jim Powers .... **James Manley**
Psicosis, Psychosis .... **Dionico Caltellanos**
Scott Putski, Konan 2000 .... **Scott Bednarski**
Flyboy Rocco Rock, Cheetah Kid .... **Ted Petty**
Tommy Rogers .... **Thomas Couch**
Pretty Paul Roma .... **Paul Centopani**
Playboy Buddy Rose .... **Paul Perschman**
Dark Patriot .... **Doug Gilbert**
Macho Man Randy Savage .... **Randy Poffo**
Madusa, Alundra Blaze .... **Deborah Micceli**
Louie Spicolli, Rad Radford, Mercenary .... **Louis Mucciolo**
Scott Steiner, Big Poppa Pump .... **Scott Rechsteiner**
Rick Steiner .... **Rob Rechsteiner**
Razor Ramon, Diamond Studd .... **Scott Hall**
Lord Steven Regal, Steve Regal .... **Darrin Matthews**
The American Dream Dusty Rhodes .... **Virgil Runnels, Jr.**
Jake "The Snake" Roberts .... **Aurelian Smith, Jr.**
Axl Rotten .... **Brian Knighton**

Ian Rotten .... **Jon Willams**
Jerry Saggs .... **Jerry Saganovich**
Samu .... **Samula Anoia**
The Sandman .... **Tim Fullington**
Tito Santana, The Matador .... **Merced Solis**
The Original Sheik .... **Ed Farhat**
Sensational Sherri, Sherri Martel, Sister Sherri **Cheryl Russell**
Psycho Sid, Sid Vicious, Sid Justic .... **Sid Eudy**
Skip .... **Chris Candido**
Skinner, Doink .... **Steve Kiern**
Dick Slater .... **Van Richard Slater**
Richard Slinger .... **Richard Acelinger**
Demolition Smash, Moondog Rex .... **Randy Culley**
Repo Man, Blacktop Bully, Krusher Kruschev .... **Barry Darsow**
Al Snow, Leif Cassidy, Avatar .... **Allan Sarven**
Superfly Jimmy Snuka .... **James Reiher**
Dave Sullivan, EVAD, Equalizer .... **Bill Dannenhauser**
Sunny .... **Tamara Sytch**
The Star of David .... **Sammy Cohen**
Mark Star .... **Mark Ashford Smith**
Ricky "The Dragon" Steamboat .... **Richard Blood**
George "The Animal" Steele .... **James Myers**
Stevie Ray .... **Lane Huffman**
Sting, Blade Runner Flash .... **Steve Borden**
The Stomper, Mongolian Stomper .... **Archie Gouldie**
Chief Jay Strongbow .... **Joe Scarpa**
Terry Taylor, The Red Rooster .... **Paul Taylor**
Tatanka .... **Chris Chavis**
Tazmaniac .... **Steve Tazello**
Travis .... **Chad Fortune**
Tugboat, Typhoon .... **Fred Ottman**
Ultimate Dragon, Ultimo Dragon .... **Yoshihiro Asai**
The Ultimate Warrior, Blade Runner Rock .... **James Hellwig**
The Undertaker .... **Mark Callaway**
Vader, Big Van Vader .... **Leon White**
Vampire Warrior, Gangrel .... **Dave Heath**
Savio Vega, Kwang, TNT .... **Juan Rivera**
Virgil, Vincent .... **Michael Jones**
Nikolai Volkoff, Beppo Mongol .... **Josiph Peruzovic**
The Warlord .... **Terry Szopinski**

Mikey Whipwreck .... **Mike Watson**
Timothy Well, Rex King .... **Mark Smith**
Van Hammer .... **Mark Hildreth**
Jesse "The Body" Ventura .... **James Janos**
Kevin Von Erich .... **Kevin Adkisson**
Kerry Von Erich, The Texas Tornado .... **Kerry Adkisson**
David Von Erich .... **David Adkisson**
Chris Von Erich .... **Chris Adkisson**
Mike Von Erich .... **Mike Adkisson**
Yokozuna .... **Rodney Anoia**
Zeus, Ze Gangsta .... **Tom "Tiny" Lister**
Boris Zhukov .... **Jim Darrel**
Larry Zbyszko .... **Laurence Whistler**

IDENTITIES OF MASKED WRESTLERS

The following is a list of wrestlers who have grappled under a mask at times during their careers. The first name is that of the masked identity, followed by the wrestler's ring alias.

Arachnaman (WCW) .... **Brad Armstrong**
Arachnaman (Georgia) .... **Scott Armstrong**
Arachnoids .... **Headbangers**
Assassin #1 .... **Jody Hamilton**
Assassin #2 (Georgia) .... **Tom Renesto**
Assassin #2 (Mid-Atlantic) .... **Hercules Hernandez**
Assassins (Indianapolis) .... **Guy Mitchell & Joe Tomasso**
Avatar (WWF) .... **Al Snow**
Avenger (Calgary) .... **Owen Hart**
Badstreet (WCW) .... **Brad Armstrong**
Batman (WWWF) .... **Tony Marino**
Battle Cat (WWF) .... **Brady Boone**
Beetlejuice (WCW) .... **Art Barr**
Big Machine (WWF) .... **Blackjack Mulligan**
Black Blood (WCW) .... **Billy Jack Haynes**
Black Knight (WWF) .... **Jeff Gaylord**

Black Knight & Red Knight (WWF) .... **Barry Horowitz & Steve Lombardi**
Black Terror (Vancouver) .... **Bobby Graham**
Black Tiger (NJ & WWF) .... **Marc Rocco**
Black Tiger (NJ) .... **Eddie Guerrero**
Blackhearts (Calgary) .... **Tom Nash & David Heath**
Blackhearts (WCW/All Japan) .... **Tom Nash & Dave Johnson**
Blue Blazer (WWF) .... **Owen Hart**
Blue Infernos (Florida) .... **Lee & Bobby Fields**
Blue Infernos (Tennessee) .... **Gypsy Joe & Pepe Lopez**
Blue Infernos (Tennessee) .... **Gypsy Joe & Frank Martinez**
Blue Knight (WWF) .... **Greg Valentine**
Bullet .... **Bob Armstrong**
Captain USA (WCCW) .... **John Studd**
Charlie Brown (Mid-Atlantic) .... **Jimmy Valiant**
Cheetah Kid .... **Ted Petty**
Christmas Creature .... **Glen Jacobs**
Clones (Memphis) .... **Pat & Mike Kelly**
Cobra (WWF & NJ) .... **George Takano**
Conquistadors (WWF) .... **Jose Estrada & Jose Luis Rivera**
Dark Patriot (GWF & ECW) .... **Doug Gilbert**
Dark Secret (SMW) .... **Brian Armstrong**
Deadeye Dick (WCW) .... **Randy Colley**
Deadhead (USWA) .... **Ken Raper**
Destroyer (Lexington) .... **Randy Savage**
Destroyer (International) .... **Dick Beyer**
Ding Dongs (NWA) .... **Tim Evans & Richard Sartain**
Dink (WWF) .... **Tiger Jackson**
Dirty Yellow Dog (Florida) .... **Barry Windham**
Dixie Dynamite .... **Scott Armstrong**
Doink I .... **Matt Borne**
Doink II .... **Steve Kiern**
Doink III .... **Steve Lombardi**
Doink IV .... **Ray Apollo**
Doink (NWC) .... **Mark Starr**
Doom .... **Butch Reed & Ron Simmons**
Doomsday (Tennessee) .... **Glen Jacobs**
Dr. Death (Oklahoma) .... **Steve Williams**
Dr. Feel Good (Deep South) .... **Terry Taylor**
Dr. X (AWA) .... **Dick Beyer**

Dr. X (Omaha) .... **Bill Miller**
Dr. X (NWA '70s) .... **Jim Osborne**
Dr. X (WCW '90s) .... **Randy Colley**
El Medico (LA) .... **Apollo Jalisco**
Eliminators (Memphis) .... **Perry Saturn & John Kronus**
Executioner (ICW) .... **Randy Savage**
Executioners (WWF '70s)........ **Killer Kowalski & John Studd**
Executioners (WWF '90s).............. **Duane Gill & Barry Hardy**
Fantasia (WCW) .... **Brad Armstrong**
Fire Memphis) .... **Don Bass**
Fire Cat (WCW) .... **Brady Boone**
Flame (Memphis) .... **Roger Smith**
The Flame (Alabama) .... **Jody Hamilton**
Freedom Fighter (WCW) .... **Brad Armstrong**
Friday .... **Buddy Wayne**
Galaxians (Memphis) .... **Dan Davis & Ken Wayne**
Giant Ninja (WCW) .... **Ron Reese**
Giant Machine (WWF) .... **Andre the Giant**
Gobbledygooker (WWF) .... **Hector Guerrero**
Grappler (Florida) .... **Johnny Walker**
Grappler (Oklahoma/Texas) .... **Len Denton**
Grapplers .... **Len Denton & Tony Anthony**
Great Wizard (WCW) .... **Kevin Sullivan**
Haito (WCW) .... **Paul Diamond**
Handsome Stranger (GWF) .... **Marcus Alexander Bagwell**
Hangman (LA) .... **Neil Guay**
The Hood (LA) .... **Ron Starr**
The Hood (Portland) .... **Ricky Santana**
The Hood (World Class) .... **Jeff Gaylord**
Hornet (SMW) .... **Brian Keyes**
Hulk Machine (WWF) .... **Hulk Hogan**
Humongous (USWA) .... **Randy Lewis**
Juicer (Portland) .... **Art Barr**
Kato (WWF) .... **Paul Diamond**
Kendo the Samurai I (SMW) .... **Tim Horner**
Kendo the Samurai II (SMW) .... **Bobby Blaze**
Kendo the Samurai III (SMW) .... **Brian Logan**
Killer Bees .... **Brian Blair & Jim Brunzell**
Killer Bee (New Japan) .... **Brian Blair**
Kim Chee II (WWF) .... **Steve Lombardi**

King Killer (USWA) .... **Mike Miller**
Kowabunga Ninja Turtle (SMW) .... **Brian Hilderbrand**
Kwang, TNT .... **Savio Vega**
Lacrosse (All Japan) .... **Jungle Jim Steele**
Lady X (LPWA) .... **Peggy Lee**
LazorTron (NWA) .... **Hector Guerrero**
Leatherface (USWA) .... **Ken Raper**
Leatherface (USWA) .... **Mike Samples**
Leatherface (W*I*N*G – Original) .... **Tim Patterson**
Leatherface (W*I*N*G) .... **Doug Gilbert**
Stagger Lee (Memphis) .... **Koko Ware**
Stagger Lee (Mid-South) .... **Junkyard Dog**
Lord Humongous (Alabama mid-'80s) .... **Jeff Van Kamp**
Lord Humongous (Continental) .... **Sid Vicious**
Lords of Darkness (WWF) .... **Duane Gill & Barry Hardy**
Los Espelicitos (WCW) .... **Ricky Santana & David Sierra**
Masked Avenger (World Class) .... **Chris Adams**
Masked Bat (Tennessee) .... **Bob O'Shocker**
Masked Champion (Oklahoma) .... **Randy Colley**
Masked Destroyer (Florida) .... **Killer Kowalski**
Masked Infernos (SMW) .... **Brian Keyes & Anthony Michaels**
Masked Outlaw (NWA) .... **Dory Funk, Jr.**
Masked Rebel (Tennessee) .... **Sonny Fargo**
Masked Skyscraper .... **Mike Enos**
Masked Strangler .... **Guy Mitchell**
Masked Superstar (Mid-Atlantic, WWF) .... **Bill Eadie**
Masked Superstar II (Mid-Atlantic) .... **John Studd**
Masked Terror (AWA) .... **Jay York**
Master of Pain (Memphis) .... **Mark Calloway**
Masters of Terror (Memphis) .... **Dan Davis & Ken Wayne**
Matador (Alabama) .... **Jerry Stubbs**
Max Moon (WWF) .... **Paul Diamond**
Medics (Tennessee) .... **Tony Gonzales & Don Lortie**
Medics (Florida) .... **Billy Garrett & Dick Dunn/Jim Starr**
Mega Maharishi (PNW) .... **Ed Wiskowski**
Mephisto (Tennessee) .... **Lou Papineau**
Mephisto (Memphis '90s) .... **Romeo Rodriguez**
Mercenaries .... **Bill Anderson, Tim Patterson & Louie Spicolli**
Midnight Rider (Florida & NWA) .... **Dusty Rhodes**

Midnight Rider (Mid-South) .... **Bill Watts**
Midnight Rider (GWF) .... **Sam Houston**
Minnesota Wrecking Crew II (NWA) .... **Wayne Bloom & Mike Enos**
Miser (Lexington) .... **Angelo Poffo**
Mister M (AWA) .... **Bill Miller**
The Monster (LA) .... **Tony Rodriguez**
Aldo Montoya (WWF) .... **P. J. Walker**
Mr. J. L. (WCW) .... **Jerry Lynn**
Mr. M. (Indianapolis) .... **Hard Boiled Haggerty**
Mr. Madness (WWF) .... **Randy Savage**
Mr. R (Georgia) .... **Tommy Rich**
Mr. R. (Georgia against DiBiase) .... **Brad Armstrong**
Mr. Wrestling I .... **Tim Woods**
Mr. Wrestling (Tennessee) .... **Dick Steinborn**
Mr. Wrestling II .... **Johnny Walker**
Nightmares .... **Dan Davis & Ken Wayne**
Nightmare Freddy .... **Doug Gilbert**
Mr. Olympia .... **Jerry Stubbs**
Patriot .... **Del Wilkes**
Pegasus Kid (NJ) .... **Chris Benoit**
Phantom (WWF) .... **David Heath**
Phantoms (USWA) .... **Jerry Faith & Troy Haste**
Shanghai Pierce (WCW) .... **Mark Canterbury**
Prince Kharis (SMW) .... **Rob Mayze**
Professional .... **Doug Gilbert**
Punisher (WCW) .... **Mark Calloway**
Purple Shadow (San Francisco) .... **Bill Longson**
Rasputin (Portland) .... **Black Angus Campbell**
Red Hangman .... **Tom Rice**
Red Knight & Black Knight .... **Barry Horowitz & Steve Lombardi**
Red Knight (Memphis) .... **Del Rios**
Red Masked Marvel .... **Jack Larve**
Red River Jack (WCCW) .... **Bruiser Brody**
Red Shadow (Tennessee) .... **Dick Dunn**
Repo Man (WWF) .... **Barry Darsow**
Russian Assassin I (NWA) .... **Angel of Death**
Russian Assassin II (NWA) .... **Jack Victory**
Screaming Eagles (WCW) .... **Michael Hayes & Jimmy Garvin**

Senior X (LA) .... **J. C. Dykes**
Sensational White Phantom .... **Nick Bockwinkel**
Shadow (Alabama) .... **Norvell Austin**
Shadows (WWF) .... **Randy Colley & Jose Luis Rivera**
Shinobi the Oriental Assassin (Ohio) .... **Al Snow**
Shinobi (WWF) .... **Al Snow**
Siva (Crockett '94) .... **Tony Norris**
Spider (Indies) .... **Randy Savage**
Spider Lady (WWF) .... **Moolah**
Spiders (USWA & WWF) .... **Headbangers**
Spoiler #1 (Georgia) .... **Don Jardine**
Spoiler #2 (LA) .... **Ron Starr**
Spoiler (Memphis '84) .... **Frank Morell**
Spoilers (Florida) .... **Don Jardine & Bobby Duncum**
Spoilers (Oklahoma) .... **Don Jardine & Buddy Wolfe**
Spoilers (Texas) .... **Don Jardine & Smasher Sloan**
Starblazer (NWA) .... **Tim Horner**
Starship Coyote .... **Scott Hall**
Starship Eagle .... **Dan Spivey**
Stomper (Oklahoma) .... **John Quinn**
Student (Detroit) .... **George Steele**
Super Assassins (WCW) .... **Warlord & Barbarian**
Super Destroyers (WCCW) .... **Bill & Scott Irwin**
Super Destroyer (GWF) .... **Bill Irwin**
Super Destroyers (GWF) .... **Bill Irwin & Gary Young**
Super Destroyer Mark II (AWA) .... **Sgt. Slaughter**
Super Infernos (Memphis) .... **Doug Gilbert & Don Smith**
Super Invader (WCW) .... **Hercules**
Super Machine (WWF) .... **Bill Eadie**
Super Olympia (Alabama) .... **Arn Anderson**
Super Shockmaster (WCW) .... **Fred Ottman**
Super Zodiac I (WCCW) .... **Gary Young**
Super Zodiac II (WCCW) .... **Cactus Jack**
Superfly (World Class) .... **Kamala**
Sweet Brown Sugar (Memphis) .... **Koko Ware**
Sweet Brown Sugar (World Class) .... **Skip Young**
Sweet Ebony Diamond (NWA) .... **Rocky Johnson**
Tennessee Stud (Memphis) .... **Ron Fuller**
Tennessee Stud II (Memphis) .... **Robert Fuller**
Terrorist (AWA) .... **Brian Knobbs**

Texan (WCCW) .... **Blackjack Mulligan**
Texas Dirt (Memphis) .... **Dutch Mantel**
Texas Outlaw (Vancouver) .... **Bobby Bass**
Texas Outlaws (Memphis) .... **Doug Vines & Jeff Swords**
Texas Red .... **Red Bastien**
Tiger Mask I .... **Satoru Sayama**
Tiger Mask II .... **Mitsuharu Misawa**
Tiger Mask III .... **Koji Kanemoto**
Vader .... **Leon White**
Viper (GWF) .... **Mike Davis**
Twin Devil #1 .... **Alfonso Sanchez**
War Machine (NWA '87) .... **Ray Traylor**
White Knight (Texas) .... **Dick Steinborn**
Wild Pegasus (NJ) .... **Chris Benoit**
Yellow Dog (WCW) .... **Brian Pillman/Tom Zenk**
Yellow Scorpion (Tennessee) .... **Buck Lawson**
Yetti (WCW) .... **Ron Reese**
Zodiac (Florida '70s) .... **Bob Orton, Sr.**
Zodiac (Calgary) .... **Barry O**

WRESTLING SCHOOLS

The following is a list of wrestling schools compiled from various sources. Every attempt has been made to make the list as up-to-date as possible.

School of Hard Knocks Wrestling School
Jesse Hernandez and Bill Anderson
3265 North E Street, San Bernardino, CA 92405
(909) 886-5201

Killer Kowalski Wrestling School
P.O. Box 67, Reading, MA 01867

Ivan Koloff Wrestling School
P.O. Box 23360, Charlotte, NC 28227

Skullcrushers Wrestling School
P.O. Box 6188, Gulf Breeze, FL 32561
(904) 934-8435

Southern States Wrestling School
P.O. Box 125, Fall Branch, TN 37656
http://www.cybersports.com/ssw/school.html

Superstars Pro Wrestling Training Camp
21063 Cabot Blvd., Suite 1, Hayward, CA 94545
(510) 785-8396

The Monster Factory (Pretty Boy Larry Sharpe)
P.O. Box 345, Westville, NJ 08093
(609) 845-5330
http://www.monsterfactory.com

Mike Shaw (Bastian Booger) Wrestling School
P.O. Box 200, Skandia, MI 49885
(906) 942-7255

Warrior University
10320 North Scottsdale Road, Scottsdale, AZ 85253
(602) 566-4276

WWO Pro Wrestling Academy
Pittsburgh, PA
(513) 724-8228

Slammers Wrestling Gym
P.O. Box 1602, Studio City, CA 91614
(818) 897-6603
http://www.slammers.com/school.htm

WCW Powerplant
Atlanta, GA
(404) 351-4959

Main Event Pro Wrestling Camp (Les Thatcher)
10235 Spartan Dr., Suite D, Cincinnati, OH 45215
(513) 771-1650

Danny Davis School of Pro Wrestling
1121 Mechanic Street, Jeffersonville, IN 47130
(812) 280-7039
http://www.pages.prodigy.com/starlink/davis.htm

Institute of Professional Wrestling
10 Stemmers Run Road, Essex, MD 21221

Bonecrushers National
Pro Wrestling Training Center, Cincinnati, OH
(513) 577-4150

Roland Alexander's Superstars Training
3833 Peralta, Suite B, Fremont, CA 94536

Iron Mike Sharp's Wrestling School
Asbury Park, NJ
(908) 750-1665

Pedro Rodriguez
Unpredictable School of Pro Wrestling
75 Lewis Avenue, Brooklyn, NY 11206
(718) 599-5345

Long Island Wrestling Federation
Brooklyn, NY
(212) 479-7775

PRO WRESTLING NEWSLETTERS

Professional wrestling newsletters come and go with frequency, so the following is a list that is as up-to-date as verifiable at the time of printing. Most of the following will make sample issues available if you write to them.

Wrestling Observer Newsletter
Editor: Dave Meltzer
P.O. Box 1228, Campbell, CA 95009-1228

Figure Four Newsletter
Editor: Bryan Alvarez
P.O. Box 426, Woodinville, WA 98072

Wrestling Perspective
Editors: MacArthur & Skolnick
3011 Highway 30, West Ste. 101-197, Huntsville, TX 77340

Pro Wrestling Monthly
Editor: Greg Rufolo
568 Speedwell Ave., Morris Plains, NJ 07950

Ring Around the Northwest
Editor: Mike Rodgers
2470 S.E. Lewellyn, Troutdale, OR 97060

Wrestling Then & Now
Editor: Evan Ginzburg
P.O. Box 640471, Oakland Gardens Station,
Flushing, NY 11364
http://members.xoom.com/wtnow

Pro Wrestling Torch
Editor: Wade Keller
P.O. Box 201844, Minneapolis, MN 55420

The Wrestling Chatterbox
Editor: Georgiann Makropolous
23-44 30th Dr., Astoria, NY 11102-3252

Wrestling Lariat
Editor: Dave Scherer
P.O. Box 612, Marmora, NJ 08223

Mat Marketplace
(published infrequently)
Editor: Sheldon Goldberg
P.O. Box 2371, Jamaica Plain, MA 02130

Piledriver
Editor: Lazarus Dobelsky
Glenhuntly, Victoria 3163, Australia
Canadian Championship Wrestling
976 Miller Rd., West St. Paul, Manitoba R4A 4A4 Canada

Combat Sports
P.O. Box 161, Gracie Station, New York, NY 10028-0006

Whatever Happened To?
Editor: Scott Teal
P.O. Box 2781, Hendersonville, TN 37077-2781

Wrestling WReality Newsletter
(published infrequently)
Editor: Dr. Michael Lano
68 Sable Pointe, Alameda, CA 94502

*** ***

INDEX

C

D

H

I

J

Q

R

S

T

U

V

W